Hard to Turn:

A History of the Camp, Gabbert, Griffin, Huskey
and Webb Families of Drew County, Arkansas
and
Associated Families: Alexander, Dodson,
George, Harris, Hawkins,
Marshall, McCall & Stovall

Judy Webb Hubbell, Ed.D.

ISBN: 1481063863
ISBN 13: 9781481063869
Library of Congress Control Number: 2012922234
CreateSpace Independent Publishing Platform
North Charleston, SC

Dedication

This narrative is dedicated to my parents, Lewis French Webb and Louise Hawkins Webb, both raconteurs extraordinaire.

Lewis French Webb and Louise Hawkins Webb,
ca. 1978

"Lord, grant that I may always be right,
for Thou knowest I am hard to turn."
—A Scots-Irish Prayer

Table of Contents

Prologue

This is an amateur work of genealogy designed for members of the families discussed in this narrative and those who may be related. I have not used DNA results or anything like that. I believe I have pieced together a family history that, for the most part, is accurate. A significant amount of information is from the oral tradition. I am fortunate that my father and mother, Lewis French Webb and Louise Hawkins Webb, were and are natural and delightful raconteurs (storytellers). I will use the term "we" throughout this narrative. It simply refers to the members of the families discussed.

One of my biggest regrets in life is my failure to record my father's stories before he died. Unfortunately, all his siblings are also dead. My mother, ninety-three years old, has filled in some of the blanks encountered in researching this narrative.

Many of my sources came from interviews with individuals, and the oral tradition of family storytelling. I have used the findings of other genealogists, and the Internet has enabled me to communicate with them on message boards. I feel confident that my sources are reliable, but please remember that much of the information has been handed down through generations and cannot be documented with a strict degree of certainty. It has been like putting together a complicated jigsaw puzzle.

The findings in this research have made me proud that our families were early pioneers who helped shape this nation, the south, and more specifically, Drew County and Monticello, Arkansas. We are one of the "old families," as my mother says in describing us. We did not come through Ellis Island—we were in America long before that. We were among the first Europeans to settle in this country at Jamestown, Virginia and, before that, perhaps the lost colony of Roanoke. We were among the first white people to venture into the wilderness that was to become the Arkansas Territory.

The oral tradition, courthouse records, passenger lists of ships, and church records have provided a treasure trove of information about our families. It is important to know who we are and how we came to be who we are. It helps determine where we go in the future.

Several branches of our family, beginning with Gabbert, then Camp, Alexander, McCall, Marshall, Harris, Huskey, Griffin, Stovall, and finally, the Webbs, are discussed in this book. I have also discussed two branches of my mother's family, the Hawkinses and Dodsons. In the Dodson chapter, there is a brief discussion of the George family. I have attempted to keep this from sounding like the Old Testament of the Bible where someone "begat" someone, who "begat" someone, and so on. Unfortunately, that is about all I know about some of the earliest generations of our family.

I am an historian, so I have used an historical backdrop to stage our family's history. It is necessary to understand what was going on in the world to understand migratory patterns and settlement decisions, so if you do not enjoy history, you should put this book down. Our family helped shape the history of our nation from its infancy. I take a great deal of pride in that, and I hope you will too. I have included a list of references at the end of the narrative. I wrote this account in the first person; it seemed appropriate for a family history.

I am **Judy Carol Webb Hubbell,** and this is the story of how I came to be who I am. To help you keep track of all the "greats," I have included a parent-to-child chart at the beginning of each section.

Chapter I
The Gabberts: Our German Roots

Direct Line of Descent for the Gabberts

Mathias Gebhard and Margaretha Mueller were the parents of Petrus Gebhard.

Petrus Gabhard and wife (Unkncwn) were the parents of Johann Michael Gabhard.

Johann Michael Gabhard and Agnes Marie Boger were the parents of Peter Gebert.

Peter Gebert and Anna Barbara Machtlin were the parents of Hans Michael Gebert.

Hans Michael Gebert and Anna Sabina Nellinger were the parents of Michael George Gabbert.

Michael George Gabbert and Catherine King were the parents of Michael Gabbert, Jr.

Michael Gabbert, Jr. and Elizabeth Brown were the parents of George Gabbert.

George Gabbert and Elizabeth Phillips/Goodwin were the parents of Julia Ann Virginia Gabbert.

Julia Ann Virginia Gabbert and George Crenshaw Camp were the parents of Martha Camp.

Martha Camp and William Griffin were the parents of Virginia Griffin.

Virginia Griffin and John Webb were the parents of Lewis French Webb.

Lewis French Webb and Louise Hawkins are the parents of Arnold Ray Webb, Donald Roy Webb, Jo Ann Webb, and Judy Carol Webb.

Judy Carol Webb Hubbell and Billy James Hubbell are the parents of Jennifer Leigh Hubbell Plunkett and William Griffin Hubbell.

This story begins in 1575 in Forchtenberg, Germany, with the birth of Mathias Gebhard. I am his direct descendent. After I traced my lineage back to Mathias Gebhard, the trail went cold. I hope to learn more about his ancestors in the future.

The spelling of the surname *Gebhard(t)* evolved to *Gebert,* some-times spelled *Gabbard,* and was eventually Anglicized to *Gabbert.* The name is derived from the root words *geb* meaning "gift," and *hard* meaning "brave," the gift of bravery. It was a popular sur-name in Germany during the Middle Ages because of the Catholic Saint Gebhardt, Bishop of Constance, during the tenth century (Gabbert-Giancola, 1999).

Mathaus Gebhard and Margaretha Mueller

Mathaus Gebhard was born in 1575 in Forchtenberg, Germany, and died around 1633. In 1600, he married Margaretha Mueller, born around 1579 in Steinheim, Lippe, Germany. It is believed they married in Am Kocher, Germany. Mathaus Gebhard and Margaretha Mueller were the parents of Petrus Gebhard. Petrus was the oldest of Mathaus Gebhard's four children, and I am one of his direct descendants (Giancola-Gabbert, 1999). The follow-ing are the children of Mathaus Gebhard and Margaretha Mueller: Petrus Gebhard, born August 21, 1607; died July 17, 1668; Maria Gebhard, born February 23, 1604/1605; Barbara Gebhard, born August 29, 1610; Leopoldine Gebhard, born September 22, 1613 *(Individual Record: Petrus Gebhard,* 2008).

Historical Background

Forchtenberg, an old walled village, has medieval roots as far back as AD 700. Archeological excavations show that Forchtenberg was inhabited by the Celts as far back as 2000 BC during the Iron Age of Europe. It was officially recognized in AD 1298. About one-third of the town was destroyed during World War II. Forchtenberg was located in the region of Germany west of the Rhine River and north of the French border called the Palatinate.

The historical background of this region helps us understand why so many of these people immigrated to America during this time. Many of the German settlers in colonial America were refugees from the Palatinate. Germans were the largest non-English group in colonial America.

The Palatinate was devastated by almost constant warfare, often over differences in religious beliefs. Our ancestor, Petrus Gebhard, became caught up in these religious disputes. He had his surname officially changed to *Gebert* and his Christian name changed to Peter after he was rebaptized as a Protestant (Gabbert-Giancola, 1999).

It is believed that he was the first in his family to break from the Roman Catholic Church and convert to the Lutheran faith during the Protestant Reformation (Gabbert-Giancola, 1999), a religious movement led by a German monk, Martin Luther. Luther's revolt was set into motion on October 31, 1517 when he posted his list of *Ninety-five Theses* that challenged the practices of the Roman Catholic Church. The Protestant leader, John Calvin, had gained many supporters in Switzerland; Calvinism was the forerunner of the Presbyterian Church.

The Huguenots, Protestant believers in France, gained many followers. In England, King Henry VIII broke away from the Roman Catholic Church out of his desire to divorce his Catholic wife, Catherine of Aragon, the daughter of the powerful Spanish rulers Ferdinand and Isabella, and marry Anne Bolyn, who he believed would give him a male heir. Henry VIII created and became the head of the Church of England.

By 1560, Europe had a large Protestant population. To recoup losses and convert new members, the Catholic Church launched the Catholic Reformation to counter the Protestant movement.

Wars of Religion

People and nations divided along religious lines, plunging Europe into a period of more than one hundred years of warfare. Germany suffered greatly; the country was left in ruins with a heavy toll in human lives. In 1547, the powerful ruler, Catholic

Emperor Charles V, defeated the German princes. The German treasury was depleted from the constant warfare, but the princes retained a great deal of political power. The German princes and Charles V reached an agreement called the *Peace of Augsburg*, under which each German prince could decide the religion for his territory. The resulting peace was shaky at best (Reich, 1905).

The most brutal of the religious wars, the Thirty Years War (1618–1648), turned much of Germany into a wasteland. Military forces plundered towns and killed everyone suspected of having Protestant leanings. One-fourth to one-third of the German population died from direct military causes or from illness and starvation before the war ended in 1648 with the signing of the *Treaty of Westphalia* (Spahn, 1912).

The Palatinate continued to suffer. During the War of the League of Augsburg, King Louis XIV of France invaded the Palatinate in 1688 with an army of fifty thousand men. One day of fighting saw twenty-three towns and villages burned, sending peasants into the fields to freeze or starve (Green, 1904).

During the War of the Grand Alliance (1689–1697), the armies of Louis XIV marched into the Palatinate, spreading death and destruction. Lord Thomas Babington Macaulay (1900) described the unspeakable suffering of the region:

> *"The French commander announced to near half a million of human beings that he granted them three days of grace, and that, within that time, they must shift for themselves. Soon the roads and fields, which then lay deep in snow, were blackened by innumerable multitudes of men, women, and children flying from their homes. Many died of cold and hunger; but enough survived to fill the streets of all the cities of Europe with lean and squalid beggars, who had once been thriving farmers and shopkeepers. Meanwhile the work of destruction began. The flames went up from every market-place, every hamlet, every parish church, every country seat....The fields where the corn had been sown were*

ploughed up. The orchards were hewn down. . . .The magnificent Cathedral of Spires perished, and with it the marble sepulchers of eight Caesars. The coffins were broken open. The ashes were scattered to the winds."

In addition, the people were heavily taxed, and many felt deep resentment over unfair taxation. The first wave of immigration to the American colonies began after Germany experienced an extraordinarily severe winter in 1708–1709. In October 1708, the Arctic cold descended. The Palatinate of Germany, famous for its fine wines, saw its vineyards and fruit trees ruined. Cattle froze to death in the barns. It was said that birds fell from the air, frozen, and fires would not burn outdoors. Many people perished from the brutal cold and starvation. Until that time, the Palatinate was a prosperous area of flat valleys and gently rolling limestone hills (Pray, 1972).

Meanwhile, the region was terrorized by the War of the Spanish Succession (1701–1714). In 1707, the French army marched through the Palatinate, leaving a trail of destruction.

Petrus Gebhard and Wife (Unknown)

During this turbulent time, Petrus Gebhard was born in 1607 in Forchtenberg, Germany. He died in 1668 Schwaigern, Baden, Germany, at sixty-one years old. Petrus married around 1635 and apparently moved from his place of birth. Petrus (Peter Gebert) and his wife had eight children (Gabbert-Giancola, 1999):

Wolfgang Gebert, born January 23, 1635/1636

Michael Gebert—This Michael may have died as an infant, because the next child listed is also named Michael.

Michael Gebert, born June, 18, 1637

Peter Gebert, born August 3, 1640, and died August 10, 1740, lived to be one hundred years old.

Johann Michael Gebert, born December 1642 in Schwaigern, Germany; died August 4, 1691 in Schwaigern.

Maria Margaretha Gebert, born December 14, 1644

Barbara Gebert, born August 26, 1647

George Mathias Gebert, born December 17, 1649

Johann Michael Gebert and Agnes Boger

My family is descended from Johann Michael Gebert, who married Agnes Marie Reufflin Boger, February 14, 1666/1667 in Schwaigern, Germany. Agnes Marie Reufflin Boger was born March 17, 1668/1669. They had eleven children (Gabbert-Giancola, 1999):

Maria Margaretha—died at two years old

Peter, born March 17, 1668/1669 in Forchtenberg, Germany; died August 17, 1728 in Schwaigern, Germany

Johan Michael—died at one year old

Agnes Marie, born April 15, 1676

Jakobus—died at two months old

Maria Magdalena, born August 15, 1679; died January 26, 1688/1689

Jakob, born August 1, 1681; died March 14, 1745/1746

Mathias died at twenty-six days old

Peter Gebert and Anna Barbara Machtlin

My family is directly descended from Peter Gebert and his wife, Anna Barbara Machtlin, daughter of Ulrich Machtlin. They were married on May 24, 1698 in Schwaigern, Germany. They had six children (Gabbert-Giancola, 1999):

Johann Friedrich Gebert, born April 10, 1699 in Schwaigern, Germany; died in 1790 in Frederick County, Virginia

Hans Peter Gebert, born July 28, 1700 in Schwaigern, Germany

Hans Michael Gebert, born November 17, 1702; died February 1747/1748 in Frederick County, Virginia.

Anna Barbara Gebert, born December 12, 1704

Hans George Gebert, born May 29, 1707

Hans Ulrich Gebert, born September 17, 1709; died June 10, 1710 at nine months old

Chapter 2
The Geberts Sail to America

Hans Michael Gebert and Anna Sabina Nellinger

Four generations of Gebhards/Geberts—Mathius, Petrus, Johann Michael, and Peter—endured war, famine, and religious persecution in Germany. Two of Peter Gabert's sons, Johann Friedrich Gebert and Hans Michael Gebert, decided to seek a fresh start in America. My family is descended from Hans Michael Gebert and his wife, Anna Sabina Nellinger, the daughter of Hans Jorg Nellinger and Anna Sabina Hartmann. Hans Michael and Anna were married, August 19, 1727 in Schwaigern, Germany. Hans Michael Gebert was a hand weaver by trade which, under normal circumstances, would have made him a solid member of the middle class. However, the times were far from normal, so he may have been impoverished when immigrating to America (Gabbert-Giancola, 1999). By this time, Europe was dominated by the political philosophy of absolutism, the belief that the monarch had absolute authority over his or her subjects. The rulers of the small German states were ruthless, suppressing revolts and collecting high taxes.

During this time, Great Britain was colonizing the New World. William Penn, who had a German mother, and founded the colony of Pennsylvania and the city of Philadelphia, made several visits to the Palatinate. The royal charter for Pennsylvania was granted by the British Crown in 1681. Penn advertised in the Palatinate in an effort to gain colonists for Pennsylvania. He billed Pennsylvania as a place of refuge for persecuted Protestants. He promised equal rights to all regardless of race or religious belief (Garman, 1999); (Pray, 1972). It is interesting that Penn owned slaves, a practice somewhat difficult to reconcile with his Quaker beliefs and political views.

Pamphlets were distributed up and down the Rhine River extolling the availability of land in Pennsylvania as well as in other colonies. In 1663, Penn made a peace treaty with the Delaware Native Americans. By 1776, Pennsylvania had one hundred thousand Germans, making the Germans the largest non-English group in colonial America (Garman, 1999).

Against this political backdrop, Hans Michael Gebert and his brother, Johann Friedrich Gebert, fled Germany and took their families on a dangerous journey to the New World. It is not known what prompted the brothers to make this decision, but there were plenty of potential reasons for their decision. At the time, Germany was occupied by the French army. There had been a mass emigration of the Palatine Germans to Pennsylvania for almost thirty years before the Gebert brothers made their journey. They left their homeland and much of their property behind, sailing down the Rhine River by barge to Rotterdam, then booking passage on the ship *Pennsylvania Merchant* as indicated by the passenger list of this vessel.

The trip down the Rhine to Rotterdam took several weeks by foot, wagon, and riverboat, and was dangerous; few could have made it without help. An underground railroad of sorts was established by Protestant families along the Rhine to give sanctuary to the refugees. Refugees established tent cities at Rotterdam where they waited to load onto ships. Unsanitary conditions and disease took a great toll.

Their first stop was in Dover, England, where they were cleared through customs and had their names officially recorded on the passenger list. The journey from England to Philadelphia usually got underway in early summer to take advantage of calmer seas and good weather. The ships arrived in the New World in the autumn with the hardships of winter ahead for the immigrants (Brobst, 1999).

The cost of passage was five to ten pounds sterling, a high price at the time. Children were half price, but few under the age of seven survived the trip (Brobst, 1999). The ships were overcrowded and unsanitary, the drinking water was polluted, and the food was vermin-ridden. Cunfer (1987) offers the following account from another family's history of the trip from Europe to America:

> "It was a severely harsh trip, taking from six weeks to six months, on filthy ships which were hardly seaworthy and with passengers packed 'like herrings' and exposed to rats, disease, thirst, and starvation. Their provisions fell short, and the last eight weeks they had no bread; but a pint of grouts (crushed oats) was all the allowance for five persons per day. They all ate rats and mice they could catch. The price of a rat was 18 pence, a mouse was 6 pence, and water 6 pence a quart."

Cunfer (1987) continues the dreadful description from the Brobst family account:

> "The pitiful signs of distress on the journey should have given any traveler pause: smells, fumes, horrors, vomiting, various kinds of sea sickness, fever, dysentery, headaches, heat, constipation, boils, scurvy, cancer, mouth-rot. . .so many lice, especially on the sick people, that they have to be scrapped off the body.

Parents must often watch their offspring suffer miserably, die, and be thrown into the ocean."

If a ship was delayed by weather, the passengers often ran out of food and drinking water. The end of the dangerous journey found Hans Michael Gebert, Johann Friedrich Gebert, and their families in the British colony of Pennsylvania. They arrived in Philadelphia, "the city of brotherly love," September 10, 1731. Most of the one hundred seventy five passengers were Palatine Germans (Passenger List, n. d.) From 1682–1776, Pennsylvania became the central point of emigration from Germany, France, and Switzerland (Rupp, 1876).

According to one source, most German immigrants after 1727 came as indentured servants in extreme poverty, and families were often broken up by the purchasers (Morris, 1963). Indentured servants, or bond slaves, had to work for a master for an agreed number of years to repay their debt. Ship captains were often unscrupulous, forcing the refugees to sign agreements to pay a fee to disembark upon their arrival in America. Most refugees could not read English and had no idea what they were signing. Those who could pay the fee to disembark could leave the ship immediately. Those who could not pay were held until a person bought the bond for the full amount owed the ship. These indentured servants were often mistreated by their masters; for example, some masters would make their servants work extra years to pay for room and board. The usual amount of time that Palatines spent indentured was four years. Many children who were orphaned or separated from their families had to serve until they were twenty-one years old. It is not known if Hans Michael and Johann Friedrich Gebert and their families became indentured servants; from the list of Hans Michael Gebert's children, it does not appear that their family life was disrupted after their arrival in Pennsylvania. They may have had more financial resources than most refugees because of their solid middle-class status as drapers and weavers.

As the German immigrants got established in the colonies, they helped other Palatines. They monitored the schedules of ship arrivals and often bought family members out of bond slavery. These German immigrants referred to Germany, their homeland, as Deutshland and their German language as Deitsch. The English incorrectly referred to these immigrants as "Dutch;" this is why these German immigrants to Pennsylvania were given the misnomer of "Pennsylvania Dutch" (Gabbert-Giancola, 1999); (Kerchner, 2008).

The colony of Pennsylvania allowed religious freedom to protect Penn and his fellow Quakers, a Protestant religious sect that preached nonviolence. By 1700, it was the third largest and richest colony in America (Bodnar, 1973). Freedom of religion was granted to all citizens, a right that must have seemed precious to the Geberts after the religious wars in Europe. Hans Michael Gebert and his wife, Anna, had eight children:

> Johann, born in Coventry, Chester County, Pennsylvania
>
> Caterina, born 1728 in Schwaigern, Germany
>
> Anna Elizabeth, born March 2, 1728/1729; died May 14, 1729
>
> Julian, born 1730
>
> Gotlieb, born June 22, 1730; died in 1815 in Kanawah County, Virginia/West Virginia.
>
> Bernhardt, born 1731
>
> Jacob, born in 1732 in Pennsylvania; died 1810 in Montgomery County, Pennsylvania.

> Michael George, born November 23, 1735 in Trapp, Chester County, Pennsylvania; died in 1790 in the Watauga Settlement around the Holstor River in what would later become eastern Tennessee (Carter County).

Michael George Gebert and Catherine King

My family is directly descended from Hans Michael Gebert's youngest child, Michael George Gebert. Michael George Gebert and his older brother, Jacob Gebert, have the distinction of being our first Gebert ancestors born in America. Michael George Gebert made his living as a weaver and a tenant farmer (Gabbert-Giancola, 1999).

Scots-Irish and German descendents from colonists in Pennsylvania, Maryland, and Virginia were some of the first settlers in the Piedmont. They traveled the Great Wagon Road and came in search of more affordable land to grow corn for their own use, wheat and tobacco to sell, and cattle that they drove northward to markets (Hendricks & Hendricks, 1995). The new frontier offered the independence that was central to their value system.

A major attraction of North Carolina was confiscated land for sale, more and better land available for the same or less money but with more hazard of war. In 1778, Michael Gebert received a grant of two hundred acres of North Carolina land on the south side of the Catawba River in Burke County (Burke County, North Carolina land record 901, 278). Because "improvements" are listed on the property, it is believed that he was there for at least a year prior to 1778.

By 1780, Michael George Gebert left North Carolina to avoid the tax collector (see the section on the Regulator Movement later in this chapter) and pushed westward to Tennessee. He settled in the Watauga Settlement in what would become Carter County, Tennesse (Gebert, n. d.), defying King George III of Great Britain and his *Proclamation of 1763* that strictly prohibited colonists from traveling west of the Appalachian Mountains (Kindig, 1999).

The Watauga Settlement was the first permanent settlement in America outside the thirteen original colonies. In 1722, the Watauga settlers wrote and adopted a constitution, the first by independent white people in what would become the United States of America (Dixon, 1989); (Ramsey, 2007). The constitution was thoroughly democratic, and free of religious tests and class distinctions. The British Secretary of State for Colonial Affairs, the Earl of Dunmore, wrote his superiors that the Watauga constitution was a dangerous example to the colonists in forming governments distinct from, and independent of, the Crown (*A Little History*, n. d.). Bogan (2004) states that "the Wataugan constitution and the records of their government have perished." When the Association dissolved, the documents fell into private hands. They are known through the Wataugans' own brief collective testimony and the testimony of early historians of Tennessee. Bogan goes on to explain, "The Wataugan Association was one of the most comprehensive democratic agreements ever penned in the New World, free of religious tests, and class distinctions."

The Watauga Settlement had direct ties with the Regulators, and was located on the Watauga River, a tributary of the Tennessee River. The Transylvania Company, headed by Richard Henderson, made the largest private real estate transaction in United States history when it purchased twenty million acres of land in this area from the Cherokee Native Americans for two thousand pounds and eight thousand pounds in goods, March 17, 1775 (*Transylvania Company*, 2008).

Daniel Boone was a land agent for Henderson. He used the Watauga Settlement as his headquarters to negotiate the land deal. This included land on the Cumberland and Kentucky Rivers. Amid these dealings, settlers purchased the right to remain on Cherokee lands on which they had settled, known as the Watauga Settlement (*Transylvania Company*, 2008).

One of the great Cherokee chiefs, Dragging Canoe, vigorously opposed the sale of Cherokee ancestral hunting grounds and warned that the whites were purchasing a "dark and bloody ground" (Smith, n. d.). At the conclusion of the *Transylvania Treaty of 1775*, Dragging Canoe proved to be prophetic about the fate of Native Americans. Concerning the sale of Cherokee lands, he spoke these haunting words (*Dragging Canoe*, n. d.):

> *"Whole Indian nations have melted away like snowballs in the sun before the white man's advance...Where are the Delawares? They have been reduced to a mere shadow of their former greatness. We had hoped that the white men would not be willing to travel beyond the mountains. Now that hope is gone. They have passed the mountains, and have settled upon Cherokee land. They wish to have that action sanctioned by treaty. When that is gained, the same encroaching spirit will lead them upon other land of the Cherokees, new cessions will be asked. Finally the whole country...will be demanded and the remnant of Ani-Yunwiya, THE REAL PEOPLE, once so great and formidable, will be compelled to seek refuge in some distant wilderness. There they will be permitted to stay only a short while... the extinction of the whole race will be proclaimed."*

Dragging Canoe and his warriors waged war against the white settlers for the next twenty years. The British government encouraged the Cherokee to wage war against the white settlers, and supplied them with ammunition, guns, and other supplies, instructing them to drive out the settlers or drop them dead in their tracks (Smith, n. d.).

The fledgling army of the colonists built Fort Watauga as a base from which to defend the frontier against the British and the hostile Native Americans. In July 1776, the settlers at the fort withstood a two-week siege by the Cherokee. When the siege was broken, the settlers, led by John Sevier, invaded the Cherokee main villages and burned them, making the area immediately surrounding the settlement safe from the Cherokee (Peters, J. & Peters, D., 1996). Sevier went on to become the first governor of Tennessee.

The problems for the settlers did not end. The British Colonel, Patrick Ferguson, had threatened to march over the mountains and lay waste their land with "fire and sword." In late September of 1780, eleven hundred settlers known as the "Overmountain Men" because of their deliberate defiance of the royal mandate prohibiting them from settling west of the Appalachians, mustered at Fort Watauga and marched to King's Mountain, South Carolina to battle Colonel Ferguson and his troops (Hammett, 2000).

The Overmountain Men had no formal military training, no uniforms, no provisions, and most importantly, no orders. They used guerilla warfare tactics, and in one hour of fighting, Ferguson was killed and most of his army captured (Hammett, 2000). Ferguson and his men were trained to fight on the open field and had never encountered guerilla warriors. It is believed by many of the Camp family descendents that Nathaniel Camp, son of Thomas Camp and Winifred Starling Camp, killed the British Colonel Ferguson. Nathaniel Camp's son was in possession of Ferguson's conch shell battle horn that was later donated to the artifact collection of the Daughters of the American Revolution (*Thomas Camp Family*, 2008).

The Battle of King's Mountain proved to be one of the turning points in the Revolutionary War, saving the Patriot cause that had suffered many military setbacks in this region. This victory set off a chain of events that led to the British surrender at Yorktown in 1781 (*Historical Statements*, 1928). This historical background gives us great insight into the dangers of living on the frontier experienced by Michael George Gabbert and the other pioneers in the Watauga Settlement.

Michael George Gebert married twice. He married Catherine Grindstaff around 1755 in Harrisonburg, Rockingham County, Virginia. Grindstaff was born in 1740 in Burke County, North

Carolina. She married Michael George Gebert when she was fifteen years old. They had six children, and Catherine Grindstaff Gebert died at twenty-four years old, after nine years of marriage, in 1764. It is uncertain what caused her death; she probably died giving birth to her sixth child, John Gebert, in 1764 (*Family Group Record: Michael George Gebert*, 2008).

Around 1765, Michael George Gebert married Catherine King. They had two children, Michael, Jr. and Henry. Another source (*Ancestors of Jason Richard Cassell*, 2004) states that they had three children: Michael, Jr., Henry, and Jacob. My family is descended from Michael Gebert, Jr.

The Regulator Movement

I was intrigued when I read that Michael George Gebert left North Carolina in the mid-1700s to avoid the tax collector, because I, too, dislike the tax collector. I found that Michael George Gebert was likely part of the Regulator Movement. This movement in North Carolina was a type of rebellion by colonists in the inland region, or the back country, of North Carolina where the land was not as fertile as in the coastal region. They were taxed the same as the coastal farmers and felt it was unjust. They were upset about officials who charged them excessive fees, falsified records, and engaged in other forms of corruption. The movement's name reflected the people's desire to regulate their own affairs. The movement erupted in violence on several occasions. The public protests began in 1764, and by 1770, officials feared for their safety (*North Carolina Regulators*, 1902); (Powell, n. d); (*Regulator Movement*, 1980).

The Regulators asked to meet with colonial Governor William Tryon but were ignored. They traveled to Hillsborough where the governor lived and camped nearby. On May 16, 1771, they sent word that they wished to meet with the governor. Tryon agreed this time but only if they surrendered their arms, a condition that infuriated the Regulators. Tryon sent word that the Regulators must disperse immediately or they would be fired upon, to which the Regulators famously replied, "Fire and be damned." This threat was the catalyst for the Battle of Alamance, a two-hour engagement. Nine of the governor's men were killed and sixty-one wounded. Six of the Regulators were hanged for treason, but on Tryon's recommendation, the rest were pardoned by King George III of Great Britain. Some consider the Battle of Alamance as the first bloodshed of the American Revolution (Foote, 1846).

Tryon issued pardons for those who swore oaths of allegiance to the royal government. Around sixty-four hundred rebels swore the oath. Many of the Regulators simply moved westward (Powell, n. d.), as Michael George Gebert chose to do. It is not known if Michael George Gebert considered himself a Regulator or if he was a participant in the Battle of Almance. Apparently, he was unhappy enough with the taxation of the colonists in western North Carolina that he moved westward to escape paying high taxes. Like most colonists, he probably had little interest in government and simply wanted to be left alone.

Michael Gebert, Jr. and Elizabeth Brown

My family is directly descended from Michael Gebert, Jr., son of Michael George Gebert and Catherine King, born around October 1765/1766 in the Shenandoah Valley of Virginia. It is around this time that the surname *Gebert* became Anglicized to *Gabbert*. Michael Gabbert, Jr. went with his father to Burke County, North Carolina. He married Elizabeth Brown, born around 1768 in Wilkes County, North Carolina, the daughter of Benjamin Brown and Susan Londerman Brown (*Ancestors of Kevin Dexter Marshall, Generation No. 7*, n. d.).

Michael Gabbert, Jr. migrated to Kentucky via the Wilderness Trail, the principal avenue of westward migration from about 1790–1840. Pioneers followed old buffalo traces and Native American paths, sometimes falling victim to hostile Native American tribes (*Wilderness Road*, 2007). Michael Gabbert, Jr. became one of the early settlers, and eventually a trustee, of the small town of Paoli, Kentucky, located in Cumberland County, Kentucky. Cumberland County later became Clinton County, Tennessee (*Ancestors of Kevin Dexter Marshall, Generation No. 7*, n. d.).

Michael Gabbert, Jr. next migrated to Iowa. He died about 1841 in Farm, Scott County, Iowa. Elizabeth died of smallpox on January 18, 1855. Michael Gabbert, Jr. and Elizabeth Gabbert's son, David, also died from smallpox. They were buried on the family's farm in Scott County, Iowa (*Ancestors of Kevin Dexter Marshall, Generation No. 6*, n. d.). Michael Gabbert, Jr. and Elizabeth Brown Gabbert had sixteen children; two died at birth.

My family is directly descended from George Gabbert, the twelfth child of Michael Gabbert, Jr. and Elizabeth Brown Gabbert. I found information on his brother, David Gabbert (third child), and his wife, Catherine Gabbert that I found interesting. David had red hair, like mine (*Ancestors of Kevin Dexter Marshall, Generation No. 6*, n. d.). I am including this information next in the Gabbert narrative, though we are not directly descended from David and Catherine Gabbert.

David Gabbert and Catherine Giles/Joles

David Gabbert, born January 10, 1793 in Washington County, Virginia and his wife, Catherine (Caty) Giles, born April 5, 1801 in Randolph, North Carolina, were listed as charter members of the Wolf River United Baptist Church established May 5, 1821 in Overland County, Tennessee (*Ancestors of Kevin Dexter Marshall, Generation No. 7*, n. d.). The Clear Fork Baptist Church minutes for April 1821 show David and Catherine Gabbert, as well as several other families, dismissed from membership to join a church more convenient for them (*Cumberland County, KY Archives*, n. d.). This is when the Wolf River United Baptist Church was created (*Charter*

Members, 1821). Overton County, Tennessee borders Cumberland/ Clinton County, Kentucky.

David Gabbert is described in an excerpt from *A Standard History of Champaign County Illinois* (Stewart, 1918) as red-headed, honest, unprepossessing in appearance, eccentric in manner, and a professional land-grabber. He served in the War of 1812 after enlisting in the Kentucky militia. He served in Colonel Barbee's regiment which was a part of General Harrison's brigade. David was nineteen years old in 1812. His military duty took him to the Ohio frontier.

After the war, David returned home and married Catherine Giles/Joles, referred to as Kate, Katie, and Caty. She was the daughter of Thomas Giles/Joles and Nancy Yates (*Ancestors of Kevin Dexter Marshall Generation No. 6,* n. d.). The year 1821 found David and Catherine Gabbert married and living in Overton County, Tennessee. By the 1830s, they relocated to Vermilion County, Illinois. It is believed that they died in Scott County, Iowa where they had migrated by the 1840s (Gabbert, 1990).

Chapter 3
The Gabberts Move Westward

George Gabbert and Elizabeth Phillips/Goodwin

George Gabbert, the twelth of sixteen children born to Michael Gabbert, Jr. and Elizabeth Brown, was born in 1808 in Cumberland County, Kentucky. He married Elizabeth Phillips around 1839 in Clarke County, Georgia. Some sources say Elizabeth's maiden name was Goodwin (*Individual Record: George Gabbert*, 2008).

George Gabbert was a younger son, probably a factor in the direction his life took. Under the old European idea of primogeniture, the eldest son inherited the lion's share of wealth, office, and social standing (*Primogeniture*, 2008). This idea carried over into colonial America, and was probably a strong influence in George's life.

George Gabbert was a winner in the Georgia Land Lottery of 1821. The government held a land lottery to distribute seized Cherokee and Creek Native American land to United States citizens. Georgia had conducted three previous land lotteries in 1805,

1807, and 1820. The 1821 lottery was to distribute land seized from the Creek Native Americans (*Georgia Land Lotteries*, 2007). Government deed records show that George Gabbert of Putnam County, Georgia, was awarded lot forty-six, section seven of Monroe County, Georgia in the 1821 Georgia Land Lottery (*Land Records*, 1821).

We can learn a few facts about George Gabbert's life by studying the requirements to participate in the lottery. To participate in the 1821 Land Lottery, one had to be a citizen of the United States and a resident of the state of Georgia for three years immediately preceding the *Act of 15 May 1821* that established the lottery and established Monroe and Montgomery Counties of Georgia. People prohibited from the 1821 draw included participants of previous lotteries, anyone legally drafted during the War of 1812 who refused to serve or hire a substitute, anyone who deserted the military, and anyone who left Georgia to escape the laws of the state, to avoid paying debts, or had not paid taxes. Convicts could not participate, but their children were treated as orphans and could participate. From these requirements, we can conclude that George Gabbert was a citizen of the United States who had lived in Georgia since at least 1818, was at least eighteen years old, was not an indentured servant, was not in prison, and paid his debts and taxes.

It is important to remember the British colony of Georgia was originally populated by persons who had been jailed in Great Britain because of nonpayment of debt and other crimes. The British government, because of its desire to colonize America, released a prisoner if he or she agreed to go to the New World and help colonization efforts. Georgia supplied cotton, sometimes called "white gold," the raw material for the British textile industry. Georgia also grew corn, rice, and indigo, all valued commodities in Great Britain. The British had established colonies in America for its economic gain. Colonists made money for the mother country (Stevens, 1847).

George Gabbert married Elizabeth Phillips/ Goodwin in Clarke County, Georgia, located in northeastern Georgia. The family migrated to Lowndes County, Alabama (*Ancestors of Kevin Dexter Marshall, Generation No. 7, n. d.*). George and Elizabeth Gabbert produced several children. A son, John, became a doctor but died young. My family is directly descended from their daughter, Julia Ann Virginia Gabbert. Using data from the federal census of 1870 for Drew County, Arkansas, and information from her headstone in Union Ridge Cemetery, Drew County, Arkansas, we can determine that Julia was born December 31, 1827 in Lowndes County, Alabama. The family moved to Jersey County, Illinois, and then to Hernando, Desoto County, Mississippi where George Gabbert died.

After George Gabbert's death, the family moved southwestward to Monticello, Drew County, Arkansas. Dr. Lafayette "Fay" Gabbert, George Gabbert's nephew, and son of Michael Gabbert, III, accompanied the family to Monticello.

Dr. Michael Gabbert III and Elizabeth Dennis

George Gabbert's brother, Michael Gabbert III, was born in 1799 in Overton County, Tennessee. He married Elizabeth Dennis, a widow with three children whom he reared and educated as his own. He became a doctor and practiced in Memphis, Tennessee. He was considered the best yellow fever doctor in the south but, ironically, died of that disease in 1852. At the time of his death, he was treating ninety-three cases of yellow fever and had predicted that all would recover except three. That was, in fact, the outcome. Sadly, Elizabeth Dennis Gabbert sought a divorce in 1826, an unusual turn of events for that time.

Dr. Michael Gabbert III had three stepsons who took his name: Lafayette Gabbert, Solon Gabbert, and Lycuryus Gabbert. All became medical doctors. Dr. Lafayette "Fay" Gabbert was born June 14, 1828 in Somerville, Fayette County, Tennessee, and died November 20, 1886 in Drew County, Arkansas. He acquired eighty acres of government land in Drew County in 1859 (*United States Department of Interior,* n. d.). Lafayette Gabbert is buried in Oakland Cemetery, Old Cemetery, Block One, in Monticello, Arkansas.

In *Old Times Not Forgotten,* the author discusses the early history of the town of Monticello. A story is told of three local men who, in 1878–1879, treed a bear in a large, red oak tree in the front yard of Dr. Gabbert's home on South Gabbert Street. The bear was shot, and the meat was sold in a butcher shop on Main Street (Dearmond, 1980).

Lafayette Gabbert married Mary Jane McCorkle. The daughter of Lafayette Gabbert and Mary Jane McCorkle was Loula Gabbert, who married Henry Wallace Wells. A detailed account of the wedding of Loula Gabbert and Henry Wallace Wells was reprinted in the July 21, 2010 edition of the *Advance Monticellonian* in the column, *"From the Museum,"* written by Sheila Lampkin. Lampkin acquired this account from Henrietta "Henri" Mason, granddaughter of Loula Gabbert and Henry Wallace Wells:

> *"Married at the First Presbyterian Church in this city (Monticello) on the 22nd of November, 1877, by Rev. T. P. Stone, were Miss Loula Gabbert and Mr. H. W. Wells, both of this place. The above wedding was one of the most brilliant and beautiful affairs in this city for many years. The church was handsomely decorated and festooned with flowers that contrasted with the brown walls and made a picturesque scene. The building was crowded to its fullest capacity with ladies and gentlemen to witness the ceremony. At 7 o'clock the bridegroom and bride entered the house accompanied by the following attendants (groomsmen and bridesmaids): Mr. A. A. Ramsey and Miss Columbia Wells, Mr. J. G. Taylor and Miss Lena Slemons, Mr. T. A. Patrick and Miss Blanche Matthews and Mr. A. R. Chestnutt and Miss Henrietta Wells. After the ceremony, the*

bridal party and invited guests repaired to the residence of Dr. Gabbert, the bride's father, where the newly-made pair received the congratulations of their many friends. After which supper was announced and the company entered the dining room and enjoyed one of the most sumptuous repasts ever spread in this city. The table literally groaned under the weight of good things, and everything that the heart could wish for or the appetite craves in the way of eatables was to be found on the table. After ample justice had been done to the rich viands and dainty delicacies the crowd entered the parlor where the young and gay passed several hours in the happy maze of the dance. The next day the bridal party was again feted and feasted in the home of W. T. Wells, Esquire, where bar-b-que meat, roasted turkey and chicken adorned the table besides all kinds of sweet-meats, cakes, custards, etc. The party took supper at the residence of the bride-groom where another excellent repast was served, and afterwards a few hours were given to the dance which closed the happy and liveliest occasion."

The Presbyterian Church where this wedding took place was located behind the present First Missionary Baptist Church and the Pilgrim Rest AME Church on North Bailey Street. The Old Monticello Cemetery on Wausau Street was behind the Presbyterian Church. Rev. T. P. Stone, who performed the nuptials, is discussed later in this book. Henry Wallace Wells and Loula Gabbert Wells lived in a two-story house behind the present location of the Monticello branch of the Southeast Arkansas Regional Library. Henry Wallace Wells become a prominent attorney and district judge in Monticello. Loula Gabbert Wells died at thirty years old, and Henry Wallace Wells never remarried (Lampkin, 2010). Loula Gabbert Wells and Henry Wallace Wells are buried in Oakland Cemetery, Old Cemetery Section, Block One, and were the parents of Adolphus Taylor Wells, buried in Oakland Cemetery, Pierce Addition, Block Three.

Adolphus Taylor Wells, who rose to prominence as a business-man in Monticello, was the father of a current and prominent citizen of Monticello, Henrietta "Henri" Wells Mason. Henrietta Wells married Carl Mason, a native of Iowa, who became a promi-nent businessman and professor of economics at the University of Arkansas at Monticello. Carl Mason is buried in Oakland Cemetery, Pierce Addition, Block Three. Children of Carl Mason and Henrietta Wells are Martha Mason Accettullo, Mark Mason, and Mary Jane Mason Vaughn.

As I was growing up, I was friends with Martha and Mary Jane Mason and remain so today. Martha was an attendant in my wedding in 1981, and I never realized that we had common ances-tors. Martha, Mary Jane, and I became educators—I wonder what Julia Ann Virginia Gabbert Camp and her husband, George Camp, both of whom were school teachers and our common ancestors, would have thought of us. Gabbert Street in Monticello, located two blocks east of Main Street, is named in honor of our Gabbert ancestors.

George Crenshaw Camp and Julia Ann Virginia Gabbert Camp

My family is directly descended from Julia Ann Virginia Gabbert Camp and George Crenshaw Camp. Julia was born December 31, 1827 in Lowndes County, Alabama. According to courthouse records in DeSoto County, Mississippi, Julia Ann Virginia Gabbert married George Crenshaw Camp on November 17, 1845. David J. White, Justice of the Peace, performed the ceremony (DeSoto County, Mississippi: Marriage Records Book 1 1845–1847). Julia was eighteen or nineteen years old at the time of her wedding.

George and Julia Camp were enumerated in the 1850 federal census report for Desoto County, Mississippi. Also enumerated in their household were two children, a three-year-old boy (the census indicates that the name was uncertain; however, this child was their oldest, William), and a two-year-old girl, Martha, who was to become my great-grandmother. Also enumerated in this household was Lafayette Gabbert, a twenty-one-year-old doctor born in Tennessee.

The 1850 federal census report for DeSoto County Mississippi described George Camp as forty-four years old, and a school teacher born in North Carolina. If this information is accurate, George Camp was born in 1806, only three years after Thomas Jefferson made the historic Louisiana Purchase of 1803. Mississippi and Arkansas were later to become states from this territory that more than doubled the physical size of the United States.

According to Bobby Gilliam (2012), a direct descendent of George and Julia Camp, George Camp lost a leg due to frostbite that occurred when he was traveling to a remote location to teach school. Drew County Cemetery Records (2002) lists George Crenshaw Camp's date of death as July 7, 1868. The 1850 census described Julia Camp as twenty-four years old, twenty years younger than her husband. It is likely that George Camp was a widower when he met and married Julia Gabbert.

It is not known when or why the Camp family migrated to Drew County, Arkansas, but according to the minutes of the Old Florence Cumberland Presbyterian Church of Drew County, Arkansas, George C. Camp was received in the membership of the church, March 8, 1851 by transfer of letter, indicating that the family was in Drew County by early 1851. The minutes further reveal that George C. Camp died in July 1868 at sixty-two years old, leaving Julia Camp a widow with six children.

One explanation for the family's relocation to Drew County, Arkansas may have been their desire to get out of the mosquito-infested lowlands of the Mississippi River Delta. Eastern Drew County is in the Delta, but the city of Monticello is located in the hill part of the county. Mosquito-borne illnesses such as malaria and yellow fever plagued the early pioneers in the Delta. Though the Delta has rich farmland, the early settlers had to drain swamps so that they could farm the land. Disease, insects, and flooding often made life miserable for inhabitants of the Delta. As a bride in 1981, I became a resident of McGehee, Arkansas located in the Mississippi River Delta. I can assure you that even with modern insecticides, the bugs can still make life miserable for Delta inhabitants.

It is interesting that George and Julia Camp were not in agreement about religion. The Old Florence Church records do not list Julia Camp on the membership roster. The only other Camps within the church membership were W. H. Camp and Melinda J. Camp, the children of George and Julia Camp.

It is also interesting that George and Julia Camp are not buried in the same cemetery. George C. Camp is buried in the Mt. Tabor Cemetery near the location of the Old Florence Church. Julia Camp is buried in Union Ridge Cemetery next to her oldest son, William Camp. According to the information on her headstone, Julia Camp died March 20, 1918, placing her close to ninety-one years old at the time of her death.

I asked my mother, Louise Hawkins Webb, why George and Julia Camp were buried in different cemeteries, and she told me that in those days, people were buried in the communities where they lived due to the absence of embalming. Julia left the Mt. Tabor community after the death of her husband. She relocated to the Bowser/Lacey community, probably to take a teaching position to support herself and her children. The 1870 federal census report for Veasey Township, Drew County, Arkansas, enumerated Julia Camp as head of household and described her as forty-three years old and a school teacher born in Alabama. Julia Camp was one of the first female school teachers in Drew County; the 1850 Professional Census of Drew County lists only nine teachers, all males. The 1860 Professional Census of Drew County lists eighteen teachers, only one of whom, Eliza Wilson, was female. The 1870 Professional Census of Drew County lists Julia Camp as one of twenty-two school teachers in Drew County, only six of whom were female. The other members of her family enumerated in the 1870 census report for Drew County are as follows:

William Camp, twenty-three years old, a farmer, and born in Mississippi. Private William (Bill) Camp served in the Confederate States of America Thirty-first Louisiana Infantry. This unit was formed at Vicksburg, Mississippi, during the summer of 1862. In the Battle of Chickasaw Bluff, the unit lost nine soldiers killed and sixteen wounded, and the unit was later captured defending the city of Vicksburg, Mississippi. After being exchanged for Union prisoners-of-war, the unit was placed in Thomas' Brigade, Trans-Mississippi Department, and fought in several skirmishes in Louisiana, then disbanded in the spring of 1865 when Bill Camp was eighteen years old. Bill Camp never married and drew a CSA pension in Drew County, Arkansas. He is buried next to his mother, Julia Ann Virginia Gabbert Camp, in Union Ridge Cemetery in Drew County, Arkansas.

Martha A. Camp, twenty-one years old, and a homemaker born in Mississippi.

George L. Camp, nineteen years old and born in Mississippi

Melinda J. Camp, seventeen years old and born in Mississippi

Adaline S. Camp, fifteen years old and born in Mississippi

Steven E. Camp, fourteen years old and born in Mississippi

Old Florence Church records state Melinda J. Camp joined the church by experience on July 29, 1872. On April 11, 1875, she was dropped from the church membership, having joined with the "Campbellites Church." The family believes that Julia Camp, Melinda's mother, had already joined with the Campbellites, the forerunners to the modern-day Church of Christ (Bowker, 1997). Melinda Camp was the mother of Marietta Camp Webb. This family helped form the Monticello Church of Christ in its infancy, and many of Melinda Camp's descendents are members of that church today. It is interesting that the Monticello Church of Christ is located on Gabbert Street, named in honor of Julia Gabbert Camp's forebears.

It is interesting that Martha, twenty-one years old, was unmarried, which was unusual for that time. Perhaps this was because so many young men were killed in the Civil War, and therefore there were few eligible bachelors. Arkansas lost about ten thousand men in this war (Davis, 2004). Martha Camp eventually married the man who was my great-grandfather, William George Griffin.

According to Julia Camp's granddaughter, Marietta Burks Webb (born near the "Scrouge Out" community in Drew County, July 24, 1878; died November 8, 1983), Julia was a much sought-after midwife. In *Old Times Not Forgotten* (DeArmond, 1980), Marietta Webb was quoted as saying, "She (Julia Camp) delivered in the homes by candle or lamp. She would stay two or three days just waiting for the baby. Everyone who had a baby wanted her. There was no charge. She delivered every one of mine except one; she brought William into the world when she was seventy years old." She also practiced the healing arts using herbal remedies (DeArmond, 1980). Bobby Gilliam (2012), of Shreveport, Louisiana, and a descendant of Julia Ann Virginia Gabbert Camp, states that she gathered herbs to use as medicine for her cousin, Dr. Lafayette Gabbert, and that she was very much like a pharmacist. Prior to her death in 1983, Marietta Burks Webb was one hundred five years old, making her, at that time, the oldest living person in Drew County. She married James William Webb, who died young.

The Old Florence Cumberland Presbyterian Church is one of the early churches in Drew County, and was the spiritual home of some of the Gabberts and Camps. It has great historical significance. It had several of the old, pioneer families of the area among its membership and interred in its cemetery, and it had a slave cemetery outside the boundaries of the white cemetery. None of the slave graves are marked. Many of these early settlers brought their Presbyterian faith with them from the Carolinas, Tennessee, and Kentucky where ancestry was often traced back to the highlands of Scotland and Northern Ireland where Presbyterianism was the dominant religion.

Chapter 4
The Old Florence Cumberland Presbyterian Church: Spiritual Home of Some of the Camps and Gabberts

The official minute book of the Old Florence Cumberland Presbyterian Church. Photo by Judy Webb Hubbell.

Old Florence Cumberland Presbyterian Church

The Protestant Reformation (1517–1648) ushered in radical new religious thinking in Europe. The teachings of John Calvin and his student, John Knox, planted the seeds for the Presbyterian Church in Europe. It is generally held that the Presbyterian faith was brought to America from Scotland and Northern Ireland by the Scots-Irish immigrants in the early 1700s. The event that spurred the departure of the Scots-Irish from Scotland and Northern Ireland was the *Test Act of 1704*, which required all Crown officials in Great Britain to be of the Anglican faith, thus excluding the Presbyterian Scots-Irish from political power. It stripped the Presbyterian clergy of its authority to perform marriages (Barkley, 1993). As a result, many of the Scots-Irish came to America. The first wave of these immigrants settled in the rich Shenandoah Valley of Virginia; they followed the Great Wagon Road south and gradually dispersed throughout the southern United States, taking their religion with them (Bainton, 1952); (Foote, 1846); (Leyburn, 1962); (Smith, 1999); (Sweet, 1936).

By the mid-1800s, there were enough Presbyterians in the Old Florence community of Drew County, Arkansas, to constitute an organized congregation. The Old Florence Cumberland Presbyterian Church, located in northeastern Drew County, left the official minutes of the church in a booklet that wound up in the possession of Lillie Mae Mullis of Camden, great-aunt of Monticello businessman, Sammy Mullis. When Lillie Mae Mullis died, her son, a resident of Delaware, gave the booklet to Connie Mullis as a donation to the Drew County Historical Museum. Covering the years 1847–1880, it is a treasure that is kept under lock and key in the archives of the museum (Mullis, 2010). It is amazing that this booklet survived one hundred sixty three years and remains, for the most part, legible. It is a valuable primary source document for researchers. Karen Groce (2001) transcribed the minutes and posted them on the Drew County Genweb website.

The *Drew County, Arkansas Cemetery Records* (2002) offers the following history of the church:

> *"Old Florence was once a community comprising a Presbyterian Church and cemetery, approximately four acres which was part of the Kirby place. It is not known if the land was donated by the Kirby family but is now property of Presbyterians of Monticello, Ark. Around 1890 the church was taken apart and moved to New Florence which is approximately four miles west. There was a black cemetery adjoining the white which was fenced into a pasture by Richard Pittman, son-in-law of Mr. Kirby. The headstones were eventually destroyed. It was thought to be a slave cemetery. This was told to Mrs. V. G. Moore by Ruth Posey Smith who lived near old Florence in her youth."*

The church was constituted in 1847 one year after Drew County was formed from what was then Arkansas and Bradley Counties. By September 25, 1868, the church, an integral part of this early Drew County settlement, had eighty-three members, a large congregation for the time. Though the church dissolved in the mid-1930s, the early records of the church have been preserved, giving historians a valuable primary source for genealogical information as well as insight into the culture and daily lives of these early Drew County pioneers. Old Florence was one of the first communities in Drew County; the original settlement was about three miles to the southeast on the Old Military Road (DeArmond, 1980); (*Encyclopedia of Arkansas*, 2010); (*Manuscript*, 1847–1880).

Early Settlers in Old Florence

The index of church members reflects the westward migration of settlers in the 1800s when Arkansas was part of the frontier. In her history of the Selma Methodist Church, Carolyn Haisty (2008) states that several families came from North Carolina to the often intertwined communities of Selma, Florence, and Mt. Tabor. The following families are listed in Haisty's history of the Selma Methodist Church: Hawks, Hicks, Bartlett, Ruth, Ayecock (Aycock?), Spivey, King, and Paschall.

Some of these surnames are listed in the Old Florence church records. Haisty aptly comments that the communities of Selma, Florence, and Mt. Tabor, and their families, "were and still are intertwined." Haisty explains that many of these early settlers crossed the Mississippi River by ferry to Gaines Landing. They made their way inland, and upon reaching the high ground that rises above the Delta, determined that the lush timberland and abundant wildlife made this a desirable settlement, and proceeded to carve out homesteads. The Old Florence community was located within three miles, by automobile, of where the hill portion of Drew County drops off into the flat Mississippi River Delta.

Haisty states that in 1857–1858, a wagon train led by Reverend John Harding Breedlove brought a number of settlers from Wilkinson County, Georgia to the Selma, Florence, and Mt. Tabor communities of Drew County. Breedlove's wife, Frances Elizabeth Echols, and extended family accompanied him. Haisty lists the following families who made the trip: Breedlove, Jesse Peacock, John Tillman Hoover, and James H. Bush families.

Early History of the Church

The Old Florence church kept meticulous records, going back to its inception in 1847. It was first organized as a Cumberland Presbyterian church and called Pine Grove. The church records state the following:

> "We whose names are undersigned feeling desirous to enjoy the
> means of grace and being pleased with the doctrine & discipline
> of the Cumberland Presbyterian Church do agree and covenant
> to join that church and form ourselves into a society known

by the name of Pine Grove Church under the care of Mount Prairie Presbytery and do look unto them for such supplies of the word and ordinances as God in his providence may enable this 8th day of August A. D. 1847."

On April 13, 1856, the church became known as Pine Flat. Church records state the name of Pine Flat was changed to Florence by the Bartholomew Presbytery in March 1860. The church building no longer exists, but the cemetery, though neglected, is still located in the community. It is located near the Selma community on the west side of the highway, before the Pine Hill intersection on privately owned land. A stand of trees has been left in and around the cemetery.

Pictured above: Old Florence Cemetery in the Selma community of Drew County. It is situated in a grove of hardwood trees on privately owned farm land. The church was probably located east of the cemetery, and the slave cemetery was probably behind the white cemetery. Many of the headstones are still legible but, sadly, there are

no markers in the slave cemetery. This cemetery is of great historical significance because it contains the graves of several of the early settlers of Drew County and contains a documented, though lost, slave cemetery. Photo by Judy Webb Hubbell.

Charter Members

Records of the Old Florence Church provide us with a glimpse into the lives of early Drew County pioneer families. It gives us a sense of the morals and values of rural Arkansans of that time. The church began with eleven members: Thomas P. Stone, the minister, and his wife, Winnie S. Stone, Benjamin H. Wilson, Margaret Wilson, Elizabeth Scott, William H. Paschall, Sarah Paschall, James H. Owens, Salina Owens, William E. Owens, and John Owens. Many of the descendants of these charter members live in Drew County today.

Church membership was based on receipt of a letter of good standing from another church, recommendation by a member in good standing, or through what the church called an "experience of grace." Often initials were used in place of given names, making it difficult to determine the gender of members, but the pronouns in the minutes help make some of these determinations.

The church may have been formed earlier than 1847; the church baptismal records show that D. B. Mason and his wife, M. A. Mason, had five children baptized during the years 1839–1846, indicating that the church may have existed before it joined with the Cumberland Presbyterians. The records show that the five Mason children were baptized by R. Burrow, Jno. Greer and A. Herron.

Census information chronicles the westward migration of these pioneers as the American frontier kept steadily pushing westward. John Isaac(s), a charter member of the Old Florence church, was enumerated in the 1870 federal census report for Bartholomew Township, Drew County, Arkansas, in which he was described as a forty-five-year-old farmer born in Pennsylvania. His wife,

Harriet, also a charter member, was described in the census data as a thirty-two-year-old housekeeper born in Mississippi. Their five children, ranging in age from fifteen years to two months old, were also enumerated in this household. Three of the children were born in Mississippi, and the two youngest were born in Arkansas.

John Donaldson, another charter member of the Old Florence Church, was enumerated in the 1870 federal census report for Bartholomew Township, Drew County, Arkansas, in which he was described as seventy-one years old and a farmer born in North Carolina. His wife, Nellie, sixty-eight years old, was also born in North Carolina. The births of their children chronicle their journey westward. Their daughter, Sarah, twenty-four years old, was born in Alabama, and their son, William, twenty-one years old, was born in Mississippi according to the census data.

Ministers of the Congregation

The first mention of a minister is found in the church minutes of March 8, 1851, referring to Thomas P. Stone, one of the charter members, as "minister." Stone was an early Drew County pioneer, settling on two hundred eighty acres of land acquired from the federal government between 1856 and 1896 (United States Department of the Interior, n. d.) making him a substantial landowner. It is interesting that the minister, as revealed in the minutes of September 11, 1854, was a slave owner.

Stone's first recorded baptism performed in the Pine Grove Church was that of Sarah C. Mason in 1851. The church records refer to both infant and adult baptisms. According to the records, Stone served as minister of the congregation until 1879. He died two years later. The June 1, 1881 edition of the *Arkansas Gazette* posted on the Drew County Genweb website by Jann Woodard (2001), commented on Stone's death:

> *"The Rev. T. P. Stone, more familiarly known as "Father Stone" a Cumberland Presbyterian minister, died at his residence about ten miles south of this place last Thursday afternoon. His was an eventful life. He was one of the early settlers of this county, having immigrated (sic) from Mississippi to this state about forty years ago. He is said to have preached the first sermon ever preached in Memphis. He was in his 80th year."*

J. P. Stanley, one of the church leaders, gave this account to the session about Stone's resignation and the acquisition of a new minister, J. S. Weaver:

> *"Since the last meeting of this Church our beloved pastor Rev. T. P. Stone resigned his pastoral charge and at the meeting of the Bartholomew Presbytery of the Cumberland Presbyterian Church. I secured the services of Brother J. S. Weaver for the next presbyterial year for which I promise to pay him the sum of seventy-five dollars or that Florence congregation would pay seventy-five dollars or more and I hope the members of this church will meet this obligation punctual as Bro. Weaver is in need of all the help he can get to prepare to more effectually preach the Gospel."*

Benjamin Alexander Ingram became the pastor of the Florence Cumberland Presbyterian Church in 1890. Born on October 5, 1850, in Jefferson County, Arkansas, his ministry, somewhat brief, was cut short by his untimely death due to swamp fever at age forty-two. Ingram was widely admired as a hard worker who was successful in winning converts. Some years he traveled six thousand miles on horseback. One year he was said to have preached three hundred sixty five sermons. A circuit rider, Ingram traveled sixty-five miles from one end of the circuit to another (*Cumberland Presbyterian*, 1893).

Ingram also served as minister of the Rose Hill Cumberland Presbyterian Church (*Benjamin Alexander Ingram*, 1893), a congregation that is still active in Drew County. My husband, Billy James Hubbell, and I were married at Rose Hill, February 21, 1981. Ingram's obituary appeared in the September 27, 1892 edition of the *Arkansas Gazette* that was posted on the Drew County AR Genweb website by Woodard (2001):

> "*Rev. B. A. Ingram, a prominent minister of the Cumberland Presbyterian Church died at his home near Monticello, September 22, of swamp fever. Deceased was well and favorably known throughout Southeast Arkansas, and the announcement of his death will cause a widespread sorrow. Though a comparatively young man, there is perhaps no minister who has labored more assiduously for the spread of the gospel, or done more hard service, often riding for weeks through swamps and thinly populated settlements to bring the bread of life to the needy. He leaves a wife and a large family of children with a host of friends to mourn his untimely end.*"

Benjamin Alexander Ingram is buried in Camp Ground Cemetery, also known as Mount Pleasant Cemetery, located about eight miles north of Monticello, Arkansas. The Cleveland County, Arkansas Marriage Records, 1873–1880, Book A-1, records the marriage of Benjamin Ingram, age twenty-three, and Elizabeth Trawick, age seventeen. Elizabeth T. Trawick was born in Alabama, January 23, 1856. She was left a widow with nine children, the youngest of whom was only a week old when Benjamin A. Ingram died in 1892.

The 1910 federal census report for Marion Township, Drew County, Arkansas, indicates that Elizabeth T. Ingram, age fifty-four, was head of her household. Her household consisted of Freddie May Ingram, age nineteen, Benjamin Ingram, age seventeen, Ripley Trawick, age seventy-six, and Mary Trawick, age seventy-four. Elizabeth Trawick Ingram had her parents living with her, perhaps to help with rearing her children and putting food on the table. The census report records the interesting fact that Ripley Trawick's father was born in France and his mother in Alabama. Mary Trawick's parents were both born in Alabama. This surname is sometimes spelled *Traywick.*

The 1930 federal census report for Marion Township, Drew County, Arkansas, enumerates Bennie Ingram, age thirty-seven, as the head of his household consisting of his spouse, Florence Ingram, a child, Marjorie M. Ingram, age nine, and Elizabeth T. Ingram, age seventy-four.

Marjorie M. Ingram, daughter of Bennie Ingram and Florence Rogers Ingram, went on to become a beloved citizen of Monticello. Most remember her as Marjorie Mae Bond, a talented musician and the wife of Judge Clifton Bond of Monticello. Mrs. Bond died April 9, 2011 at age ninety. Her obituary on the Stephenson-Dearman Funeral Home website states that she began playing music for First Presbyterian Church in Monticello at twelve years old. She later played for First Baptist Church of Monticello for many years and was the organist for Stephenson-Dearman Funeral Home in Monticello.

Marjorie Mae Ingram Bond graduated from Monticello High School, obtained a Bachelor of Arts degree in music from the University of Arkansas at Fayetteville, and attended the Cincinnati Conservatory of Music. She taught music at Monticello High School and at the University of Arkansas at Fayetteville. She received a Bachelor of Arts degree in English from Arkansas A & M College and was a former homecoming queen at both Monticello High School and Arkansas A & M College. She had the distinction of being the first female member of the Monticello Rotary Club. Marjorie Mae Ingram Bond and Judge Clifton Bond were married sixty-two years (*Marjorie Mae Bond: February 1, 1921–April 9 2011*).

Elizabeth Trawick Ingram, grandmother of Marjorie Mae Ingram Bond, never remarried. She died September 2, 1939, and is buried in Camp Ground Cemetery. She lived as a widow for forty-seven years (*Cumberland Presbyterian,* 1939). Two of Benjamin Alexander Ingram's sons became Cumberland Presbyterian ministers, as did three grandsons. W. T. Ingram, one of Benjamin Alexander Ingram's grandsons, served as president of the Memphis Theological Seminary from 1964–1978 (Campbell, 1985).

Deacons and Elders

The Old Florence Cumberland Presbyterian Church was governed by a body of deacons and elders. The minute book lists the following men as deacons and elders from 1847 to 1880: Amos Boyte, B. H. Wilson, W. H. Paschall, J. R. Eager, W. D. Munroe, A. G. McGowan, C. J. Bean, E. A. Howel, J. P. Tagart, Thomas Howel, J. P. Stanley, and Dempsey Touchstone. These leaders in the church were expected to live moral, upright lives and serve as an example for the congregation.

One of them struggled with temptation and periodically lapsed from grace. E. A. Howel was elected and ordained an elder on January 13, 1867. However, on April 14, 1867, Howel requested that his name be withdrawn from membership in the congregation. On October 20, 1867, Howel was again received into membership of the Florence congregation. On July 11, 1868, it was reported to church leaders that Howel was guilty of "immoral conduct." On September 12, 1869, Howel again requested that his name be dropped. A year later, on September 11, 1870, Howel was received for the third time as a member of the Florence congregation. Another report of alleged immoral conduct surfaced on July 9, 1871. Oddly, this was the date of the baptism of Howel's children, Edward A. Howel and Elizabeth Jane Howel. The minute book does not reveal the outcome of this allegation, but information is recorded in the index of deaths at the end of the minute book that Howel died on February 22, 1872, indicating he was a church member at the time of his death.

Teachings of the Church

The church required personal accountability from its members. The deacons and elders played active and critical roles in the governance of the church. Discipline was administered liberally by the ruling body, and members monitored the morality of their brothers and sisters of the church. When misconduct was reported to the governing body, action was taken.

The minute book reveals that in 1860, M. E. Paschall was reported for "disorderly conduct" and was suspended from church membership, but it was not recorded. His membership was restored August 19, 1866 and the minutes state, "his name still stands where first recorded and is now a member in full fellowship in Florence Congregation." The minutes do not reveal the nature of the disorderly conduct or the reason that his suspension was not recorded.

Drinking alcohol was not tolerated by the church. The minutes tell that two of the ruling elders were appointed to talk with W. G. Donagan who had been reported as having been intoxicated; Donagan admitted guilt. The minutes of January 13, 1867 state that "Brother Donagan confessed the crime and acknowledged sorrow and promised to refrain in the future was forgiven by the committee."

The church elders often took swift and decisive action against those who violated the rules of the church. The minutes of March 8, 1868 state that "charges were then brought before the session against Brother John T. Eager for very improper conduct and he having absconded is therefore by the session excluded from the church." A committee was appointed to talk with Eager; they reported that Eager "acknowledged himself to be unworthy of membership and sent a request to the session that his name be withdrawn from the church which request was by the session granted."

Dancing was not tolerated and seemed to be a common lapse from grace by a number of the members. The women seemed to be particularly susceptible to the temptation of dancing. The September 12, 1869 minutes state that "it being known to the session that Sister Harriet Isaack had been dancing, Elders Howel and Tagart voluntarily talked to her. She confessed she had done wrong and expressed sorrow for the same and the session forgave her."

On February 12, 1870, the minute book states that it was reported to the session that W. S. Paschall, Josephine E. Richardson, C. E. Paschall, and G. A. Hawks had been dancing. A committee was appointed to confer with them. The committee reported to the session that three of the culprits, Josephine E. Richardson, C. E. Paschall, and G. A. Hawk asked for forgiveness, but W. S. Paschall, not willing to give up dancing, requested that his name be withdrawn for the Florence congregation.

The church expected members to be conscientious about their requirements for membership. The October 13, 1872 minutes state that "Cornelia and Susan E. Hawk...joined the church and have of their own account neglected to be baptized and having since been dancing, the session thinks proper to discontinue their names as members of Florence congregation." The session was also informed that Sister G. A. Hawk had confessed to dancing (again) and promised (again) not to indulge in that activity, and was forgiven (again) by the session. However, Sister G. A. Hawk soon broke that promise. The April 13, 1873 minutes state that a non-repentant Sister Hawk "reported that she would make no promises of reformation but expected she might continue to indulge in the practice of dancing." The session suspended her from church membership.

The May 12, 1878 minutes of the session state that three women and one man, Josephine Youngblood, Anna K. Shults, C. J. Richardson, and Josephine E. Richardson had been reported for dancing. The women did not repent but requested their names be removed from the membership. Only C. J. Richardson asked for and received forgiveness by the session.

Some members experienced serious legal problems. The March 28, 1875 minutes resolved that "Brother J. T. Lytle has been convicted of grand larceny and is now confined in the state penitentiary that his name be dropped from the roll as unworthy to be a member of Florence congregation."

The August 13, 1876 minutes tell of "slanderous reports circulating against L. C. Goff," a female church member. Apparently there was some truth to the rumors; four days later, she requested that her name be dropped from the church because she was unworthy of church membership.

Male members of the congregation often struggled with immoral conduct, and it seems that the ruling elders tried to be fair in their judgments. Brethren G. D. Lytle and William Isaac were reported to the session for behaving immorally. The committee appointed to investigate the transgressions found Lytle not guilty of immoral conduct, and he was exonerated by the session. Isaac requested his name be withdrawn from the membership.

Jake Bradshaw, as related in the March 12, 1871 minutes, was charged with immoral conduct. The elders met with him, and he acknowledged his transgressions and asked for the committee to be patient with him in his attempt to reform. However, the December 1871 minutes report that Bradshaw requested that his name be withdrawn from the membership. The 1870 federal census report for Bartholomew Township enumerated Jacob Bradshaw and described him as twenty-two years old and a farmer born in South Carolina. He was the only member of his household, apparently a young man alone in the world.

Evangelistic Efforts

The church also provided a social life and entertainment for the community. The church records tell of a "protracted meeting," what would today be called a revival that commenced on Sunday, August 21, 1859. Arkansas natives can imagine how hot it must have been in late August, before the advent of electricity, in a crowded church with the preacher spouting hell fire and brimstone. According to the minutes, the protracted meeting was fruitful. Nineteen converts joined the church: W. M. Robertson, M. E. Paschall, H. J. Hawks, Eliza E. Stone, D. J. Mason, J. N. Mason, Hannah E. Donaldson, Sarah A. Donaldson, A. M. Womack, Mary J. Paschall, Artimisia R. Touchstone, D. G. Agea, Eliza A. Gabbert, J. L. Donaldson, James P. Donaldson, J. M. Townsen, A. G. McGowan, H. C. Stone, and Permelia J. Hasty.

Singing conventions, sometimes referred to as "singing schools," were a popular form of entertainment in rural communities such as Old Florence. The mother of this researcher, Louise Hawkins Webb (b. 1919) lived near the Old Florence community during the waning years of the church when she was a teenager. She worked as a live-in housekeeper for an old couple who paid her $2.50 per week. The couple was of the Pentecostal faith and often held church meetings in their home. As was the custom of the day, the live-in hired help had to obey the household rules of their employers, a vestige of the indentured servitude system. The couple did not allow Louise to socialize in the community (Webb, 2010).

"At the time, I was sweet on a boy who attended the singing school at Old Florence. I would wait until the Pentecostal church meetings got spirited, and the old woman would start dancing and shouting, then I would climb out my bedroom window and meet another girl, Bobbie White, and we would walk to the Old Florence church and enjoy the singing and see the boys we were sweet on. It was great fun. I would climb back in the window and go to bed, and the old couple never seemed to notice. Other than that, they were really good to me. Singing school was about the only entertainment we had back then," Webb stated in a 2010 interview.

Community Leaders in the Membership

Some members of the Old Florence congregation rose to respected positions in the community. Dr. James Phillip Stanley, according to the Old Florence church records, joined that congregation, October 8, 1865. He had attained the rank of Lieutenant Colonel in the Confederate Army. Dr. Stanley served in Company E, Twenty-sixth Regiment, Arkansas Infantry, and was wounded at Jenkins Ferry, April 30, 1864 (Gerdes, 2001).

Stanley's daughter, identified as Mrs. Joe Cook in a letter dated September 23, 1913, stated that Dr. Stanley was born August 29, 1833 and died September 8, 1899. Cook stated that her parents married at the beginning of the Civil War. Dr. Stanley served as a Confederate army surgeon, and he was seriously wounded by a bullet in the chest that barely missed his heart (Haisty, 2008).

Cook stated in the letter that Dr. Stanley was reared in Tennessee and his father was determined his son would become a lawyer. When the young James Phillip Stanley told his father of his desire to become a doctor, his father refused to pay for his education. To attain a medical education, young Stanley taught school to earn money. Cook stated in her letter that he graduated in 1858 from the "U of P," possibly the University of Philadelphia, as hinted in the letter (Haisty, 2008).

In the letter, Cook stated that Dr. Stanley, upon graduation, came to the Selma community of Drew County, Arkansas, and married Martha Elizabeth Howell of Selma. He was a Mason, a Knight of Honor, and the father of thirteen children, only four of whom survived him. Dr. Stanley went on to serve as the mayor of Selma and became a dry goods merchant in that community. In 1885, he became a trustee of the Selma Methodist Church. He died in Pine Bluff, Arkansas where he had moved about twenty years prior (Haisty, 2008).

Thomas P. Howell joined the Old Florence Church, October 8, 1865. He went on to form T. P. Howell and Company, a dry goods and grocery business in Selma (Haisty, 2008). Old Florence church records state that he married Elizabeth Grisham in October 1867. Haisty writes in her history of the Selma Methodist Church that Stanley and Howell owned what was considered as fine homes and that a picture of Stanley's house, which became known as the Barrett house, is displayed at the Drew County Historical Museum and Archives.

Allen D. Touchstone and Dempsey Touchstone, both large land owners and members of the Old Florence Cumberland Presbyterian Church, were pioneers who purchased government land in Drew County, Arkansas. Dempsey Touchstone purchased a total of three hundred twenty acres of land (United States Department of the Interior, n. d.). On September 1, 1860, he acquired two hundred forty acres in Drew County. He had acquired eighty acres in Lincoln County in 1859. Dempsey Touchstone, an elder in the church, died of "congestion of the kidneys" at fifty-one years old, according to church records.

Allen D. Touchstone began his land acquisition in 1857 when he purchased one hundred twenty acres in Drew County, Arkansas from the federal government. In 1858, he and five other investors purchased three hundred twenty five acres of land in the Drew, Ouachita, and Union counties of Arkansas. This parcel of land was acquired through the *Choctaw Scrip of 1842*, part of the federal government's effort to remove Native American tribes west. The land patent was signed by President James Buchanan (United States Department of the Interior, n. d.). In 1859, Allen D. Touchstone purchased another eighty acres in Drew County.

In 1861, Allen D. Touchstone acquired another one hundred sixty acres in Drew County. This piece of property had an interesting history. Allen D. Touchstone is listed as the "patentee," and William Richmond is listed as the "warrantee." Richmond had acquired the land for $1.25 per acre through the *Scrip Warrant Act of 1855* as bounty for his service as a teamster in the Mexican-American War. The land patent was signed by President Abraham Lincoln (*Land Scrip*, 2006); (United States Department of the Interior, n. d.). Allen D. Touchstone owned a total of three hundred sixty acres in Drew County plus the three hundred twenty five acres he owned jointly with partners, making him a substantial land owner.

Zachary Taylor Prewitt, a prominent citizen of Selma, married Cora B. Lobban of the Old Florence congregation in February of 1874. Their descendants married into the Taylor family, also prominent in Drew County.

George Crenshaw Camp, the great-great grandfather of this researcher, was a member of the Old Florence congregation. The minutes reveal that he joined the church by transfer of letter, March 8, 1851. George Crenshaw Camp had brought his family to Old Florence from DeSoto County, Mississippi. He died in 1868, leaving his wife, Julia Ann Virginia Gabbert Camp, to rear six children. Unlike her husband, Julia Camp was not a member of the Old Florence congregation. Julia Camp joined with the "Campbellites" (Webb, 1984), the forerunner to the present day Church of Christ (Bowker, 1997).

James Owens, a member of the Old Florence congregation, is listed in the 1870 federal census report for Marion Township, Drew County, Arkansas, and was described as a forty-year-old doctor from South Carolina. A substantial landowner, Owens purchased approximately five hundred acres of land from the federal government in 1857 and 1859 (United States Department of the Interior, n. d.). His wife, Catherine, thirty years old, was born in Arkansas according to the census information. They had four children, all born in Arkansas, ranging in age from sixteen years to one year of age. Also enumerated as a member of the household was sixteen-year-old Lacy Raymond, a white female, who was a household servant born in Mississippi.

A migrant from Tennessee listed on the church's membership index was Pattie Wells, enumerated in the 1870 federal census report for Marion Township, Drew County, Arkansas, and described as twenty-eight years old. Her husband, not listed as a member of the church, was William Wells, a lawyer from Tennessee. Five children were enumerated in their household ranging in age from nine years old to one year old, all born in Arkansas. The Wells family grew to a position of prominence in Monticello and Drew County. Both are buried in Oakland Cemetery, Old Cemetery Section, Block One, Monticello, Arkansas.

Marriages and baptisms were faithfully recorded, leaving genealogists valuable family information. The records of the Old Florence Cumberland Presbyterian Church state that Elizabeth Donaldson married T. J. Gabbert, and that Elizabeth Donaldson Gabbert died young, November 26, 1858.

The records reveal that Harriet Harrell was married in 1867 to J. L. Tillar, whose family founded the community of Tillar in eastern Drew County, near the Old Florence Community. James P. Tillar and Fannie E. Tillar were also on the membership roster (DeArmond, 1980); (Haisty, 2008).

The African Diaspora Reflected in the Church Membership

In keeping with the customs of the Antebellum South, the Old Florence Cumberland Presbyterian Church admitted both Caucasian and African-American members. The minutes of September 11, 1854 state that "Rose, a colored sister, servant of T. P. Stone," the minister, was received as a member of this society by recommendation from her master. It would be interesting to know if Rose joined of her own accord or if her master required her to join. The minute book sheds no light on this question. The minute book further records that in 1856, Mary Jane, servant girl of the Wiley Estate, joined the congregation by an experience of grace. The minutes of October 9, 1859 reveal that Charlotte, servant of J. M. Taylor, also joined the church by an experience of grace.

After the Civil War (1861–1865), the Florence church continued to admit African-American members. The October 14, 1866 minutes state that "Elvin, a black woman, was received by experience." The November 10, 1867 minutes state that a committee was appointed to "investigate a matter of disorderly conduct supposedly committed by Elvin, a colored sister, and to report at the next meeting." The February 9, 1868 minutes state that the committee appointed to investigate the allegations against Elvin reported that she "acknowledged the crime and promised to be more orderly in the future." Elvin applied for a letter of "dismission" in 1872 and was granted the letter by the session. Perhaps Elvin used her newfound freedom to join a church comprised exclusively of African-Americans.

Mary Jane and Charlotte were suspended from membership in the Old Florence Church because they had been "for years removed from the jurisdiction of Florence society." Rose, Mary Jane, Charlotte, and Elvin are the only African-Americans mentioned in the minute book. They are referred to only by their given names. The absence of a surname is a painful reminder of the effects of the African Diaspora and how it stripped African-Americans of personal identity or family history. It is interesting that the church minutes never used the term "slave" but instead used the term, "servant," a common euphemism among slaveholders.

Slave Cemetery at Old Florence

Several of the more expensive, high-quality markers that remain in the Old Florence cemetery can still be read, a testament to the affluence of some of the members. However, time and neglect have eroded the information on several of the stones. Many of the early settlers in the Old Florence community were buried in the church's cemetery, and a slave cemetery is said to have existed beyond the fence that once surrounded the white cemetery, but there are no markers indicating such (Smith, 1982 quoted in *Drew County Arkansas Cemetery Records*, 2002). Unfortunately, these graves have been lost over the years. Technology that can locate lost graves exists; it works on the same principle as an x-ray machine (*Genealogical Computing*, 2004). Though the identities of the skeletal remains can probably never be ascertained, the use of this technology would help substantiate the long-held belief that the Old Florence Church was the site of a slave cemetery.

The Civil War and the Church

Arkansas lost approximately ten thousand men between the ages of fifteen and forty, about twelve percent of its population, in the Civil War (*Civil War Timeline*, 2010), and Drew County lost its share. The Old Florence church records state that J. N. Mason died early in the war in Virginia on September 9, 1861. This is the only information given in the minutes about the death of J. N. Mason, but the minutes reveal that J. N. Mason was one of the converts who joined the church as a result of the "protracted meeting" in August 1859.

Jesse N. Mason

Jesse Mason held the rank of Sergeant in the Confederate army and served in Company D, Selma Rifles, Third Regiment, Arkansas Infantry. This regiment was mustered in at Lynchburg, Virginia in June of 1861, and consisted of men from Ashley, Drew, Desha, Hot Spring, Union, and Dallas Counties of Arkansas. Mason was reported "sick" in August 1861 and has no further record (Gerdes, 1998). Apparently he died of disease, a fate of many Civil War soldiers. Mason was born in Tennessee around 1839 and was enumerated in the 1860 federal census report for Desha County, Arkansas. He was a farmer.

Jabez H. Mason

The minutes state that Private Jabez H. Mason was killed in the Battle of Corinth, Mississippi on October 3, 1862, after surviving the bloodbath at the Battle of Shiloh, Tennessee in April of 1861. Private Mason served in Company F, the Dixie Guards, Ninth Regiment, Arkansas Infantry (Gerdes, 2003).

Henry James Hawks

Henry James Hawks enlisted in the Confederate Army at Monticello, Arkansas, February 14, 1863. He served as a Private in Company F, the Dixie Guards, Ninth Regiment, Arkansas Infantry. He died in a hospital in Jackson, Mississippi on April 29, 1864 (Gerdes, 1998); (Gerdes and Howerton, 2003).

James P. Donaldson

James P. Donaldson's story is especially sad. Donaldson, apparently an excellent soldier, was promoted quickly in the Confederate Army. He enlisted June 20, 1861 as a Private in Company D, Selma Rifles, Third Regiment, Arkansas Infantry. He was promoted to Second Corporal on September 21, 1861, to First Corporal in January 1863, to Third Sergeant in May 1863 and finally to Second Sergeant in May of 1864. The Third Arkansas participated in many battles in the campaign of Northern Virginia (Second Bull Run Campaign), such as Harper's Ferry, Sharpsburg, Maryland, Gettysburg, Pennsylvania and Chickamauga, Georgia, to name a few (Gerdes, 2002). Donaldson came close to surviving the entire war but was captured toward the end in Virginia on October 7, 1864. He died at Point Lookout, Maryland, military prison on April 21, 1865, and was buried there (*Descendants*, 2009). Point Lookout had an intended capacity of ten thousand, but more than fifty thousand men were held prisoner there. Inmates froze to death, starved, and died from disease (*Point Lookout Prison Camp*, n. d.). The war ended with the Confederate surrender at Appomattox Courthouse, April 9, 1865, a few days before Donaldson's death (*Civil War Timeline*, 2010). Donaldson was also one of the converts who joined the Old Florence church as a result of the August 1859 "protracted meeting."

David P. Phillips

David P. Phillips enlisted in Company D, Selma Rifles, Third Arkansas Infantry, on June 20, 1861. He was promoted to Fourth Sergeant and died on furlough at Memphis, Tennessee on February 27, 1862. He was born in Tennessee and was enumerated in the 1860 federal census report for Desha County, Arkansas. He was described in the census data as an overseer, probably on a large plantation. The Selma Rifles had eighty-three men on their roster, and only eight were still alive at the end of the war (Gerdes, 2002).

Phillips joined the Old Florence Church on March 8, 1851 along with his wife, Sarah Phillips, and George C. Camp. The three promised to produce letters of "dismission and recommendation" from Mississippi. The Camp and Phillips families are enumerated in the 1850 federal census report for DeSoto County, Mississippi. In the census data, David Phillips was described as thirty-three years old, and his wife, Sarah was described as nineteen years old. Both were born in Tennessee. Phillips was an overseer in Mississippi. David and Sarah Phillips were the only two members of their household, and according to the census report, both were literate. It was common for several families to pull up stakes and move westward together. Apparently the Camps, Gabberts, and the Phillips came to Drew County together, probably to acquire government land, and the Phillipses may have been related to the Gabberts and the Camps.

A. M. Womack

The minutes state that A. M. Womack, also a convert from the 1859 evangelistic effort, died in the war in 1859. This cannot be correct, because the Civil War did not begin until April 12, 1861, when Confederate forces fired on Fort Sumter, South Carolina.

Womack's religious conversion occurred the same year as his death; perhaps he was ill and knew that his death was imminent.

The Old Florence Presbyterian Church gradually died out during the 1930s. It helped shape the community, culture, and economy of Drew County, and that influence is evident today. Many of the descendants of the church's congregation remain citizens of Drew County, Arkansas. The minutes contain an index of church members, a list of marriages, a list of baptisms, and a list of deaths. This minute book is a wonderful primary source document for researchers.

This Woodmen of the World marker is somewhat illegible. It marks the grave of John T. Mason, but it is difficult to see the dates. The Mason family were early pioneers of Drew County and charter members of the Old Florence Church. This is the fanciest marker remaining in the cemetery. Photo by Judy Hubbell.

Chapter 5
The Camps/Campes/Kemps/ Kempes Our English Roots

Note: The Camps liked the name *Thomas* just as the Gabberts liked the name *Michael.* I tried to avoid confusion by assigning numerals to each *Thomas.*

It is generally accepted that the Camps are of English origin. The name *Camp* is sometimes spelled *Campe* or *Kemp* in historical documents. Other variations of the name are *de Campos, Kempe, Kampe, and de Campe.* The following is a parent-to-child linear chart of direct descent.

Direct Line of Descent for the Camps

William Campe I and wife (Unknown) were the parents of William Campe II.

William Campe II and wife (Unknown) were the parents of Henry Campe.

Henry Campe and Mary Tishunt were the parents of Thomas Campe.

Thomas Campe I and Margery Bannister were the parents of William Campe III.

William Campe III and Mary Farmer were the parents of Thomas Camp II.

Thomas Camp II and Sarah Williamson were the parents of Thomas Camp III.

Thomas Camp III and Catherine Barron were the parents of Thomas Camp IV.

Thomas Camp IV and Mary Marshall were the parents of Thomas Camp V.

Thomas Camp V and Margaret Carney were the parents of Stephen Camp.

Stephen Camp and Anne Alexander were the parents of George Crenshaw Camp.

George Crenshaw Camp and Julia Ann Virginia Gabbert were the parents of Martha Camp.

Martha Camp and William George Griffin were the parents of Virginia Griffin.

Virginia Griffin and John Webb were the parents of Lewis French Webb.

Lewis French Webb and Louise Hawkins are the parents of Arnold Ray Webb, Donald Roy Webb, Jo Ann Webb, and Judy Carol Webb.

Judy Carol Webb and Billy J. Hubbell are the parents of William Griffin Hubbell.

The Gabbert branch of our family originated from the middle class of Germany and remained middle class for most of its history. The Camps, however, originated from the English nobility according to some sources. In *Peerage and Baronetage of the British Empire* (1832), Burk states:

> *"This family, deriving its name from the Saxon word Kemp [meaning] combat has been of long standing in the counties of Kent, Essex, Suffolk and Norfolk. We meet with two very eminent churchmen of the name; John Kemp, L.L.D., Archbishop of Canterbury; and Thomas Kemp, his grace's nephew, who was consecrated Bishop of London in 1449."*

Fred H. Kemp (1902) states the following:

> *"[T]he name Kemp is widely distributed in the British Isles, chiefly in the Eastern and Southern counties of England, notably Norfolk, Suffolk, Essex, Kent, Middlesex, Sussex, Surrey, and Hampshire. Further the popular etymology of Kemp is as the Anglo-Saxon word 'Campa' — a champion in modern spelling."*

> *He lists the following spellings of the name: Kemp, Kempe,*
> *Kempt, Camp and Campe.*

William Kempe was Shakespeare's comedian and a celebrated dancer who is said to have danced from London to Norwich in nine days. John Kemp, a weaver, is believed to have settled in Carlisle around 1335; the author states that *Kemp* is an archaic spelling of *comb* and is a technical term in the weaving industry that denotes a bristly hair found in wool. It is recorded that Stephen Kemp in 1127 was fined for leaving the King's Court. Elizabeth Kemp was Lady of the Bedchamber to Elizabeth of York, the consort of King Henry VII of England (Copinger, 1904).

An early variation, AD 1086, of the spelling of this surname was *de Campo*, contained within the *Domesday Book* of William the Conqueror after the Norman Conquest of England. The spelling of the surname evolved. There was an instance in 1624 where the author of a will spelled his name Thomas *Campe*, while his son who witnessed the will spelled his name Thomas *Kempe* (Copinger, 1904).

There are several references to pre-English ancestors in *The Camp Bulletin* (1924), a family history publication. This particular one focuses on the history of the weaving and textile business:

> *"In a work, the alien immigrants to England is (sic) a fac*
> *simile of the patent granting protection by King Edward III,*
> *1055 AD to John Kempe, who seems to have been a capitalist*
> *in the weaving business. He was granted the right to come to*
> *England from Flanders (a major city in Holland) with a large*
> *company of workers to establish the weaving industry. The name*
> *was the Germanic form of Camp."*

The Camp forebears were in the draping and weaving business as early as AD 1055. Lawrence Camp was an investor in the Jamestown Company discussed later in this chapter. This is interesting because most of the branches of our family that followed the Southern frontier of migration were directly tied to this industry through cotton farming and, after the Industrial Revolution, working in the textile industry.

My parents raised cotton and worked at Burlington Industries, a textile mill in Monticello, Arkansas. At one time, my father, Lewis French Webb, held the elected office of Shop Steward in the Monticello local of the United Textile Workers of America labor union. My father often spoke of representing his union at their national convention in Atlantic City, New Jersey. He had no luggage, so he carried his clothing in paper grocery sacks. Several members of my father's family worked for Burlington. If you trace that back to AD 1055, it is a long legacy of textile manufacturing.

There were many generations of Camps all over Europe. In Hotten's *List* (1874), there is an entry where Isack Kemp, age twenty-three, sailed from London to Virginia in 1635. It stated he had taken the *Oaths of Allegiance and Supremacy* before leaving London.

When King Henry VIII was denied a divorce from Catherine of Aragon by the Roman Catholic Church in favor of his new love, Anne Boleyn, he broke from the church, formed the Church of England, proclaimed himself head of the Church of England, granted himself a divorce, and married Anne. He required the clergy to take an *Oath of Allegiance and Supremacy* to him and his church, an act that renounced Catholicism and papal authority. Those who refused were beheaded. Subjects of the king who wished to succeed economically and politically found it necessary to take the *Oath* (Jokinen, 2003).

Sir William Berkeley, the colonial governor of Virginia, recruited Royalist elite, or cavaliers, for the English colony. As part of his colonization efforts, he encouraged the cavaliers, or supporters of King Charles I, to migrate to Virginia in large numbers. As a reward for settling in Virginia, Berkeley rewarded them with high political offices and grants of large estates. In this way, Berkeley created an oligarchy of an elite group that ran the colony of Virginia for many generations. The migration of the English cavaliers to Virginia continued from 1642 to 1676 (Fischer, 1989).

In his appeal to younger sons who would not inherit because of the law of primogeniture, Berkeley (1914) referred to the Kemps when he stated:

> *"A small sum of money will enable a younger brother to erect a flourishing family in a new world; and add more strength, wealth, and honor to his native country, than thousands did before, that dyed (sic) forgotten and unrewarded in an unjust war. . .men of as good families as any subjects in England have resided there, as the Percys, the Barkleys, the Wests, the Gages, the Throgmortons, Wyatts, Digges, Chichelys, Moldsworths, Morrisons, Kemps, and hundred others which I forbear to name, lest I should misherald them in this catalogue."*

The first members of the Camp branch of our family came from England and settled in Virginia. I was able to trace our direct line of descent back to William Campe I. Many records of genealogical value were destroyed in the Great Fire of London of 1666 that destroyed eighty percent of the city (Robinson, 2004).

William Campe I and Wife (Unknown)

William Campe I was born around 1414 in Essex County, England, and died around 1456 in Clavering, Essex County, England. London is located in Essex County. He was the father of William Campe II (*William Camp Family History Wiki*, 2011).

William Campe II and Wife (Unknown)

William Campe II was born in 1450 in Essex County, England, and died in 1493 in England. He was the father of Henry Campe (*William Campe*, 2011).

Henry Campe and Mary Tishunt

Henry Campe was born in 1475 in Nazeing, Essex County, England. He married Mary Tishunt in Nazeing, Hertfordshire, England. He died in 1539 in Nazeing, Essex County, England. Henry Campe and Mary Tishunt had the following children: Isabella, John, Thomas, Robert, and Nicholas (*Henry Campe*, 2011). Our family is descended from Thomas Campe.

Thomas Campe I and (First) Joan Boreham and (Second) Margery Bannister

Thomas Campe I was born around 1507 in Nazeing, Essex County, England; he died June 15, 1560 in Roydon, Essex County, England. In 1532, he married Margery Bannister. His occupation was yeoman, or a person who operated a small farm and belonged to a class of English freeholders below the gentry. Thomas Campe I had at least six children (*Person Sheet, Thomas Campe*, 2009):

>   **Richard Campe, born in 1533 in Nazeing, Essex County, England; died around 1584**

>   **William Campe, born in 1535 in Nazeing, Essex County, England; died around 1601**

>   **Joan, born around 1535 in Nazeing, Essex County, England**

>   **Mary, born around 1535 in Nazeing, Essex County, England**

>   **James Campe, born 1539 in Nazeing, Essex County, England; died in 1607**

Robert Campe, born May 11, 1537 in Roydon, Essex County, England; died July 21, 1608 in Roydon, Essex County, England

I have no explanation why three of these children were born in 1535. Perhaps they were the result of a multiple pregnancy, but it is more likely that the dates are incorrect. Thomas Campe I apparently prepared his will while literally on his death bed. The will for Thomas Campe of Roydon, Yeoman, June 15 1560, reads (Emmison 1982; Essex Wills (England), Vol. I, 1558–1565):

> *"To Richard my eldest son my tenement called Snowes with appurtenances in his tenure; my tenement called Cramphornes with appurtenances in the tenure of John Skete; lands called Cottlands (5 acres); 1 acres in Nazeing Mead called Cottlands Mead; my leases (small parcels of meadow) in Nazeing Marsh; 2 acres of arable in Common (open) Field at Priest Field Corner; and 1 acre of land at Birch Croft Gore."*

> *"To James my son my tenement called Dawnes with appurtenances in the tenure of John Skranges, parcels of land late Robert Nicoll's, i.e. Broad Field 4 acres and 1 acre, a parcel of land called Napsys (1 acre), my tenement in Roydon Street free*

> *and copy in the tenure of Stephen Leonard, my part of the lands called Baldwynes free and copy in the tenure of Sheles, a parcel of land called Jacket Hatch and two parts of the tenement of late Richard Lonnesdayle's with appurtenances in the tenure of Runyon Warde, and 2 acres of mead in Nazeing Mead in the tenure of John Yngold."*

> *"To William my son my tenement called Ruddockes with appurtenances; a parcel of ground called Grovelees with appurtenances (30 acres), and a parcel of ground called Nicolles (20 acres). Provided that Margery my wife shall have and enjoy*

Ruddockes, Grovelees, and Nicolles for her use until Michaelmas 1562; after that term one-half of Ruddockes for her life."

"To Robert my son my tenement called Tylers with appurtenances late in the tenure of Ralph Wheatley; my tenement called Sydges (Fydges?) both free and copy with appurtenances in the tenure of Edward Davye, my tenement called Quarnes with appurtenances in my tenure, 1 acres in Stony Shott and 7 roods in Thorndon in my occupation, and my tenement free and copy with appurtenances called Hertes Horne in the occupation of John Yngold."

"To Thomas Campe, the younger, son of Thomas Campe deceased, my lands wherein Thressher dwelleth."I have surrendered the copyhold lands into the lord's hands by tenements of his manor."

"To the poorest sort of householders in Nazeing and Roydon 12d a house and to the next sort of poor 8d a house."

"To my godchildren 12d apiece."

"To Besse Baker my servant, John Baker and Joan Borne each an ewe."

"My will is that my wife pay to Joan and Mary my daughters at marriage 23 pounds apiece. The residue of my goods to my wife whom I make my executrix."

"I desire my brother John Bannyster to be my overseer, and for his pains 10s."

Witnesses: John Bannyster, Ranulph Blethym, John Goodge, Thomas Coke, Thomas Morefield.

Proved 30 July 1560

There seems to be some confusion as to the identity of the wife or wives of Thomas Campe. He specifically mentions his wife, Margery, in his *Last Will and Testament*. Joan Boreham was probably his first wife because one of Thomas Campe's daughters was named Joan. Joan Boreham was the daughter of John and Elizabeth Boreham.

William Camp III and Mary Farmer

William Campe III, born around 1560 in London, England, and Mary Farmer, born around 1563, in London, were married around 1584. They had at least four children. They may have had other children, but the Great Fire of London of 1666 destroyed birth records (*English Camp/Kemp Ancestors,* 2001).

> **Thomas Camp II, born around 1633, Essex County, England**
>
> **Lawrence Camp, born around 1635, Essex County, England**
>
> **Richard Camp, born around 1637, Essex County, England**
>
> **Nicholas Camp, born around 1639, Essex County, England**

In 1637, Nicholas and Thomas Camp were called to jury duty in Essex County, England; these are the two brothers who immigrated to America (Andrea, 1947). We are directly descended from Thomas Camp II, born around 1633. Thomas's brother, Lawrence Campe, was a prosperous member of the *Company of Honorable Drapers and Weavers* (*English Camp/Kemp Ancestors,* 2001), a livery company or craft guild somewhat like modern-day labor unions. This made Lawrence Campe a prominent member of the middle class, probably the upper middle class, of London. Curl (2001) summarizes the history of London's Livery Companies:

> "The ancient Livery Companies of the City of London had their origins before 1066, and were very similar to the many fraternities, guilds, or mysteries that flourished throughout Europe for many centuries. The Companies get their name from the mode of dress, the wearing of a Livery, often of peculiar magnificence, which was a badge of membership of a particular Company. These organizations were concerned with trade and its proper regulation, with the giving of alms and support of charities, and took part in religious observances, yet were secular in character. When craftsmen, dealers and merchants obtained charters for managing their callings; they formed fraternities (the membership of which contributed money to a common stock), and could make laws by licence (sic) of the Crown. During the Middle Ages the 'Chief Mysteries' or 'Great Companies' merged as the wealthiest and most influential, paying the highest annual sums (called fermes) to the Crown,... there were twelve Great Companies, which bore the brunt of all levies on the City by the Government. These are, in order of precedence, the Mercers', Grocers', Drapers', Fishmongers', Goldsmiths', Skinner, Merchant Taylors', Haberdashers', Salters', Ironmongers', Vintners', and Clothworkers' Companies, and they comprised... the most eminent citizens among their members."

Considered to be a wealthy man, Lawrence Campe endowed a scholarship for poor students at a university and gave seven thousand pounds to found an "alms house" or poor house in his home county. He was the builder and patron of the Church of All-Hallows-In-The-Wall, where he is buried (*English Camp/Kemp Ancestors*, 2001). The church of All-Hallows-in-the-Wall escaped the Great Fire of London in 1666. It is located in a street that runs along the south side of London's medieval Roman wall that was built around AD 200. Part of the church literally stands on the Roman wall. By 1765, the church was in a state of disrepair, and parishioners obtained an Act of Parliament in 1765 to demolish and rebuild it. A portion of the wall can still be seen in the churchyard (*All Hallows*, 2006); (*All Hallows: London Wall London EC2*, n. d.).

Many of London's churches were bombed during World War II; All-Hallows-in-the-Wall was restored and today is a Guild Church. It no longer has parish responsibilities and is the headquarters of the Council for the Care of Churches. Among other things, it houses a contemporary art gallery. The church is open to the public on Fridays from 11:00 a.m. to 3:00 p.m. (*All Hallows on the Wall: Visitor Information*, n. d.).

Lawrence Campe never had children. Several wise investments made him wealthy. He invested in the fund to colonize Virginia, an investment somewhat similar to a modern-day publically traded stock company. In John Burke's *History of Virginia, Vol. 1 appendix* (1805), Lawrence Campe is referred to as a "Member of the Great Charter of the Virginia Company."

The seventeenth century saw great colonization efforts in America. King James I of Great Britain granted a royal charter to the Virginia Company, May 23, 1609. Jamestown, Virginia, in the Chesapeake region, became the first permanent British colony in America and was owned by the Virginia Company. On May 6, 1607, three ships, the *Susan Constant, Godspeed*, and *Discovery*, brought one hundred fifty adventurers to Cape Henry of the Chesapeake Bay area for the purpose of finding treasure and wealth in the New World and to spread Christianity (*Jamestown*, 2001).

Our First Ancestors in America

The colonization of Virginia became a prosperous business venture for the British government. The colony experimented with growing tobacco and was successful in this endeavor. By 1612, it had developed a sweeter tobacco that proved to be a great cash crop (Mann, 2007). Other crops such as corn grew well in Virginia. There was an abundance of fish and game, and virgin forests provided raw materials for building.

Because of his stock in the Virginia Company, Lawrence Campe was entitled to draw six hundred acres of land in Gloucester County, Virginia. His brother, Thomas Camp II, inherited this land upon Lawrence's death. His brother, Nicholas, inherited Lawrence's land holdings in New England. His brother, Richard, inherited Lawrence's land in England and remained in England (*English Camp/Kemp Ancestors*, 2001). My family is directly descended from Thomas Camp II.

Thomas Campe II and Sarah Williamson

Thomas Campe II was born around 1633 in Essex County, England, and married Sarah Williamson around 1653. They had a son, Thomas Camp III, born in 1661 in Nazeing Parish, Essex, England (*Carpenter and Garrett Family*, 2002). It is located on the North Sea and the Thames River estuary. Thomas Camp III died in 1711 in King and Queen County, Virginia (*Thomas Camp*, n. d.).

The seventeenth century was a period of great conflict in England. When King James I took the throne, England was torn apart over religious divisions between Protestants and Catholics. Civil war erupted in England (Lambert, n. d.). In 1665, the Bubonic Plague, sometimes called the Black Death, swept through the country, resulting in about one hundred thousand deaths. A similar epidemic had swept through England in 1348, killing thirty to fifty percent of the population. The capital city of London was particularly hard hit by the disease. The following year, 1666, the Great Fire of London, destroyed eighty-seven churches and many birth, baptismal, and death records traditionally kept by churches (Alagna, 2003).

In the region of Essex, Thomas Camp's home, paranoia over suspected witches resulted in forty executions (Carlson, 2004); (Muhlberger, 1999). This same "witch hunt" spilled over into the Massachusetts colony in America (city of Salem) and became known as the infamous "Salem Witch Trials" (Linder, 2007). History teaches us that Thomas Camp probably had several good reasons to immigrate to the American colonies.

Thomas Camp III married Catherine Barron in 1689 in James City, Virginia. She was the daughter of Andrew Barron and Mary Ewens Barron. Catherine Barron was born around 1672 in Jamestown, Virginia. Both Thomas and Catherine Camp died in King and Queen County, Virginia, he in 1711, and she in 1715 (*Thomas Camp*, 2001). Robert Barron, born in 1595 in England, was the father of Andrew Barron. Robert Barron immigrated to James City, Virginia where he died. Phillip Barron was the father of Robert Barron (*One Great Family*, 2011).

It is believed that Thomas Camp III had come to Virginia to manage his holdings inherited from his brother. The name Thomas Camp first appeared in records for New Kent County, Virginia as early as 1679. He amassed sizeable land holdings by 1687. He was a self-sufficient farmer and considered to be a large scale farmer for that time. When he married Catherine Barron of Jamestown, Virginia, they made their home on the Mettapony River in New Kent County, Virginia, later to become King and Queen County, Virginia. In 1704, Thomas Camp was listed in the *True Account of Lands* as recorded by Sheriff Robert Bird. Catherine and Thomas Camp III had at least two children, Thomas Camp IV and Mary Camp (*Camp*, 2001). My family is directly descended from Thomas Camp IV and his wife, Mary Ida Marshall.

Chapter 6
The Marshalls and Our Family's Role in the American Revolution

Direct Line of Descent for the Marshalls

Nicholas Marshall and Ann Doane were the parents of Thomas Marshall I.

Thomas Marshall I and Ellen (Unknown) were the parents of Thomas Marshall II.

Thomas Marshall II and Mary Cotton were the parents of Thomas Marshall III.

Thomas Marshall III and Mary Fitzgerald were the parents of Thomas Marshall IV.

Thomas Marshall IV and Martha Jane Sherwood were the parents of Mary Ida Marshall.

Mary Ida Marshall and Thomas Camp IV were the parents of Thomas Camp V.

Thomas Camp V and Margaret Carney were the parents of Stephen Camp.

Stephen Camp and Anne Alexander were the parents of George Crenshaw Camp.

George Crenshaw Camp and Julia Ann Virginia Gabbert were the parents of Martha Camp.

Martha Camp and William Griffin were the parents of Virginia Griffin.

Virginia Griffin and John Webb were the parents of Lewis French Webb.

Lewis French Webb and Louise Hawkins are the parents of Arnold Ray Webb, Donald Roy Webb, Jo Ann Webb, and Judy Carol Webb.

Judy Webb and Billy Hubbell are the parents of William Griffin Hubbell.

The surname Marshall is English or Scottish in origin. The meaning of the name comes from the Old French *mareschal* meaning "mare" (horse) servant. It applies to a wide variety of occupations related to the care of horses such as a farrier (one who shoes horses), groom, or horse doctor. When surnames originated, the "marshall" was one of the most important servants in the houses of nobility. Other spellings include *Marshal* and *Marshale* (*Marshall Family*, 2009); (*Marshall-Name Meaning & Origin*, n. d.). The Marshalls were first found in Wiltshire, England, the location of Stonehenge, the mysterious circle of stones, after the Norman Conquest in 1066 (Gerson, 1995); (Wiltshire, 2008).

Hotten's *List* (1874) includes several of the first Marshalls to come to this country between 1634 and 1636. Matthew Marshall, age thirty, took the *Oath of Allegiance and Supremacy* at the Port of London before embarking upon the ship *Bonaventure* for Virginia.

Hotten (1874) lists Francis Marshall, age thirty, as taking the *Oath* and embarking upon the *Planter* for Virginia. William Marshall, age forty, embarked for New England on the *Abigail*; Henrie Marshall, age thirty-five, embarked for Virginia on the *Assurance*; Walter Marshall, a lad of seventeen, embarked for Virginia on the *Primrose*; and fourteen-year-old, Jo Marshall, set out for New England on the *Hopewell*. All the Marshalls were travelling alone, seeking a better way of life, and probably leaving nothing behind in England.

The Enclosure Movement

What made Europeans set out on such a dangerous, uncertain journey? There were a number of potential reasons. Conditions in Europe accounted for much of the colonization of America. Peasants were treated cruelly in England. When Henry VIII broke away from the Catholic Church, he seized millions of acres of land from the monks and nuns and granted large estates to his favorite noblemen. The landlords, in an effort to make as much money as they could, as quickly as they could, enclosed the estates and turned them into sheep farms. They drove the peasants from what had been "common land" from which they had earned a living, to starve or find a new livelihood elsewhere. This became known as the Enclosure Movement (Bradley, 1918). The production of wool had become more profitable than the production of grain crops (Slater, 1913).

In the early eighteenth century, large series of private acts of enclosure covered some seven million acres before the *General Enclosure Act of 1845*. Small tenant farmers had to choose between becoming landless laborers and migrating elsewhere. Hardworking peasants no longer had common land to share. The tenant farmers who tried to hang on to their way of life faced high rent from greedy landlords (Slater, 1913). Many peasants wound up in debtor's prison where conditions were squalid. When jails became overcrowded and colonists were needed, debtors and other criminals were offered the opportunity to immigrate to America. Most were eager to embark on the journey (Slater, 1907).

I traced the Marshall direct line of descent for my family back to Nicholas Marshall and Ann Doane.

Nicholas Marshall and Anne Doane

Nicholas Marshall from whom my family is directly descended was born around 1500 at Tydd Saint Mary, Lincolnshire, England. He married Anne Doane around 1519 when she was about fifteen years old. Her father was Thomas Doane. She was also from Tydd Saint Mary, Lincolnshire, England. Nicholas Marshall and Anne Doane had at least three children (*Family Group Record: Nicholas Marshall*, 2007):

John Marshall I was born around 1520 at Tydd Saint Mary, Lincolnshire, England.

Thomas Marshall I was born in 1523 at Abbots Ann, Hampshire, England, and was married around 1541 to a woman named Ellen (Unknown).

Anne Marshall was born around 1524 at Tydd Saint Mary, Lincolnshire, England.

My family is descended from Thomas Marshall I and Ellen Marshall. They had one son, Thomas Marshall II (*Ancestors of William Kirk Kottmeyer*, 2007).

Thomas Marshall I and Ellen (Unknown)

Thomas and Ellen Marshall had one son, Thomas Marshall II, born in 1545 at Abbots Ann, Hampshire, England. He died on March 19, 1618 at Downton, Wiltshire, England (*Ancestors of William Kirk Kottmeyer*, 2007).

Thomas Marshall II and Mary Cotton

Thomas Marshall II married Mary Cotton around 1569. Mary Cotton was born in 1553 at Abbott's Ann, Hampshire, England. Her parents were Henry and Margaret Cotton. The following are the children of Thomas Marshall II and Mary Cotton (*Family Group Record: Thomas Marshall*, 2007):

Thomas Marshall III was born in 1570 at Abbotts Ann, Hampshire, England, and died March 19, 1618.

John Marshall II was born in 1572 at Abbotts Ann, Hampshire, England.

Elizabeth Marshall was born in 1574 at Abbotts Ann, Hampshire, England.

Ann Marshall was born 1576 at Abbotts Ann, Hampshire, England.

Mary Marshall was born in 1578 at Abbotts Ann, Hampshire, England.

Lucy Marshall was born 1580 at Abbotts Ann, Hampshire, England.

My family is directly descended from Thomas Marshall III.

Thomas Marshall III and Mary Fitzgerald

Thomas Marshall III was born in 1570 at Abbotts Ann, Hampshire, England. He married Mary Fitzgerald, born in 1574 in Ballymocadamcast, Kerry, Ireland, around 1595. Her parents were Maurice Fitzgerald and Wife (unknown). They had one child, John Marshall III born in 1596 at Isle of Wight, Virginia (*Family Group Record, Thomas Marshall and Mary Fitzgerald*, 2007).

John Marshall and Jane McCarthy (Second Wife)

John Marshall was born around 1596 in England or Ireland. He served as a Captain of the Cavalry in the army of Charles I of England. The defeat of the Royalists in the English Civil War by the New Model Army headed by Oliver Cromwell may have been the event that sent John Marshall to the American colony of Virginia. He may well have fled for his life. King Charles was beheaded, and Cromwell took over the government and destroyed anyone who got in his way (Plant, 2007).

John Marshall was married five times (*Individual Record: John Marshall*, 2009). My family is descended from his second wife, Jane McCarthy, born in 1596 in Clodane, Ireland. John Marshall and Jane McCarthy were married around 1623 in Ireland. They migrated to Virginia and settled in Westmoreland County. John Marshall fought in the Indian Wars in Virginia and was prominent in Bacon's Rebellion (Virkus, 1998).

Bacon's Rebellion was a revolt in colonial Virginia led by a young, wealthy Englishman, Nathaniel Bacon. The movement was spurred by high taxes, low tobacco prices, and resentment of special privileges given to those close to the colonial governor of Virginia, Sir William Berkeley. Part of what precipitated the revolt was Berkeley's failure to defend against the Native American tribes. Bacon led two unauthorized, but successful, expeditions against the Native Americans (*People and Events*, n. d.).

John Marshall died in Isle of Wight County, Virginia, November 8, 1688 (Virkus, 1998). He had at least four children, birth dates unknown: Humphery Marshall, John Marshall III, Robert Marshall, and Thomas Marshall IV (*Family Record Group, John Marshall and Jane McCarthy*, 2009). My family is directly descended from their youngest son, Thomas Marshall IV.

Thomas Marshall IV and Martha Jane Sherwood

Thomas Marshall IV was born in 1660 in Culpepper County, Virginia. Thomas Marshall IV and Martha Jane Sherwood were married April 30, 1690 in Richmond County, Virginia. Martha Jane Sherwood was born in 1662 at Sittenburne Parish, Old Rappahonnock, Virginia to Phillip Sherwood and Martha Pendleton. Thomas Marshall IV died on May 31, 1704 in Westmoreland County, Virginia. Martha Jane Sherwood Marshall died July 4, 1749 in Culpepper County, Virginia. They had nine children, one of whom was Mary Ida Marshall, born 1697 in Westminster County, Virginia, and died in 1738 in Caroline County, Virginia. She married Thomas Camp III around 1715 (*Family Group Record: Thomas Marshall and Martha Jane Sherwood*, 2008).

Chapter 7
The Camps and the American Revolution

Thomas Camp IV and Mary Ida Marshall

Thomas Camp IV was born in 1691 in King and Queen County, Virginia. He has the distinction of being our first *Camp* ancestor born in America. He died in 1751 in Culpepper County, Virginia (*Thomas Camp II Family*, 2001). Thomas Camp IV married Mary Ida Marshall around 1715 in Westmoreland County, Virginia. Mary was born in Westmoreland County in 1697, and died in 1757 in Culpepper County, Virginia. They had four sons (*Thomas Camp II Family*, 2001):

> Thomas Camp V, born February 8, 1716/1717 in King and Queen County; died 1798 in Rutherford County, North Carolina

> John Camp, born 1719 in Virginia; died between 1720 and 1809

Marshall Camp, born 1721 in Virginia; died between 1722 and 1811

Ambrose Camp, born 1723, Spotsylvania County, Virginia; died March 17, 1769, Culpepper County, Virginia

John Camp and Marshall Camp are said to have been officers in the Revolutionary Army of Virginia, but Thomas Camp V was too old to serve (*Thomas Camp Family*, 2005). My family is directly descended from Thomas Camp V.

Thomas Camp V and (First) Winifred Starling (Second) Margaret Carney

Thomas Camp V, born February 8, 1717 in Culpepper County, Virginia, married Winifred Starling, of Welsh descent; she was born around 1720 in Accomack County, Virginia. Thomas Camp V and Winifred Starling married in 1737 in Halifax or Accomack County, Virginia. She was the daughter of Richard Starling. She bore Thomas Camp fourteen children. Winifred Starling Camp died in 1761 at forty-one years old in Culpepper County, Virginia. Although we are not descended from Winifred Starling, but from Thomas Camp's second wife, Margaret Carney, I will discuss the children of Thomas Camp and Winifred Starling because of their heavy involvement in the American Revolutionary War (*Thomas Camp Family*, 2005).

Of the fourteen children of Thomas Camp and Winifred Starling Camp, five served in the American Revolutionary War. However, at least one, John Camp, is believed to have fought on the side of the British. The Daughters of the American Revolution (DAR) has rejected membership applications of individuals descended from John Camp; they must prove he was not a British Loyalist. No one has applied under his name since 1991, although he was originally listed as an accepted patriot by the DAR in 1938 (*Ancestral Rolls, South Carolina DAR*, 1938).

In January of 1783, the sheriff of Rutherford County, North Carolina issued a summons for one hundred sixteen individuals to appear and answer to the charges of treason, felony, and forfeiture. Included in this list were John Camp, Sr. and his sons, John Camp, Jr., James Camp, and Starling Camp. The Camps did not show up to disprove the charges. Rutherford County had the reputation of being one of the strongest Tory regions of the state (*John Camp Family*, 2006).

The following are the fourteen children of Thomas Camp and Winifred Starling, and a brief discussion of each (Price, 1963); (*Thomas Camp Family*, 2005):

> *Edmund Camp was born in 1739, and died in 1834 in Franklin County, Georgia. He served as an ensign during the American Revolution; he enlisted in the North Carolina militia as a private, and was promoted to rank of ensign in June 1776; he had twenty-two or twenty-three children by two wives. He lived to be ninety-five years old, and is buried at Camp Cemetery, Stephens County, Georgia. He married Mary Ragsdale in 1760 in Virginia; Mary Ragsdale was the daughter of Benjamin Ragsdale and Martha Jones; he later married Elizabeth Carney, around 1784 in Pendleton District, South Carolina. Elizabeth Carney was the sister of Margaret Carney, Edmund Camp's stepmother.*

> *Mary Camp, born around 1740 in Orange or Culpepper County, Virginia; she married Thomas Tarpley (Price, 1963), and died around 1786, and is buried in Charlotte County, Virginia.*

> *Reverend Joseph Camp, also a medical doctor, was born around 1741 in Orange County, Virginia. He died before January of 1820, probably in Pulaski County, Kentucky; he*

was a Baptist preacher in the Broad River Baptist Association. He was arrested by the British General Cornwall as a spy for the colonists. He married (First) (Unknown) Roundtree, and (Second) Susannah Tate.

Lucy Camp was born around 1742 in Orange County, Virginia; she married Dennis Hearn.

John Camp, Sr. was born in 1743 in Orange County, Virginia, and died in 1818 in Jackson County, Georgia, and is buried in Lebanon Methodist Church Cemetery, Laurens County, South Carolina. He was a lieutenant who fought in the Battle of King's Mountain. He is suspected on fighting on the side of the British. He married Mary "Minnie" Tarpley, his cousin, on January 30, 1764. Her brother, Reverend James Tarpley, was the founder of the Methodist faith in Virginia.

Nathaniel Camp was born in 1745 in Orange County, Virginia, and died after January of 1832 in Gwinnett County, Georgia; he served as a corporal in the Revolutionary Army, and fought in the Battle of King's Mountain, where, according to family lore, he may have killed the British General Ferguson. Nathaniel Camp's son had Ferguson's conch shell battle horn which later became part of the collection of the Daughters of the American Revolution; he married Winifred Tarpley of Richmond County, Virginia, born June 9, 1748.

Thomas Camp VI was born in 1747, in Orange County, Virginia, and died after 1811 in Walton County, Georgia. He fought in the Battle of King's Mountain; however, it is not known if he was a Patriot or a Tory. He married Nancy Anne Tarpley, born October 6, 1750, in Richmond County,

Virginia. Thomas and Nancy Anne Camp are buried in Old Bethlehem Cemetery, Walton County, Georgia.

Starling Camp was born in 1749 in Orange County, Virginia, and died in 1851. If these dates are correct, Starling Camp lived to be one hundred two years old. He, too, was suspected of being a Tory.

Hosea Camp was born February 25, 1751 in Culpepper County, Virginia, and died, date unknown, in Fayette County, Georgia. He served in the American Revolutionary War; it is not known if he was a Patriot or a Tory.

William Camp was born August 1, 1753 in Culpepper County, Virginia, and married Rebecca Wofford, born around 1750 in Prince George's County, Maryland. She died in 1827 in York County, South Carolina, and is buried at Buffalo Church, York County, South Carolina.

Alfred Camp was born in 1755, and married (Unknown) Jennings. They are buried in Campbell County, Georgia, death dates unknown.

Benjamin Camp was born in 1757 in Culpepper County, Virginia, and married Elizabeth Dykes. Camp died around 1832 in Walton County, Georgia.

Elizabeth Camp was born in 1759 in Culpepper County, Virginia, and died around 1850 in South Carolina. She married Reuben Brock II of Orange County, North Carolina around 1777 in North Carolina. Brock was an American Revolutionary War soldier. He enlisted June 1, 1776 in the North Carolina Cavalry, and served six months. The United States Congress on June 7, 1832 passed legislation to provide for *military pensions for war veterans. On September 27, 1832, Reuben Brock, seventy-eight years old, waived these benefits. According to pension records, Brock did not see actual combat but served as a scout. After his first enlistment was completed, he was drafted to serve three months in the South Carolina militia but paid for a substitute and, therefore, relinquished all claims for a pension (Southern Campaign, 2009). Reuben Brock was the son of immigrants from the Holy Roman Empire. Elizabeth Camp lived to be ninety years old. Reuben and Elizabeth Brock are buried in Barker's Creek Baptist Church Cemetery, Anderson County, South Carolina.*

Joel Camp was born in 1761 in Culpepper County, Virginia, death date unknow.

Four of the fourteen children of Thomas Camp and Winifred Starling married Tarpleys; these were the children of James Tarpley and Mary Camp Tarpley. These four marriages resulted in four sets of double first cousins.

All the children of Thomas Camp and Winifred Starling Camp had professions. Several were carpenters, and several became noted preachers. Most embraced the Baptist or Methodist faith. It is also believed that at least one of them, perhaps more than one, served in the British army during the Revolutionary War. This has never been disproved. Frontier farmers often had no real interest in politics, and conveniently switched sides in the war when it was to their advantage. They were self-sufficient and mostly wanted to be left alone. They viewed the war as a conflict between the wealthy plantation owners and the British government. Most of the frontier farmers wanted to escape from any kind of government and be completely independent.

Winnifred Starling Camp probably died in 1761, probably bearing her youngest child, Joel, or shortly thereafter (*Thomas Camp Family*, 2005).

Thomas Camp V and Margaret Carney

My family is directly descended from Thomas Camp V and his second wife, Margaret Carney, born June 20, 1744 in Limerick, Ireland. They married in Virginia in 1762. Thomas Camp and Margaret "Margie" Carney Camp were colorful characters. Thomas Camp was born February 8, 1716/1717 in King and Queen County, Virginia, and died January 8, 1798 at Island Ford on the Broad River, between North and South Carolina. Margaret was eighteen years old when she married forty-five-year-old Thomas who had twelve children from a former marriage. She was nineteen years old when her first child was born, and forty-two years old when her twelfth and last child was born. Thomas Camp was sixty-nine years old when his last child was born. Margaret Carney Camp died at eighty years old, outliving Thomas Camp by twenty-six years. We are directly descended from Stephen Camp, the sixth of Thomas and Margie Camp's twelve children. The following are the children of Thomas Camp and Margaret Carney Camp (*Thomas Camp Family*, 2005):

> Crenshaw "Granger" Camp was born January 5, 1763, in Culpepper County, Virgina, and died in 1808, in Rutherford, North Carolina. He never married, and willed everything to his siblings.

> James Camp was born in 1765 in Orange County, North Carolina, and married Sarah Jennings of Nottaway County, Virginia. He died in 1817 at Spartanburg, South Carolina.

> Daniel Camp was born on April 2, 1766 in Rutherford County, North Carolina, and died on April 2, 1798 in Rutherford County, North Carolina. He married Sarah McKinney.

Lewis Camp was born on January 16, 1768, and married Joanna Neal of Charlotte County, Virginia.

Adam Camp was born in 1769, and died in infancy. He is buried in State Line Baptist Cemetery, Cherokee County, South Carolina.

Stephen Camp was born September 17, 1771, and died in 1846 in Rutherford County, North Carolina. According to the August, 1932, Vol. I, No. 17 *Camp Bulletin*, Stephen Camp, as a ten-year-old boy, accompanied his brother, Benjamin, and other members of the community to the Battle of Cowpens where he held their horses during the battle. He received an injury that crippled him for life. He married Anne Alexander who was born in 1771. She was the daughter of Colonel Elias Alexander, Jr. of the Revolutionary Army, and Nancy Agnes McCall.

Larkin Camp was born in 1773, and died in infancy. He is buried in State Line Baptist Cemetery, Cherokee County, South Carolina.

Unity Camp was born in 1775. She married Samuel Broadway, and they had no children.

Ruth Camp was born on September 30, 1780, and died in 1852. She married Daniel Patterson, and they had no children.

Aaron Camp was born in June, 1778 in Rutherford County, North Carolina. He married

(First) Frances Willis Terrill, and (Second) Sarah Byars Suttle. He died on July 6, 1861, in Ringgold, Georgia.

George Camp was born on September 24, 1782, in Rutherford County, North Carolina. He married Mary Norman. George Camp died in 1835 in Tennessee.

Joshua Camp was born on July 10, 1786, in Rutherford County, North Carolina, and died on January 9, 1849 in Rutherford County, North Carolina. He married Nancy Neal Gregory.

It is interesting that the two daughters born to Thomas Camp V and Margaret Carney Camp died with no children. Thomas Camp V was a millwright by profession and built and owned the first grist and saw mill in Rutherford County, North Carolina. The mill no longer remains, but the small falls in the river where the mill was located can still be identified. He settled at Island Ford, about ten miles down the Broad River in the forks of Camp Creek and the Broad River. The family burial ground is on the opposite side of the river across the falls. Thomas Camp V and Margaret Camp are buried there along with many of his descendents. Thomas Camp's headstone of plain blue granite rough hewn stone bears the simple inscription "T. Camp, born 1717 Died 1798." Thomas Camp's *Last Will and Testament* was dated January 8, 1798 and is recorded in North Carolina Archives, Raleigh North Carolina, in Rutherford County Wills, 1784-1833, Ace-Haw, Vol. I, p. 29.

There are several land records of Thomas Camp V; a 1779 record shows Thomas claiming two hundred acres of land in Tryon County, and later, another one hundred acres. A 1780 Orangeburg District, South Carolina deed book dated March 21, 1780, shows

Thomas Camp owning eighty acres on Sandy Run, a north branch of White Oak Creek in Rutherford County, North Carolina.

Thomas Camp was said to be a genial host in the old Virginia style of hospitality, entertaining many notables of the day. Family lore describes him as having been a handsome man with a powerful physique, amiable disposition, very religious, and a hard worker.

During the Revolutionary War, Thomas Camp had sons in both armies, so he did not take sides, but his second wife, Margaret, was a staunch rebel, probably due to her Irish ancestry. The English and the Irish have a long history of strife and hatred. Her twelve children were too young to serve in the Revolutionary War, and because of her political position, their farm was often robbed by the British, and the mill and their home were burned by the British. Their home stood at the halfway point between the British and Patriot armies. It was not unusual for farmers in the Carolinas to frequently switch sides in the conflict to avoid foraging expeditions by the British, as well as loss of life and property. After the war, Thomas and Margie Camp moved closer to Island Ford and made their last settlement (*Thomas Camp Family*, 2005).

Margaret "Margie" Carney Camp was a remarkable person. She was born on June 20, 1744, in the aftermath of the Forgotten Famine of Ireland in 1740–1741 (Dickson, 1997). This famine was caused by extremely cold weather that killed both root and cereal crops. This was the same Arctic cold that descended on all of Europe, as discussed in the Gabbert section of this narrative. The Forgotten Famine is so named because, in historical accounts, it is usually eclipsed by the Great Famine, also known as the Potato Famine of 1847–1849 (Henahan, n. d.).

Margaret "Margie" Carney immigrated to America between birth and eighteen years old with her parents. The voyage across the Atlantic was dangerous, and it is likely that her family was impoverished. If so, they probably sold themselves as indentured servants or bond slaves to pay for their passage to America. Approximately one-half of the settlers in the Southern colonies came as indentured servants (*Southern Colonies*, n. d.). When their indentures were fulfilled, they were given a small tract of land.

Margie Camp's family probably came to America for a fresh start and the promise of prosperity and food on the table. At eighteen years old, she married a forty-five-year-old widower with twelve children ranging in age from twenty-three years (older than she was at the time) to two years. She had her first of twelve children one year later (*Thomas Camp Family*, 2005).

Margie was a large woman; she may have known hunger in her younger years, but apparently she did not lack for food in her adult years. Margie did not join the Baptist Church until she was old and helpless, though she always attended church meetings. She said she would not be baptized until she felt she was a fit subject for the church. It took four ministers to baptize her in the Broad River, and she had to be baptized in her rocking chair bcause of her size. She had a reputation as a good woman, and a mother who was honest and industrious with sharp business acumen, character traits she passed on to her children. She outlived Thomas Camp by twenty-six years (*Thomas Camp Family*, 2005).

The following is the *Last Will and Testament of Thomas Camp:*

1798, Jan 8- Last Will and Testament of Thomas Camp is recorded in North Carolina Archives, Raleigh North Carolina in *Rutherford County Wills, 1784-1833, Ace-Haw,* Vol. I, page 29:

> *"In the Name of God Amen*
>
> *I Thomas Camp of Rutherford County of No-Carolina being Sick and weak of Body but of perfect mind and memory thanks be to God Calling to mind the Mortality of my Body and knowing that it is appointed for all men onst to Die Do make and ordain this my Last Will and Testament that is to Say as Tuching Such Worldly Estate where with it has Pleased God to bless me in this Life I give Didmise & Dispose of the Same*

in the folowing maner and form First I give and Bequeth to Margret my Dearlly beloved wife all my Stock and household furniture (Excep a horse Colt that I gave to my Son Aaron and one heffer to my Daughter Ruth) and the Land that I live on She is to keep in Peaceable posesion as Long as she Lives for hur benefit and the benefit of the three youngest Sons till they become of age and at hur Decease if before they become of age then a reasonable a Lowance till they Should becom and when they becom of age & if not She is to Continue in persision till hur Decease then the hole of My Property to be Equally Divided Amoungst my Children as folows after giving to my Sons Edward John Thomas William& Josephe Nathen& Benjaman five Shillings starlin Each & to my Daughter Lusey Hearn the same & to (my Son Aaron(lined out)) my Daughter Ruth a feather Bead the rest of all my property to be Equally Diveded amoung my Last wifes Children viz, Cranshw James Daniel Lewis Stephen Aaron Unica Ruth George & Joshua I hereby utterly Disalow revok and Disanul all and Every other former will by me in any waise made rattifiong & Confirming this and no other to be my Last Will and Testament in witness whereof I have hereunto Set my hand and Seal this Eighth Day of January iun the yeare of our Lord one thousand Seven hundred and Ninty Eight and I appoint Crashaw Camp and Daniel Camp my Executors to this my Last will and Testament."

Signed Sealed Published . . . Thom Camp (Seal)

Pronounst & Dclelardby the Sd Thomas Campas his Last will and Testament in the Presence of us who in his Presence & in the Presence of Each other have hereunto Subscribed our Names

John McKinney
David Patterson
Benjm. Hix

Thos Camp's last Will and Testament. Proved in open Ct. April Term 1798

There are also several land records relating to Thomas Camp:

1779: Old First Register, Rutherford County, North Carolina. No. 507 (Granted Nov. 2, 1779). Thomas Camp claiming 200 acres of land in Tryon County on the south side of Main Broad River (?) hawkins shoal on said River including his own improvement. January 2, 1779.

No. 508. (granted) Thomas Camp claiming 100 acres of land in Tryon County on the south side of Main Broad River above pools Branch including John Wilson's improvement. January 20, 1779.

1780: Orangeburg Dist., South Carolina:

Deed Book JL, page 181. Dated March 21, 1780, recorded March 26, 1794. Christopher Hicks, Orangeburg District, South Carolina, to Thomas Camp of Rutherford County, North Carolina, for 80£ land on Sandy Run, a north branch of White Oak Creek in Rutherford County. Witnesses: Cranshaw Camp and Daniel Camp. Deed Book 10-11, page 91. Dated April 12, 1795, recorded December 26, 1798.

Thomas Camp to William Womack, both of Rutherford County, North Carolina, for 20 lb. 100 acres in Rutherford County on both sides of Obed Hill's Creek. mentions Elizabeth Armstrong's corner. Granted Thomas Camp November 28, 1792.

Witnesses: Isaac Safield, Daniel Webb, and William Smith.

My family is directly descended from Thomas and Margie Camp's sixth child, Stephen Camp who married Anne Alexander. The Alexander branch of our family is rich in the history and heritage of our nation. The Alexanders played a proud and prominent role in gaining independence for this country, and were the consummate political activists in addition to being largely responsible for the establishment of the Presbyterian Church in America.

Chapter 8
Norsemen to Scottish Royalty and Nobility: Our Scottish Roots and the Alexanders

NOTE: I am skeptical of the accuracy of this direct line of descent from Somerled through Donald, Lord of the Isles because of the scarcity of written records during this time. I suspect most of it is legend, but it is interesting. From Donald on down to the present, I feel fairly comfortable about its accuracy.

Direct Line of Descent for the Alexanders

Somerled of Argyll and Ragnhilda of Argyll were the parents of Ranald, Lord of the Isles.

Ranald, Lord of the Isles and Fonia (Unknown) were the parents of Donald, Lord of the Isles.

Donald, Lord of the Isles and daughter of Walter High Stewart were the parents of Angus Mor, Lord of the Isles.

Angus Mor, Lord of the Isles and wife (Unknown) were the parents of Angus Og, Lord of the Isles.

Angus Og, Lord of the Isles and daughter of Campbell were the parents of John, Lord of the Isles.

John, Lord of the Isles and Margaret Stewart were the parents of Donald, Lord of the Isles.

Donald, Lord of the Isles and Mary Leslie were the parents of Alexander McDonald, Lord of the Isles and Earl of Ross.

Alexander McDonald and wife (Unknown) were the parents of Alexander Alexander.

Alexander Alexander and Elizabeth (Unknown) were the parents of Thomas Alexander, Baron of Menstrie.

Thomas Alexander and Wife (Unknown) were the parents of Andrew Alexander, Baron of Menstrie.

Andrew Alexander and Catherine Graham were the parents of Alexander Alexander, Baron of Menstrie.

Alexander Alexander and Elizabeth Douglas were the parents of Andrew Alexander, Baron of Menstrie.

Andrew Alexander and Wife (Unknown) were the parents of Alexander Alexander, Baron of Menstrie.

Alexander Alexander and Elizabeth Forbes were the parents of William Alexander.

William Alexander and Wife (Unknown) were the parents of Alexander Alexander, Baron of Menstrie.

Alexander Alexander and Marion Graham were the parents of William Alexander.

William Alexander and Janet Erskine were the parents of John Alexander.

John Alexander and Agnes Graham were the parents of William Alexander.

William Alexander and Araminta Liston were the parents of Andrew Alexander.

Andrew Alexander and Jane McKnitt were the parents of Elias Alexander, Sr.

Elias Alexander, Sr. and Ann Taylor were the parents of Elias Alexander, Jr.

Elias Alexander, Jr. and Agnes McCall were the parents of Anne Alexander.

Anne Alexander and Stephen Camp were the parents of George Crenshaw Camp.

George Crenshaw Camp and Julia Ann Virginia Gabbert were the parents of Martha Camp.

Martha Camp and William G. Griffin were the parents of Virginia Griffin.

Virginia Griffin and John Webb were the parents of Lewis French Webb.

Lewis French Webb and Louise Hawkins are the parents of Arnold Ray Webb, Donald Roy Webb, Jo Ann Webb, and Judy Carol Webb.

Judy Carol Webb and Billy James Hubbell are the parents of William Griffin Hubbell

❦

This branch of my family descended from Scottish royalty and nobility. According to F. W. Thorlton, author of *They Came from Ireland* (2007), the Alexanders can be traced back to Alfred the Great, William the Conqueror, Charlemagne, and the Stuart dynasty of Scotland and England. The early generations do not have the Alexander surname; it evolved over time.

Our Alexander Lineage

In 7500 BC, the first evidence of human settlements in Scotland was found at Kinloch, Isle of Rhum, in Lochaber. By 3000 BC, there was evidence of an agricultural society of cave dwellers. Burial urns containing charred human remains were found around 2000 BC. Fortifications were being built by 1000 BC. Many generations of warrior-kings followed, and my family descended from these warriors. Lochaber is an important location for these warrior-kings. It is also the location of the infamous bombing of Pan Am flight 103, December 21, 1988, in which a bomb planted by terrorists exploded, killing two hundred forty three passengers and sixteen crew members (Rosenberg, 2010).

Feudalism and Manorialism

It is necessary to understand feudalism and manorialism to understand this chapter. Feudalism was the political and military system of the Middle Ages, while manorialism was the basic economic system. Essentially, the king was the owner of all the land, and he granted lands to nobleman in exchange for loyalty, military service, and often high taxes. The grantor of the land was the lord, and the grantee was the vassal. One could be both lord and vassal if one received a grant of land and in turn granted it to another. It was considered to be an honorable and sacred relationship, and only members of the nobility could be lords or vassals (Hanes, 1997).

The king kept about one-third of the land for his own use called the *domain*. Peasants farmed the land, and were considered to be part of the land, and could not be sold away from the land. These peasants were called *serfs*. They were not slaves, but they were not entirely free, but were described as "semi-free," a somewhat contradictory term (Hanes, 1997). The share cropping system of the American South had its origins in manorialism.

NOTE: The following information was gathered from these sources: (MacPhail, 2003); (MacPhee, 2004); (Rogers, 1877); (Sellar, 1966); (*Somerled*, n. d.); (*Somerled, Lord*, 2000); (Williams, 1999).

Somerled of Argyll, King of the Isles and Ragnhilda, Daughter of the Norse King Olaf/Olave I (Olaf the Red)

Somerled was born around 1113 in Morvern, a peninsula on the west coast of Scotland, and is believed to have been descended from Viking, Celtic, and Pict Kings of Ireland, Scotland, and the Isles. Somerled came to power by defeating the Norse King of Man in 1156, thus gaining independence for southwestern Scotland that lasted for over four centuries. It is believed that Somerled was descended from Vikings as well as Norsemen. His grandfather had been defeated by the Norse and exiled to Ireland. When Somerled was a child, he and his family were exiled to Ireland as well. His father raised an army of five hundred warriors and returned to regain his lands but was killed in battle. Somerled, who can best be described as a hunter-gatherer, lived in the caves of his homeland after the death of his father and survived by hunting and fishing.

Somerled lived and died a warrior. In 1135, he led a rebellion against Norse control, a somewhat ironic turn of events as Somerled was of Norse descent. The rebellion was successful and Someled gained Morvern, Lochaber, and the northern part of Argyll, and as a result, became known as the Thane/Thegn of Argyll. One who served as a *thane* was a Scottish feudal lord, an important official of the king, usually in a military capacity, and was considered to be a member of the nobility (*Thane*, 2009). This probably gained Somerled favor with King David, I of Scotland because it ridded him of the Norse enemies.

Somerled made a politically advantageous move when he married Ragnhilda around 1140, daughter of the Norse King Olaf/Olave, known as Olaf the Red. Oral tradition tells the story of how Somerled won the hand of his wife through trickery. Somerled drilled holes in his future father-in-law's ship and plugged them with a substance that dissolved after a short while in the water. A relative of Somerled told King Olaf that he would fix the problem if he would grant Somerled his daughter's hand in marriage, and

Olaf agreed. The holes were repaired, and Somerled wedded the king's daughter around 1140.

In 1143, King Olaf was murdered by the sons of his brother, Harold. Somerled's brother-in-law, Godfrey, ascended the throne after the death of his father, Olaf. Godfrey the Black, as he was known, was cruel to his people and was unpopular. In 1158, there was an uprising against Godfrey of which Somerled was a backer. Somerled had a fleet of ships fitted with rudders, the latest in naval technology, and was able to defeat Godfrey. The kingdom formed by Somerled was independent of Norway and Scotland.

King Malcolm IV of Scotland began to see Somerled as a threat. In 1160, Malcolm and Somerled met in a decisive battle at Argyll. Afterward, an uneasy peace grew between the two kingdoms. In 1164, Somerled landed fifteen thousand troops from one hundred sixty four galley ships with the intention of capturing Renfrew in the heart of Malcolm's kingdom. Before Renfrew could be captured, Somerled was assassinated by one of his nephews, Maurice MacNeil, who had accepted a bribe from Malcolm to kill him. The oral tradition tells that when King Malcolm and his nobles came to view the body, one of the nobles kicked the corpse with his foot. MacNeil, the assassin, was overcome by the shame of his act. He confessed his sin and stabbed in the heart the man who had kicked the corpse of Somerled (Lee, 1920).

Somerled was buried at the monastery of Saddell, or on the Isle of Iona; accounts differ. Somerled had one son by a previous marriage, Gillecallum, his heir, who was killed at Renfrew. Somerled and Ragnhilda had six sons, and one daughter: Dougall (Dufgall, King of Inessgall), Angus (Engul), Prince of Man, Olave, Prince of the Isles, Ranald, Lord of the Isles, Beatrice, Prioress of Iona, and Alan who probably died as an infant, or died young.

My family is descended from their fourth son, Ranald/ Reginald, from whom the Clan of Donald is descended. Bryan Sykes, a professor at Oxford University conducted a DNA study in

2005 from which he concluded that around a half million persons living today are descended from Somerled.

Ranald/Reginald, Lord of the Isles and Fonia of Moray

Ranald, sometimes called Reginald, married Fonia of Moray, granddaughter of Fergus, Prince of Galloway around 1155. Ranald assumed the title "Lord of the Isles" or received it from his followers. He and his two brothers were considered "Kings of the Isles." However, Ranald eventually drove his brother, Angus, and his sons out of Bute and Arran, islands in the west of Scotland. The death of Angus and his sons resulted in Ranald and his brother, Dougall, controlling the mainland and island possessions (Paul, 1908).

In 1180, perhaps out of guilt he felt for his treatment of his brother, Ranald completed the Abbey of Saddell and granted to the monks certain lands. Some researchers believe that at this time, Ranald had his father's bones exhumed from the Isle of Iona and interred at Saddell Abbey. It is believed by some that Somerled had begun the Saddell Abbey and Ranald finished it. Ranald became a monk of Paisley and granted to the monastery eight cows and two pennies for one year and one penny in perpetuity for each house in his territories from which smoked issued. Ranald enjoined his dependents to afford protection to members of the monastery. Fonia became a nun and paid a tithe of her goods to the religious community. Ranald and Fonia's entrance into the religious community was probably more for protection than from any sort of religious conversion. Ranald died in 1207 leaving his lands to his three sons, Donald, Roderick, and Dougall. Roderick was infamous for his acts of piracy (Paul, 2008).

My family is directly descended from Donald, Lord of the Isles who married a Stewart woman. From Donald descended the powerful Clan of Donald, considered the most powerful of the ancient Highland clans. At one time they virtually controlled the entire western seaboard from the Butt of Lewis in the north to the Mull of Kintyre in the south, almost a third of the Kingdom, along with possessions in Northern Ireland (MacDonald, n. d.).

Donald, Lord of the Isles and Wife (Unknown, perhaps Stewart)

Donald, Lord of the Isles, was born around 1190 and died around 1269. Some sources say he married a daughter of Walter, High Stewart of Scotland; others say he married his cousin. An interesting story is told about Donald, but it is probably a myth. It seems that Donald engaged in a contest with a rival clan for possession of a certain piece of land. It was agreed that whoever put his hand on the shore first would win the property. According to the story, Donald's ship was overtaken before he reached shore, so he cut off his left hand, threw it to the shore, and was declared the winner (Paul, 1908).

Donald lived the stormy, violent life of a warrior king, and committed acts that caused him to have a guilty conscience. It is said that he made a pilgrimage to Rome accompanied by seven priests to confess his sins and receive forgiveness by the Roman Catholic Church. Like his father, Donald became a monk and his wife became a nun. He established an annual gift to the monks of Paisley Abby of eight cows and one penny for every house in his territory from which smoke emitted from the chimney, and one-half merk of silver from his own house (Paul, 1908).

It is believed that his father, Ranald, had granted a charter to the Paisley Abby around 1180. When Donald died, he was buried on the Isle of Iona. He had a son, Angus Mor, Lord of the Isles. One source says that Alexander, the brother of Angus Mor, Lord of the Isles, is the progenitor of the Alexanders of Mensrie, the Earls of Stirling, and the Alexanders, Earls of Caledon (Paul, 1908).

Angus Mor, Lord of the Isles (Big Angus) and Daughter of Sir Colin Campbell of Lochawe

Angus Mor, son of Donald, Lord of the Isles, was born around 1249 and died around 1301. Angus Mor had allied himself early with King Hacon of Norway because Alexander III of Scotland had ravaged his lands in 1255. Alexander III of Scotland opposed even nominal suzerainty of Norway over the Hebrides, an archipelago off the west coast of Scotland. *Suzerainty* (2009) is a term of feudal law used to describe persons or states in positions of superiority or over-lordship. Alexander's opposition provoked the launching in 1263 of the Norwegian Fleet of King Hacon consisting of one hundred sixty ships carrying a force of twenty thousand men, and its anchoring off Largs, a town about thirty-three miles from Glasgow, Scotland.

Parties were sent in advance to pillage the countryside of Kintyre and Bute. Angus Mor, Lord of the Isles, sometimes called "Big Angus" was technically a vassal of King Hacon of Norway, and he sent word that he was prepared to submit himself to Norway to save his lands from being plundered. Hacon sent a reply that the plundering would stop the next day at noon, and in the meantime, Angus Mor and several noblemen should present themselves in person to his camp (Lee, 1920); (MacDonald, n. d.); (MacPhail, 2003).

Angus Mor and his men came the next morning, surrendered their lands, swore allegiance to his feudal obligations, and gave hostages along with twelve hundred head of cattle to Hacon who, in turn, told them they would be included in a treaty of peace with Alexander III, if such an accord could be reached. Negotiations broke down, and the Battle of Largs ensued. A full scale war developed, and Alexander III of Scotland was victorious and became the overlord of Angus Mor, Lord of the Isles. Angus Mor was said to be on friendly terms with the Scottish king by 1264. In 1266, there was a formal cession of the Hebrides to Scotland (Graham, 1885).

In 1295, following family tradition, Angus Mor became a monk and granted to the Convent of Paisley one penny annually for each house in his territories, and a half a merk of silver from his own mansion. He granted to the monks of Paisley the church at Kilkerran. Angus Mor, Lord of the Isles, had three sons, Alasdair Og, Angus Og, and John Sprangach (John the Bold). Angus Mor died around 1301 (Lee, 1920); (MacDonald, n. d.); (MacPhail, 2003).

Angus Og, (Angus the Young) Lord of the Isles and Agnes, Daughter of Guy O'Cahan of Ulster, Northern Ireland

Angus Og, Lord of the Isles, married Agnes, a daughter of Guy O' Cahan of Ulster, Northern Ireland. He became the sixth Lord of the Isles after his elder brother, Alexander, fought on the losing side against famous Robert the Bruce. Angus Og received all his brother's forfeited land. Angus Og sheltered Robert the Bruce at the lowest point in his political career. He led a small army of five thousand men and was instrumental in Bruce's defeat of the English under Edward II at Bannockburn in 1314 that won independence for Scotland. As a reward, Bruce proclaimed that Clan Donald would forever occupy the honored position on the right wing of the Scottish army. Angus Og and Agnes had a son, John, Lord of the Isles. Angus Og died in 1336 and was given a royal funeral on the sacred Isle of Iona (Lee 1920); (MacDonald, n. d.); (MacPhail, 2003).

John, Lord of the Isles and Margaret Stewart

John, Lord of the Isles, was born around 1334. He was known as Good King John of Islay because of his generosity to the Church and is said to have been the most distinguished of his line because of his diplomacy and farsightedness (Paul, 1908). John found it politically expedient to be friendly with the English Crown. However, this did not place him in good stead with David Bruce when he returned from France to claim his father's throne. John had to forfeit several of his lands, but when David Bruce decided to invade England, he wanted solidarity, so he pardoned John and reinstated his lands. During the fighting that followed, John was taken prisoner (Paul, 1908).

The English king released him after a few months and gave him a safe pass home. Two years later, he took an active role in promoting a treaty for the liberation and ransom of David Bruce. After procuring a divorce from a previous wife, John married Margaret Stewart, a move that gained him more favor from the English king (Graham, 1885); (Paul, 1908).

By 1364, John held the prestigious position of High Steward of the King's Household but fell from grace with the English Crown because of his refusal to pay a tax he felt was oppressive. After several years of open but successful defiance, an agreement was reached in 1363 in which John swore his allegiance to the king and had his lands restored to him (Paul, 1908).

John had five sons by two wives. Rogers (1877) states John's second wife was Margaret, daughter of Robert II of Scotland, and grandson of famous Robert the Bruce. Donald, his eldest son by his second marriage, succeeded him as Lord of the Isles. Rogers further states that John's third son by this marriage, Alexander, Lord of Lochaber, had a son, Alexander, who founded the house of Alexander.

Donald, Lord of the Isles and Lady Margaret Leslie, Countess of Ross

Donald, Lord of the Isles, was also known as Donald of Harlaw, Lord of Lochaber. Born around 1359, Donald was a famous chieftain and was educated at Oxford. He inherited the lordship in 1386. He fought against Black Angus MacKay, Earl of Farr, in the Ross Highlands, defeated him and forced him to marry his daughter, Elizabeth. However, he was unsuccessful in his bid to obtain the great Earldom of Ross through his wife, Lady Margaret Leslie, Countess of Ross, daughter of Sir Walter Leslie and Euphemia Ross, Countess of Ross (MacPhail, 2003). At the bloody Battle of Harlaw in 1411, he was defeated and then returned to the Isle of Islay. He died in 1423 at his castle (Paul, 1908).

Donald and Lady Margaret had four children: Alexander, his successor, Angus, Bishop of the Isles, an unnamed son who was a monk, and a daughter, Anna (Paul, 1908). MacPhail (2003) lists seven children of Donald and Lady Margaret: Alexander, his successor, Elizabeth who was forced to marry Black Angus MacKay when he was defeated in battle by her father, Angus, Bishop of the Isles, an unnamed son who was a monk, a daughter, Anne, a daughter, Mariotta who married Alexander Sutherland, and an unnamed daughter who married Dugald Campbell.

Alexander McDonald, Lord of the Isles and Tenth Earl of Ross and Spouse (Unknown)

Donald had a son around 1400, Alexander McDonald, who succeeded him as Lord of the Isles. Alexander's life was that of a violent warrior-king who was often ruled by his emotions. The first written record relating to Alexander McDonald is his presence and participation in the trial and condemnation of the Regent, his two sons, and the Earl of Lennox (Paul, 1908). One of the feudal obligations of a vassal to his lord was participation in court matters. The lord often held court proceedings and was the only law enforcement entity during the Middle Ages; his vassals often acted as jurors (Hanes, 1997).

The following year, King James, in an effort to restore order in the Scottish Highlands in the aftermath of the war with Alexander's father, Donald, Lord of the Isles, traveled to Inverness with a formidable army and held a Parliament there. Among the forty persons summoned to Parliament was Alexander, Lord of the Isles. He was imprisoned, and others were executed. Alexander was released after two months; when his mother died, he became the legal Earl of Ross, a coveted title. Alexander was not grateful for the royal favor but immediately went out and raised an army of ten thousand men, and marched on the mainland of the king, burning the town of Inverness to the ground and laying waste to the king's lands. He was not successful in taking the castle at Inverness. Alexander and his troops returned to Lochaber, followed by an army led by King James himself. As the royal army approached, two clans, the Cameron and the Mackintosh, deserted from Alexander's ranks, and joined the king and his troops (MacPhail, 2003); (Paul, 1908).

Alexander was forced to ask the king for a peace treaty, but the king would settle for nothing less than unconditional surrender. Alexander would not agree to unconditional surrender; he retreated and was chased down by the royal army to Holyrood Castle at Edinburgh, Scotland. Holyrood was established as a monastery by King David I of Scotland, and from the middle of the fifteenth century, it was used as a residence by Scottish kings. The castle lies in ruins today (Hunter-Blair, 1910); (Paul, 1908).

Again, Alexander tried to come to terms with King James but was refused. Alexander then threw himself on the king's mercy. On August 27, 1429, before the high altar of Holyrood Church, Alexander, upon his knees, clad only in his shirt and drawers, presented his drawn sword to King James in the presence of the queen and the noblemen (MacPhail, 2003); (Paul, 1908).

King James spared the life of Alexander due to his complete, utter submission; however, Alexander was imprisoned at Tamtallan Castle under the charge of the Earl of Angus. In a parliament held at Perth in 1431, a free pardon was granted to Alexander, the Earl of Ross. He died in 1448/1449. Alexander married Elizabeth Seaton, daughter of Alexander Seaton, Lord of Gordon and Huntly with whom he had children. He also had children out of wedlock by his mistress (MacPhail, 2003).

NOTE: At this point, there is some dispute about the line of descent. Alexander McDonald had a son, John, who was the last "Lord of the Isles" and was married to Lady Elizabeth Livingstone. Because of bad decisions, he had to forfeit the lordship to the Crown in 1493. He then lived for several years as a monk in Paisley, and died in 1498. One source says Alexander of Lochalsh (Alexander Alexander) is the son of Alexander McDonald (Parran, 1935). Other sources say Alexander of Lochalsh (Alexander Alexander) is his nephew. When John lost the title "Lord of the Isles," the family lost the McDonald surname. The McDonald dynasty came to an end, and the house of Alexander was established (Bannerman, 1977); (Cannon, 2004); (Dunbar, 1981); (Gregory, 1975); (MacDonald, C., 1950); (MacDonald, H., 1914); (Munro, 1986). This is why the surname becomes *Alexander* and not *McDonald* (MacPhail, 2003); (Paul, 1908).

John, Lord of the Isles and Elizabeth Livingstone

John, son of Alexander McDonald, squandered a great inheritance. He was forced to marry a woman he did not love, Elizabeth Livingstone, who accused him of trying to murder her while she was pregnant. Throughout his life, he methodically alienated everyone close to him.

John made a deal with King James III of England, the *Treaty of Westminster,* in which John agreed to help the Crown conquer and partition all of Scotland. John's illegitimate son, Angus Og McDonald, commanded an army that took up arms against his father and the king. Angus Og McDonald forced John from his position of leadership of the clan and from his home, forcing John to take shelter under an old boat.

John's ships met his son's ships in the Battle of Bloody Bay. The battle was a victory for Angus Og McDonald who continued to dominate the politics of the Clan of Donald until the time of his murder in 1490. John lived in obscurity until the death of Angus Og. When he emerged from the shadows, he seemed to be under the control of his nephew, Alexander of Lochaber. John died in Dundee, Scotland in 1503. In 1540, James V reserved the title of *Lord of the Isles* for the Crown (Bannerman, 1977); (Cannon,

2004); (Dunbar, 1981); (Gregory, 1975); (MacDonald, C., 1950); (MacDonald, H., 1914); (Munro, 1986). Charles, Prince of Wales, today carries the title *Lord of the Isles (Charles, Prince of Wales, 2006)*.

Alexander, Lord of Lochaser/Lochaber

Alexander, Lord of Lochaser/Lochaber, was also known as Alexander MacAlexander and as Alexander Alexander. His father, or a close relative, Alexander McDonald, made war against the King of Scotland and, as a result, was banished. Alexander lost his surname due to his father/relative's banishment. He had two sons, Angus and Alexander (Rogers, 1877).

Alexander Alexander and Elizabeth (Unknown), Founder of the House of Alexander

According to Rogers (1877) and Parran (1935), Alexander was the true founder of the House of Alexander. He was born around 1400 and died around 1480. He obtained lands in Menstrie from the noble House of the Argylls. He and Elizabeth had a son, Thomas Alexander, Baron of Menstrie, born around 1445 in Menstrie, Parish of Logie, Clakmannshire, Stirling, Scotland.

Thomas Alexander, Baron of Menstrie and Spouse (Unknown)

Thomas Alexander, Baron of Menstrie, was born around 1445 in Menstrie Parish of Logie, Clakmannshire, Stirling, Scotland. Records of March 1505 (*Chartulary of Cambuskenneth Abbey*, p. 86) show a *Thomas Alexander of Menstrie* as one of the sixteen arbitrators in a boundary dispute over forty acres of land. It seems that the dispute had arisen between the Abbot of Cambuskenneth and Sir David Bruce (Rogers, 1877).

Records also indicate that on August 25, 1529, the family entered into a feudal agreement with their cousins, the Campbells. As part of the agreement, they were given farmlands, a mill, and a bog at Menstrie. A bog provided fuel called peat that is used for heating; it was sometimes the only source of fuel for ancient Scots and Irish. Peat is a very early stage of coal deposits (*Ireland Information Guide*, n. d.). Annual payments were to be made to the Campbells with wheat, oats, sheep and capons, or roosters whose reproductive organs have been removed. This agreement is on file in Scottish Public Record Office in Edinburgh, Scotland.

There is a statement about the Alexanders inheriting Temple lands at Menstrie in 1537 and again in 1553. Menstrie is a small village northeast of Stirling, in Scotland's smallest county, Clackmannanshire, and sits at the foot of the Ochil Hills. Another source states that the Alexanders held Temple lands twenty years later. There is a charter from King James V dated April 15, 1530 in Stirling, Scotland, confirming the gift of Menstrie for a payment of twenty-four barrels of corn. Thomas Alexander was the father of Andrew Alexander, Baron of Menstrie (*Alexander Genealogy*, 2008).

Menstrie Castle

It is believed that Menstrie Castle was constructed around 1322. It is actually not a castle but an excellent example of a baronial mansion house. Douglas Campbell, a cousin to the Alexanders, was perhaps the first owner and inhabitant. The Earls of Argyll resided at Menstrie Castle, a three-storey castellated house, until 1526 when title was transferred to the Alexanders. It is famous for being the birthplace of the First Earl of Stirling. Title to the house passed to the Holburne family in 1649. In 1719, title passed back to the Alexanders. It fell vacant in the late 1800s. It became so dilapidated that it was almost demolished but for the efforts of actor and conservationist Moultrie R. Kelsall. His efforts resulted in the castle being listed as a building of national importance that cannot be altered or demolished without official permission. It has been restored to its present state, and subdivided into flats and holiday accommodations (Mack, 2007); (*Places to Visit*, n. d.).

Andrew Alexander, Baron of Menstrie and Catherine Graham

Andrew Alexander, born around 1446, succeeded his father as the Baron of Menstrie. He married Catherine Graham around 1470, and had two sons, Alexander and Andrew. Andrew entered the church. In a sasine/seisin, a feudal legal document, dated November 15, 1529, he is referred to as "Andreas Alexander, presbyter," meaning an officer, minister, or priest in the early Christian church (*Presbyter*, 2009); (Rogers, 1877).

In a charter dated April 8, 1526, the Earl of Argyle granted to Andrew Alexander and his wife, Catherine Graham, lands in Menstrie, in life-rent, and to their son and heir, Alexander Alexander, in fee. *Life-rent* is a Scottish legal term meaning that an individual could have full use of the land and retain the income from it but that individual could not transfer the land to another individual (*Life-rent*, 2009).

Alexander Alexander, Baron of Menstrie and Elizabeth Douglas

Andrew Alexander died prior to 1527 and was succeeded by his son, Alexander Alexander who was granted lands called the Main of Menstie. Annual rent was to be paid in the form of twenty-four bolls of corn, twenty-four bolls of barley malt, and twenty-four bolls of oat meal and other agricultural commodities. A handy conversion table (*Scottish Weights and Measures*, n. d.) states that the boll was the Scottish basic unit of measure of dry capacity. For barley, oats, malt, and corn, a boll was the equivalent of five bushels three pecks, nearly six bushels in the English system. Barley malt was used to produce Scotch whiskey. Alexander Alexander was granted other lands for the annual payment of one penny. Alexander Alexander married Elizabeth Douglas, daughter of Sir Robert Douglas of Lochleven. Alexander and Elizabeth had two sons, Andrew and William, and two daughters, Marion and Isabel (Rogers, 1877).

Andrew Alexander, Baron of Menstrie and Spouse (Unknown)

Andrew Alexander succeeded his father as Baron of Menstrie in 1544. He died young, only a short time after his father's death. Andrew Alexander left two sons, Alexander and John, and was succeeded by Alexander (Rogers, 1877).

Alexander Alexander of Menstrie and Elizabeth Forbes

Alexander Alexander was simply Alexander Alexander of Menstrie. There is a legal document in the Rogers book (1877), written in the Scottish dialect, which is nearly a foreign language. I muddled through the document, and I believe the title of *Baron* was lost. However, *Alexander Genealogy* (2008) lists Alexander Alexander as Baron of Menstrie. Alexander and Elizabeth Forbes were the parents of three sons, William, James, and John, and three daughters Elizabeth, Marion, and Janet (Rogers, 1877).

William Alexander of Menstrie and Spouse (Unknown)

William Alexander was the father of Alexander Alexander, according to Rogers (1877). However, *Alexander Genealogy* (2008) lists another son, Thomas.

Alexander Alexander of Menstrie and Marion (Unknown)

Alexander Alexander and Marion (Unknown) were married around 1540. According to Rogers (1877), they were the parents of one son, William Alexander, and two daughters, Janet and Christian. William Alexander was later to become Sir William Alexander, First Lord of Stirling.

Sir William Alexander, First Lord of Stirling and Janet Erskine

Sir William Alexander, First Lord of Stirling, lived from approximately 1567–1640. When William's father died, he and his two sisters were left in charge of his grand-uncle, James Alexander, a Burgess of Stirling. William Alexander probably attended Glasgow University and perhaps the University of Leiden. He took the traditional Grand Tour of Europe with the Seventh Earl of Argyle. As a reward, he was given the entire barony of Menstrie (Clemens, 1914); (Taylor, 1889); (*William Alexander*, 1911).

He married Janet Erskine, daughter of Sir William Erskine of Balgonie, around 1601–1604 (*William Alexander*, 1911). Sir William Alexander, First Earl of Stirling, was a poet and statesman whose tragedies preceded and influenced the famous English playwright, William Shakespeare. He was an associate of Shakespeare, Johnson, Dryden, and Spenser. His kinship to the Argyles gave him access to the Scottish Court and won him an introduction to the king. He served on the Privy Council, became a friend and confidant to King James VI, and was appointed as tutor for the king's eldest son and heir to the throne, Prince Henry. He became a gentleman usher to Prince Charles, the son of James VI, and was knighted by King James in the early 1600s, probably 1609–1611. King James asked for Sir William's help in translating the Bible. Sir William translated the Psalms of David in the King James Version of the Bible. He was knighted in 1613 (*Alexander Genealogy Chart*, n. d.); (Clemens, 1914); (Taylor, 1889); (*William Alexander*, 1911). He received a grant of lands in Canada in 1621 that he named Nova Scotia, meaning "New Scotland." Sir William served as Secretary of State for Scotland from 1626 to his death and was given the title Earl of Stirling in 1639 (*William Alexander*, 1911).

He met and married Janet Erskine shortly after he returned from the Grand Tour. Janet was described as being musically talented and aristocratic. Her family had been keepers of Stirling Castle and protectors of princes of the realm. William and Janet had seven sons and three daughters. They were married forty years, and Janet outlived William. In spite of his shining career, Sir William was bankrupt in his later years. He died in London in September 1640, impoverished and hounded by creditors. Janet had to apply for a Crown pension to live on during her remaining years (*Alexander Genealogy*, 2008).

William Alexander, Second Lord of Stirling

The Second Lord of Stirling is not in the direct line of descent in my family; however, I am including this brief discussion. William Alexander, Second Lord of Stirling, 1726–1783, was Surveyor-General of New Jersey. He also fought in the Franco-Indian War of 1755 with Governor General Shirley of Massachusetts. The two men went to Scotland to claim the Earldom of Stirling and the lands granted to the First Earl of Stirling. He reclaimed the title but not the lands and returned to America and served as a Brigadier General in the American Revolution. He served under General George Washington and was praised for his bravery in the Battle of Long Island. He married Sarah Livingston, sister of the governor of New Jersey, and they had two daughters. A heavy drinker, he died a few days after the American Revolutionary War was won (Lawrence, n. d.). William Alexander was praised posthumously by Congress in 1783, and two portraits of him hang in public places, Independence Hall in Philadelphia, and Town Hall, Stirling, Massachusetts (*Alexander Genealogy Chart*, n. d.).

My family is descended from the fourth son of Sir William and Janet Erskine Alexander, John Alexander, born around 1590–1606 in Menstrie.

Captain John Alexander and Agnes / Catherine Graham, and the "Irish Plantations"

John Alexander, born around 1590 in Menstrie, Stirling, Scotland, married Agnes Graham. However, Chapman (1939) says her name was Catherine Graham, daughter of John Graham of Gartmore, Scotland. In the early 1600s, John Alexander went to Ireland with a large number of other Presbyterians, and settled in Londonderry, Northern Ireland, as part of the "Irish Plantation" (*Culp Notes*, 2001).

The Irish Plantations were colonization efforts by the English, with the intention of subjugating the unruly Irish. Colonists were "planted" in English lands. The Plantation of Ulster took place in the northern Irish province during the early seventeenth century in the reign of James I of England, a Protestant. The idea was conceived to "plant" the counties of Ulster (Northern Ireland) with a variety of persons of different nationalities and religions. Scottish Protestants were given lands that were confiscated from Irish Catholic landowners. To carry out this "plantation" idea, James I confiscated large tracts of land and banished the owners. He parceled out the land to certain proprietors, most of whom were English or Scots (Ford, 1915); (*Irish Plantations*, n. d.).

The Plantation of Ulster ensured that at least half of the settlement would be Scots (Robinson, 1994). Ulster was "planted" this way to avoid rebellion. Ulster had proved to be the most resistant of Irish provinces and in the past had been outside English control. King James VI of Scotland became King of England in 1603, uniting the two crowns. The English Crown found the native Irish difficult to govern. They were often antagonistic, combative, and lawless. The Irish constantly demanded freedom and self-government (Ford, 1915). To this day, hostilities between the English and the Irish run high.

The Scots-Irish were so called not because they married the Irish, but to distinguish themselves from the Irish. The Scots had no love for the English or the Irish; in fact, each group disliked, and in some cases, hated, the other two groups. The Scots-Irish who migrated to America had no great love for the British government whose injustices had caused them to migrate to Northern Ireland (Canny, 2003). Consequently, the Scots-Irish colonists were solidly allied to the Continental Army during the American Revolutionary War.

John and Agnes/Catherine Alexander immigrated to America around 1659 where they obtained a grant of fifteen hundred acres of land in Northampton County, later to become Accomac County, in the Shenandoah Valley of Virginia. In 1664, John Alexander obtained a grant of one thousand four hundred fifty acres, making him one of the largest land owners in the American colonies (Parran, 1935).

John Alexander also bought land in Stafford County, which later became King George County. John Alexander built a home that he called Salisbury that overlooked the Potomac River and was near the main highway, the Ridge Road that was more of a trail used by the Native American tribes than a highway. In Accomac County, John Alexander purchased more land and bought and shipped tobacco. He gained fifteen hundred acres as a reward for transporting thirty persons to the colony of Virginia (Chapman, 1939).

In Stafford County, John Alexander was a community leader who was appointed Justice and High Sheriff. He presided at the first court of Stafford County, May 27, 1664. This was considered to be a post of honor because it was the highest gift of the Council. John Alexander served in this position without remuneration, and it carried the honorary title of Captain. Alexandria, Virginia was named for the John Alexander family (Chapman, 1939).

In 1664, Captain John Alexander was given the responsibility of supervising the building of the first county courthouse for Stafford County, Virginia. He was made vestryman, the first in the county, of Potomac Parish, November 8, 1666, and was reelected in 1667. There was no church building at that time so services were held at private homes. The colonies in America were divided into parishes. The vestryman performed many civic duties and was held accountable to the government. To be a vestryman, one was required to be a resident freeholder of the parish. This became the permanent home of the Alexander family, a family that became numerous, prominent, and influential. Five generations of Alexanders lived there. John Alexander was a surveyor by profession. He and Agnes/Catherine Graham had eight children. John Alexander died in 1677. My family is descended from William Alexander, son of John and Agnes Alexander (Chapman, 1939).

The Southern Frontier

It is important to understand the impact and history of the American frontier in the development of the United States. The frontier was usually regarded as a westward movement, but before this movement began, an important southern migration occurred. The southern frontier existed for more than seventy years as Scots-Irish and Germans from Pennsylvania settled around Cecil County, Maryland, and then followed the Great Wagon Road through the Shenandoah Valley of Virginia and western North Carolina (Caruso, 1963).

These settlers were separated from English towns and settlements in Virginia by the Blue Ridge Mountains. The southern exodus resulted in settlements along the road that led south to North Carolina and later to settlements in Kentucky and Tennessee (*The Scots-Irish from Ulster*, n. d.). Most of the branches of my family followed the southern frontier, many of them ultimately settling in Drew County, Arkansas.

The *Advance Monticellonian*, in its May 15, 1894 edition, mentions Reverend S. C. Alexander, pastor of the Presbyterian Church in Monticello, Arkansas. This particular Alexander was a grandson of John McKnitt Alexander, later discussed in this narrative. He lived in Pine Bluff according to *The History of Mecklenburg County from 1740 to 1900* (1902). Most likely he was a circuit rider preacher who moved from congregation to congregation. *The History* (1902) described him as an evangelist who had preached in many of the southern states, and was somewhat well known. The Monticello, Arkansas First Presbyterian Church, located on North Main Street, is housed in the building that was once the Mack Wilson Hospital. For many years, an inscription over the front entrance to the church read "Mack Wilson Hospital." Unfortunately, the church has removed the inscription.

William Alexander, Sr. and Araminta Ann Liston

William Alexander, Sr. was born in 1624 in Erindy, Donegal County, Ulster, Ireland. He married Araminta Ann Liston, born around 1630 in Raphoe, Donegal, Ulster, Ireland. William Alexander, Sr. immigrated to America from Scotland sometime before 1675 and settled in Somerset, Maryland. He was an extensive trader of lands. William Alexander, Sr. remained in Somerset, and called his home Raphoe. William and Araminta Alexander had seven sons and two daughters. My family is descended from their son, Andrew Alexander (Butterworth, 1909); *Descendants of John Alexander*, 2008).

Andrew Alexander and (First) Abigail McKnitt (Second) Anne Anderson Taylor

Andrew Alexander was born around 1648 in Raphoe, Donegal, Ulster, Ireland. He is described as Andrew Alexander, the farmer, to distinguish him from other Andrew Alexanders. Andrew married Abigail McKnitt who was born in 1667 in Stirling, Scotland. Andrew and Abigail Alexander had two children: Abigail, born September 15, 1677, and Elias, born February 26, 1679. There is some debate about which wife was number one, and which wife was number two. Abigail was probably his first wife because their daughter is named for her mother. Andrew had other children, as well. My family is directly descended from Elias Alexander, Sr. (*Elias Alexander, Sr.*, n. d.); (Virkus, 1998).

Elias Alexander, Sr. and (First) Sophia Alexander (Second) Ann Taylor

The first wife of Elias Alexander, Sr. was his cousin, Sophia Alexander, daughter of his uncle, Joseph Alexander and Abigail McKnitt Alexander. She was born around 1687 in Maryland. Joseph Alexander's will, dated 1726, refers to his son-in-law, Elias Alexander. Elias Alexander was born February 26, 1679 in Somerset County, Maryland. He died around 1750 in Frederick County, Maryland (*Alexander Pioneers*, 1920).

Elias Alexander, Sr. has the distinction of being our first Alexander ancestor born in America. Elias and Sophia Alexander had six children: Arthur, Ezra, Abigail, William, Abraham, and Zebulon (*Alexander Pioneers*, 1920); (*Neel Family Bible*, 1785); (Stafford, A. & Stafford, E., 1951). Ann Taylor was the second wife of Elias Alexander. She may have been related to his mother who had the same name. Elias and Ann Alexander had seven children: Esther, Judekiah, Andrew, Isaac, Mary, Elias, Jr., and Francis (*Alexander Genealogy*, 2008); (*Elias Alexander, Sr.*, n.d.). My families is directly descended from Elias Alexander, Jr. Elias Alexander, Sr. and Sophia Alexander were the parents of two signers of the famous Mecklenburg Declaration of Independence, Abraham Alexander and Ezra Alexander, and were the grandparents of two other signers, Adam Alexander and Charles Alexander (*Alexander Genealogy*, 2008).

Chapter 9
The Alexanders' Role in the American Revolution

Colonel Elias Alexander, Jr. and Agnes McCall

Elias Alexander, Jr. was a colonel in the American Revolutionary War, serving under General Nathaniel Greene, according to *Daughters of the American Revolution*, vol. 41. He was born in Pennsylvania in 1746, immigrated to Maryland, and then to North Carolina where he died in 1826. He married Nancy Agnes McCall, daughter of James McCall and Janet Harris McCall, around 1768 (*Family Group Record: Elias Alexander and Nancy Agnes McCall*, 2008). His brother, Captain Isaac Alexander, also served in the Revolutionary War (*Southern Campaign*, n.d.). Elias Alexander Jr. and Agnes Alexander had eleven children. My family is descended from their eldest daughter, Anne Alexander, who married Stephen Camp, son of Thomas Camp and Margaret Carney Camp. Stephen Camp, crippled from the Battle of Cowpens (*Camp Family Bulletin*, 1932) must have been a charming young man to win the hand of the aristocratic daughter of Revolutionary War hero, Colonel Elias Alexander, Jr. (*Family Group Record: Stephen Camp and Anne Alexander,* 2008).

Several Alexanders were prominent in the American Revolution. Two of them are Elias Alexander's half-brothers, and several were his cousins. Though they are not in our line of direct descent, I will discuss them because of their prominent roles in gaining our nation's independence.

Our family has deep roots in Mecklenburg County, North Carolina where many of the Alexanders settled. The county has a rich history, part of which is the *Mecklenburg Declaration of Independence of May 20, 1775.* Several prominent Alexanders were among the signers of this historic document. The *Mecklenburg Declaration of Independence* was a resolution proclaimed by leading citizens of Mecklenburg, declaring themselves "independent of the Crown of Great Britain" (*Celebrating the Mecklenburg Declaration,* 2004); (Graham, 1905); (Thorlton, 1996).

Over the months leading up to this watershed event, the citizens of Mecklenburg grew increasingly opposed to the British Parliament's powers of taxation and regulation of internal affairs of the Colonists. When word of the Battle of Lexington reached Mecklenburg County, the Colonists elected delegates to draw up a resolution proclaiming their freedom from the British Crown.

There is some controversy over the authenticity of the *Mecklenburg Declaration.* Some believe it never existed. The Public Library of Charlotte and Mecklenburg County, North Carolina has an excellent website, *Celebrating the Mecklenburg Declaration of Independence.* It has the text of the document and biographical sketches of the signers. The site is easy to navigate and informative. It presents both sides of the argument surrounding the document.

I believe the document is authentic because there are so many other well-documented details about the document and the signers, but I will leave it to my readers to decide about the document's authenticity. I will summarize this controversy as succinctly as possible. Legend has it that the original *Mecklenburg Declaration* was signed by twenty-seven prominent citizens of Mecklenburg County, North Carolina, May 20, 1775, six of whom were Alexanders. Colonel Abraham Alexander was chairman, and John McKnitt Alexander was secretary. Also among the signers were Colonel Adam Alexander, Ezra Alexander, Hezekiah Alexander, and Charles Alexander. John McKnitt Alexander and Hezekiah Alexander were brothers. Abraham Alexander and Ezra Alexander were brothers, and half-brothers of Elias Alexander, Jr. from whom we are descended, and Adam Alexander and Charles Alexander were brothers (*Celebrating the Mecklenburg Declaration*, 2004); (*Childress/Mathis Family Tree*, 2008); (Coffey, 1956); (Graham, 1905).

There is no original copy of the document because the original draft and other records passed to the hands of the group secretary, John McKnitt Alexander, and were destroyed in a fire at his home in 1800. The "old secretary," as he was called, attempted to recreate the original document from memory (Graham, 1905). Many of the original signers and their family members have provided testimony in support of the document's existence and authenticity (*Celebrating the Mecklenburg Declaration*, 2004). This interesting question is presented on the library's website (2004):

> "*If this declaration actually existed, then it would have predated the National Declaration of Independence which was written by Thomas Jefferson in 1776 by more than a year. View a recreation of the Meck Dec document yourself. Do you think Jefferson borrowed from any of its concepts or wording? Or was it the other way around?*"

Controversy brewed around this question. In 1819, Dr. Joseph Alexander submitted a copy of the *Mecklenburg Declaration* for publication in the *Raleigh Register* newspaper. He had transcribed it from a copy written by his father, John McKnitt Alexander. The elder

Alexander had written the copy from his notes after the fire. John Adams read the document that had been published in the *Essex Register* in Massachusetts in June 1819. He was so impressed that he sent a copy to his friend, Thomas Jefferson, with whom he had corresponded over a lifetime (Graham, 1905). Jefferson, with a vexed air, wrote back to Adams that he believed the document to be "spurious" (Cappon, 1988). In 1907, William Henry Hoyt (1907) wrote a book, the premise of which was that the declaration was "spurious."

Mud-slingers circulated rumors that Jefferson had plagiarized some of the *Mecklenburg Declaration* in drafting the *Declaration of Independence*. Jefferson's supporters responded by accusing the Alexanders of forgery, taking the position that the *Mecklenburg Declaration* never existed. Many persons still hold that position; however, in North Carolina, the *Meck Dec* is still widely celebrated (*Celebrating the Mecklenburg Declaration,* 2004); (Thorlton, n. d.). The flag of North Carolina and the State Seal of North Carolina bear the date of the *Mecklenburg Declaration,* May 20, 1775. If you have doubts about the authenticity of the "Meck Dec," it would probably not be a good idea to voice that opinion in Charlotte, or in Mecklenburg County, North Carolina. Its residents are proud of the legacy of the historic document. Several United States Presidents, including Eisenhower, Ford, Taft, and Wilson, have been guests at the annual celebration (*Celebrating the Mecklenburg Declaration of Independence,* 2004).

The one hundred ninth Congress of the United States, on May 10, 2005, passed a resolution celebrating the two hundred thirtith anniversary of the *Mecklenburg Declaration of Independence* and honoring the leaders who created and signed this significant document (*Congress of the United States,* 2005). The Alexander signers of the Mecklenburg Declaration of Independence were half-brothers and first cousins of Colonel Elias Alexander, Jr. from whom my family is directly descended.

Colonel Abraham Alexander

Colonel Abraham Alexander (1717–1786), son of Elias Alexander, Sr. and Sophia Alexander, and half-brother of Colonel Elias Alexander, Jr. was elected chairman of the *Mec Dec* group. Born in Cecil County, Maryland in 1717, Abraham was a cooper (barrel maker) by profession. After he married, Abraham Alexander moved to a frontier area, Mecklenburg County, North Carolina (King, 1956).

Abraham Alexander started out in Mecklenburg on the wrong side of the law, which was not unusual on the frontier. He was a participant in what was dubbed the "Sugar Creek War of 1765." The colonial Governor, Arthur Dobbs, and his friend, Henry McCulloh, a representative of Lord Selwyn who claimed much of the land, were partners in the land speculation business. They accused the Mecklenburg settlers of being "squatters" and set about to survey the boundaries of their land so they could charge rent to the settlers, many of whom were indeed "squatters" (Morrill, n. d.). The independent-mindedness of the settlers became apparent when a group of the settlers, led by Thomas Polk, warned McCulloh to back off or run the risk of bodily harm. McCulloh ignored their threat and called the band of men "blockheads." Abraham Alexander and the other men were disguised as Indians, striped with black paint when they attacked McCulloh and his men. McCulloh retreated to New Bern, North Carolina (Foote, 1846).

William Tryon became Royal Governor of the Colony of North Carolina in 1765, and settled the land disputes. He appointed Thomas Polk and Abraham Alexander to study the situation and make a recommendation for a settlement. Not surprisingly, they determined that McCulloh's claims for Lord Selwyn were invalid because they had not attracted a sufficient number of settlers to their property. Therefore, they had to sell their land to the settlers or to the Royal government. Tryon donated part of the land formerly owned by Lord Selwyn for the county seat. He placed Polk and Alexander in charge of creating the town in 1768; it was to be called *Charlotte*, in honor of the Queen of Great Britain (Foote, 1846).

Abraham Alexander lived three miles northwest of Charlotte, the present location of the Charlotte Country Club, and was a leading member of the community, serving as an elder in the Presbyterian Church at Sugar Creek (Foote, 1846). He was a founder of the Steele Creek Presbyterian Church. He amassed a fortune in real estate and was related to many prominent citizens. He was a large slaveholder, imbuing him with great social status in the colonial south (Foote, 1846).

In 1762, Abraham Alexander was appointed a justice of the peace and a commissioner in charge of erecting a courthouse and other public buildings. In 1769 and 1770, he served as a representative in the North Carolina Assembly. An early environmentalist, Abraham Alexander sponsored a bill to protect the Catawba River that was an important source of food for the frontiersmen (Foote, 1846); (King, 1956). Abraham Alexander was one of the trustees who established the city of Charlotte as the county seat of Mecklenburg County. He became one of the trustees of the Queen's Museum, an educational institution in Charlotte. Today it is known as Queen's University of Charlotte, a private, Presbyterian-affiliated university (King, 1956). He was an honored chairman of the inferior court both before and after the Revolution (King, 1956). Abraham Alexander was also a surveyor (*Celebrating the Mecklenburg Declaration*, 2004).

Abraham Alexander was active in the agitation leading up to the American Revolutionary War. He was a lieutenant colonel of the militia, a member of the Colonial Assembly in 1771, chairman of the county court, and a member of the Committee of Safety of Mecklenburg County (*Daughters of the American Revolution*, 1952). His age prevented him from fighting in the Revolution (King, 1956). When King George III of Great Britain, in an address to Parliament, suspended the constitution of the colonies, the *Mecklenburg Declaration of Independence* was born, with Abraham Alexander serving as chairman of the group of delegates who drafted the resolution. The *Mecklenburg Declaration* is significant because it was the first step in any of the colonies to establish a nation independent of Great Britain. Abraham Alexander is buried in the Sugar Creek Presbyterian Church Cemetery in Charlotte, North Carolina (Graham, 1905).

Captain Ezra Alexander

Ezra Alexander, a brother of Abraham Alexander, and another half-brother of Elias Alexander, Jr. from whom my family is directly descended, was another signer of the *Mecklenburg Declaration of Independence*. He was born in Frederick or Cecil County, Maryland, February 26, 1740. In 1754, he came with other members of his family to Mecklenburg County. As an adult, he was granted several hundred acres of land and established his home near an area now known as Pineville, and was a slave owner. He was appointed Overseer of Roads in 1778. During the Revolution, he served in several campaigns including the Battles of Ramseur's Mill and Hanging Rock and was promoted to the rank of captain (*Celebrating the Mecklenburg Declaration*, 2004); (Coffey, 1956).

Ezra Alexander was buried in the cemetery of the Ezekiel Polk family near Pineville, North Carolina. The cemetery was lost over the years to the forest. Around 1950, squirrel hunters found it buried deep in the woods near Sugar Creek. A double grave stone marking the graves of Ezra Alexander and his wife, Mary Polk Alexander, is said to be quite beautiful and was imported from a northern stone cutter. In 1954, the *Mecklenburg Declaration of Independence* chapter of the Daughters of the American Revolution unveiled a monument to Ezra Alexander for his patriotic contributions to Mecklenburg County. They placed it next to the grave of his son, Augustus Alexander, in Sharon Presbyterian Church Cemetery due to the inaccessibility of the Polk Cemetery (Coffey, 1956).

John McKnitt Alexander

John McKnitt Alexander was secretary of the delegation that wrote the *Mecklenburg Declaration of Independence*. The records of the meeting, along with the original draft, passed into his possession and were destroyed when his home burned in 1800. John McKnitt Alexander was the son of James Alexander and Margaret McKnitt, born June 6, 1733, and reared in Pennsylvania. He came to Mecklenburg County when he was twenty-one years old. He was a tailor by profession and took cattle and hides in exchange for work. He would take the cattle and hides to Philadelphia and purchase cloth and other fine materials to make suits for a wealthy group of customers. He was also appointed as a surveyor by the British Crown and is believed to have surveyed much of the land claimed by early settlers in the area (*Celebrating the Mecklenburg Declaration*, 2004); (*Daughters of the American Revolution*, 1952); (Graham, 1905).

John McKnitt Alexander built a home of field stone in 1774, nine miles northwest of Charlotte, in the Hopewell section of Mecklenburg County, and his home became a general meeting place for the more intelligent and patriotic citizens for miles in all directions. The dwelling, in the 1950s, was the oldest house standing in Mecklenburg County; five chapters of the Daughters of the American Revolution in Charlotte restored the house in the 1950s (*Daughters of the American Revolution*, 1952).

In 1954, the *Charlotte Observer* ran a feature story with photographs of the John McKnitt Alexander home place. One of the pictures shows the last original building of the John McKnitt Alexander plantation; it is the two hundred-year-old cabin of a slave named Wynn. The article also discusses and provides a photograph of the spring near the house where John McKnitt Alexander and other patriots met to discuss the *Mecklenburg Declaration of Independence* and British oppression in general. John McKnitt Alexander was a hospitable host and often served corn liquor or apple brandy that he distilled on his plantation. The corn liquor was said to be so hot that it strangled an unwarned guest (*News from Massachusetts*, n. d.).

John McKnitt Alexander was a member of the Provincial Assembly in 1772 and a member of the Committee of Safety in 1775 (*Celebrating the Mecklenburg Declaration*, 2004); (*Daughters of the American Revolution*, 1952). He was a substantial landowner whose property was estimated at ten miles square; his plantation was known as Alexandria (*News from Massachusetts*, n. d.).

John McKnitt Alexander served in the Colonial Congress. He helped organize the Hopewell Presbyterian Church, donating the land, and served as a ruling elder. He served as treasurer of the Presbyterian Synod which included what are now the states of North Carolina and South Carolina. He was a staunch patriot and owned many slaves. He ordered his slave and foreman, Cato, to burn down his barns and granary rather than let them fall into the hands of the British Army when it invaded Charlotte in 1780 (*Hornets' Nest*, n. d.). John McKnitt Alexander is believed to have served as an army scout for General Greene and was with General Greene when the British General Cornwallis surrendered at Yorktown (*Daughters of the American Revolution*, 1952).

His civic leadership was evident when he served as Mecklenburg's Register of Deeds from 1788 to 1792. He was elected to the North Carolina State Senate, serving as the first state senator from Mecklenburg County and the House of Commons. He was also a member of the convention that wrote the *North Carolina State Constitution*. John McKnitt Alexander had two daughters who both married Presbyterian ministers. He sent his son, Joseph McKnitt Alexander, to what is now Princeton University to study for the Presbyterian ministry. John McKnitt Alexander is buried in the Hopewell Cemetery (Graham, 1905).

Hezekiah Alexander

Hezekiah Alexander was a brother of John McKnitt Alexander. Born in Cecil County, Maryland, he married Mary Sample, and migrated to North Carolina in 1754 with his brother James McKnitt Alexander and their widowed sister, Jemima Sharpe, and her six children. Before coming to North Carolina, he lived for a time in Cumberland County, Pennsylvania where he owned land until 1773.

Records show that Hezekiah Alexander was an administrator and councilor and was the first appointed Magistrate in Mecklenburg County. He was a blacksmith by trade (Mobley, 2003). He served in the Revolutionary War as paymaster of Colonel Thomas Polk's regiment. Records also reveal that he purchased land in Mecklenburg County in May of 1765 and more land in 1767 on Alexander's Creek. He also purchased land in Gaston County on the Broad River. He and his wife, Mary, had eleven children. Hezekiah Alexander was an elder in the Sugar Creek Presbyterian Church which he had helped organize. Four or five miles east of Charlotte, he built a two-story home of native stone in 1774 on which the date is cut; it contained a full basement where the family stored food. The exterior of the home displayed a carving of a fish, the secret symbol of the Presbyterians of Ireland and Scotland.

The story is told of the day the British raided the basement and took all the food they could carry and destroyed the rest. They stole jars of honey and broke what they could not carry on a large rock outside the basement. Mary Alexander had to hide her children in the weeds to keep the British from kidnapping them and holding them for ransom (Alexander, 1908); (*First Generation,* n.d). Today, the home has been restored by the Daughters of the American Revolution and is the oldest house now standing in Mecklenburg County. The Hezekiah Alexander home site had been designated an historic site open to the public as part of the Charlotte Museum of History. Hezekiah Alexander was a calm and steadying presence during

The American Revolution when the British were burning homes and personal belongings. He is buried in the Sugar Creek Cemetery (*Celebrating the Mecklenburg Declaration,* 2004); (*Daughters of the American Revolution,* 1952); (Graham, 1905).

Major Thomas Alexander

The 1840 Census of Pensioners for Mecklenburg County, North Carolina lists Major Thomas Alexander, eighty-seven years old, as drawing a pension for military service in the American Revolutionary War.

The Alexanders and Slavery

Hezekiah Alexander was affluent, one of the elite and influential artisan-planters in Mecklenburg County. He employed his sons and nephews as teamsters to haul flour, furs, cattle, and pinkroot, a drug used to treat hookworms, to Philadelphia. These goods were commodities traded for manufactured goods and slaves. Slaves were social status symbols on the colonial frontier, and Hezekiah Alexander used his slaves as labor in his business enterprises (Foote, 1846). Hezekiah Alexander owned as many as thirteen slaves, placing him in the top one percent of slaveholders in late eighteenth century Mecklenburg County, North Carolina (Hendricks, C. & Hendricks, J., 1995). His will outlines the value of his slaves and who received the slaves upon his death (Ferguson, 1993). The following lists the slaves of Hezekiah Alexander and their disposition upon his death (*Will of Hezekiah Alexander*, Mecklenburg County Will Book A, pg. 20):

> Sam, a field hand, was willed to Hezekiah's wife, Mary, upon his death (Ferguson, 1993).

> Abram, a field hand, was willed to Hezekiah's wife, Mary, upon his death.

> Jack was willed to William Sample Alexander upon the death of Hezekiah Alexander.

> *Mary was sold by James Ranklin Alexander to John Parks* before the death of Hezekiah Alexander.

Ann was willed to Silas Alexander upon the death of Hezekiah Alexander.

Jean and her three children, plus her future children, were willed to Esther Alexander Garrison, upon the death of Hezekiah Alexander. Her three children are listed as Sarah, Frank, and Nancy.

Hannah was willed to Keziah Alexander upon the death of Hezekiah Alexander.

Nance is listed in the inventory of the estate of Hezekiah Alexander in 1801. As a child, her value was cited as one hundred fifty dollars. She became the property of Mary Alexander Polk upon her marriage. The 1797 codicil of the will of Hezekiah Alexander, written when Mary was deceased, makes Nance the property of Mary's husband, Charles Polk.

Rachel is listed in the inventory as a child valued at one hundred thirty dollars.

Unnamed girl is listed in the inventory. She was purchased at a vendor ("vendor" is probably a euphemism for slave dealer) on April 4, 1799 for three hundred one dollars. She was left to Hugh Alexander, apparently as part of a debt owed to Hugh Alexander by Hezekiah Alexander.

Bet was a woman left to Hezekiah's wife, Mary, then to Joel Alexander *in Mary Sample Alexander's will probated in* October of 1805 (Will of Mary Alexander, Mecklenburg County Will Book A, p. 47); (Ferguson, 1993).

Jenny, born September 5, 1803, was the daughter of Bet and was given to Kezia Alexander, in Mary Sample Alexander's will, when Jenny was two years old.

Joel Alexander, to whom Bet was given, was the son of Hezekiah and Mary Alexander; Kezia Alexander, to whom Bet's child, Jenny, was given, was their daughter. Apparently Bet *and her child were given to different households, an act of cruelty.*

The information about the slaves of Hezekiah Alexander is offered for two reasons: to illustrate the contradiction of the idea of "freedom" in the Alexander family and to cite this chilling example of the African Diaspora and how it robbed enslaved people of their families and identities. This is a sad story, and difficult to reconcile.

The W. T. Alexander Slave Cemetery

The W. T. Alexander Slave Cemetery is historically significant in Mecklenburg County, and Charlotte, North Carolina. It is the most extensive, best preserved, and most imposing slave burial site in Mecklenburg County, and it retains its essential setting. The cemetery is located on property that was originally part of the plantation purchased by William Tasse Alexander in the early nineteenth century. The plantation originally consisted of one hundred acres, but under Alexander's ownership, it grew to nine hundred thirty-five acres, and slaves were used extensively. According to United States federal census records of the slave population of Mecklenburg County, W. T. Alexander owned thirty-three slaves in 1860, the year before the beginning of the Civil War. It cannot be determined exactly how many slaves are buried in the cemetery. It has been estimated that twenty-five to thirty slaves are interred there.

Only two headstones have been erected, one of which marks the grave of a slave named Violet. Historians believe that Violet must have enjoyed a special relationship with the family to merit a headstone. It is only fair to point out that slave masters often had sexual relationships with their female slaves, and sometimes there were offspring from these unions. That may have been the case with Violet, and could explain why she had a special relationship with the family. Violet and another slave, Solomon, are mentioned in Alexander's will; it was his desire that these two slaves remain on the plantation to care for his widow (Stathakis, 1988). Apparently Violet and Solomon lived as husband and wife, based on the inscription on the headstone placed by their children which reads, "Our father and mother." Solomon Alexander died May 18, 1864 at sixty-four years old. Violet Alexander died August 16, 1888 at eighty-three years old. Violet lived to experience freedom, but Solomon did not. This slave family adopted the Alexander surname from their masters, a common practice among African-Americans after the *Emancipation Proclamation*.

Alton Caldwell, a descendant of slaves buried in the cemetery stated that, according to his great-grandparents, Alexander was a kind slave owner who bought shoes for his slaves, allowed them to travel off the plantation, and did not discourage marriage to slaves on other plantations. He provided space for formal burial of his slaves, an exceptional practice for that time. The cemetery is located deep in the woods off Mallard Creek Church Road and is overgrown, but despite these conditions, the Alexander Slave Cemetery is the best kept of only a few remaining slave cemeteries in Mecklenburg County (*The Alexander Slave Cemetery*, 1989).

Colonel Adam Alexander

Colonel Adam Alexander, brother of Captain Charles Alexander, was also a signer of the *Mecklenburg Declaration of Independence*. Their parents were William and Agnes Alexander. He was born in Somerset County, Maryland, September 23, 1728, and died in Mecklenburg County, North Carolina, November 13, 1798. Adam Alexander married Mary Shelby of Frederick County, Maryland. He settled on Clear Creek in Mecklenburg County and was a delegate to the Catawba Native Americans. He owned and operated a store and a mill and was prosperous enough to have a second home. He owned fifty-five slaves which made him the largest slave owner in Mecklenburg County (Foote, 1846); (King, 1956).

Adam Alexander was a large landowner and a leader in the community. He served as a justice of the peace and as a member of the county court. He was a prominent member of the Clear Creek Presbyterian Church. After signing the *Declaration*, he served as Lieutenant Colonel of Minute Men in 1775 and was promoted to Colonel in 1776 (Alexander, 1897).

Adam Alexander's military experience brought him into the conflict with the Regulators, the group of rebels with whom our ancestor, Michael George Gebert, was probably associated. Recall from the Gabbert account that Michael George Gebert left North Carolina to avoid the tax collector. The Regulators were colonial rebels who were at odds with the government over excessive taxes, dishonest sheriffs, and illegal fees. The Regulators resided in western North Carolina where they were isolated and out of sympathy with the residents of coastal North Carolina. Lacking a strong leader, they never accomplished a great deal, but they did have a military encounter with the colonial militia in which Adam Alexander was an officer (*The Regulator Movement*, 2002).

Adam Alexander and many of his fellow militia men had sympathy for the Regulators and were unwilling to have a military encounter with fellow colonists. Their general, Hugh Waddell, was forced to retreat because of their sympathetic attitudes and the fact that many were falling away from his ranks and from threats of violence if he continued to advance (Foote, 1846). At the time of his death, Adam Alexander owned more than thirty books, considered to be a nice library at the time (King, 1956). He and his wife, Mary Shelby Alexander, are buried in the old Rock Springs Cemetery near where the first building of the Philadelphia Presbyterian Church stood (Alexander, 1902).

Captain Charles Alexander

Another signer of the *Mecklenburg Declaration of Independence* was Captain Charles Alexander, probably born in Somerset County, Maryland. He was the son of William and Agnes Alexander and the brother of Colonel Adam Alexander *(Daughters of the American Revolution,* 1952). Charles Alexander, a captain of a militia unit, was a true patriot, serving in the Snow Campaign under the leadership of his brother, Colonel Adam Alexander, and Colonel Charles Polk. Charles Alexander had served under Colonel Polk in the Cherokee Indian Campaign. His service in the Revolution included being an officer in the Raft Swamp Expedition with Colonel Polk's Dragoons. Unlike the rest of his staunchly Presbyterian family, he was an "unbeliever" of Christianity. He was apparently a man of substance and integrity in spite of his anti-religion views, and was frequently appointed by the Court as a bondsman and appraiser of land (*Celebrating the Mecklenburg Declaration,* 2004). Captain Charles Alexander had a son, Charles, who served with him in the Revolutionary War, sometimes in the same company. This son died in 1801. Captain Charles Alexander had a grandson who was an officer in the Mexican War (Graham, 1905).

Colonel James Harris, Signer

Colonel James Harris was another of our ancestors who signed the *Mecklenburg Declaration of Independence.* A native of Yorkshire, England, Harris settled in the Susquehanna in 1719, but it was not until sixty-five years later that the city of Harrisburg, Pennsylvania was laid out and named in his honor. He eventually settled on Clear Creek in

Mecklenburg County. In the Revolutionary War, James Harris was a major serving under Colonel Irwin. After defeating the Tories at Ramseurs, he was promoted to the rank of colonel. He was described as wealthy, successful, quiet, and a devoted Presbyterian. He served as a delegate to the Mecklenburg Convention. His younger brother, Samuel, was also a soldier of the Revolution (Graham, 1905).

Pioneers of "Freethought" in North Carolina: Charles and Ezra Alexander

It seems that Ezra Alexander and Charles Alexander liked to stir up things a bit. Recall that Charles Alexander was described as being an "unbeliever of Christianity" (Graham, 1905). Indeed he was. He and his cousin, Ezra Alexander, were leaders in the "freethought" movement in North Carolina. The Age of Enlightenment in the eighteenth century was a great force in shaping American individualism. Americans threw off the shackles of the despotism of kings and approached religious creeds with reason. From this evolved the philosophy of Deism that was adopted by many Americans such as Charles and Ezra Alexander. Deism was a creed that sought to hold the rational mind of humans as the sole means of truth and the sole guide to life (Human, n. d.).

Today, the religious right would have us believe that our founding fathers were champions of freedom of religion. It is true that many of them came to this country to find religious freedom for themselves, but were often not willing to extend that freedom to others. Many religious groups in the colonies were persecuted for their beliefs, an example of which is the Quakers who were often persecuted and driven out of settlements. The religious right is often unwilling to recognize the influence of Deism in the cultural development of individualism in our nation's history.

Deism was radically different from Christianity; at its core was the tenet of the supremacy of human reason over faith and revelation. Deism stated that God exists, but that only reason can prove his existence or design of the universe. This belief was anathema to the Christians' reliance on faith. The Deists believed that God created the universe and set it in motion to operate by natural laws, then stepped back and left it alone. Deism clashed with Christianity almost point by point. Deism denied the existence of angelic and demonic messengers, as well as miracles, and divine rewards and punishment. Deism rejected the divine appointment of human authority such as the political idea of the divine right of kings. Most inflammatory of all, the Deists rejected the divinity of Jesus Christ.

Deists rejected the idea that religious texts such as the Bible were divinely inspired. Some Deists did not accept the belief in life after death. The Deists delighted in finding contradictions in the scriptures and condemned atrocities recorded in the Bible. Today, it would be political suicide for politicians to espouse Deistic beliefs, but here is the important contribution of the freethinkers—they opposed government suppression, tyranny, and injustice, as well as the colonial government's establishment of the Anglican Church, or the Church of England, as the official religion of the colonies. The Deists were a catalyst for the establishment of true freedom of religion in America. Like the Deists, the Presbyterians, Baptists, and Quakers opposed an official state religion. This was a huge step in establishing true freedom of religion in this country. In part, we must thank the Deists for that even if we disagree with their philosophy.

Most colonial Americans were "unchurched," a fact of which most Americans are unaware. The "unchurched" were bitterly opposed to an established religion. Virginian William Byrd, in 1728, described the unchurched majority of North Carolina, saying that they "were not troubled with any religious fumes" and "did not know Sunday from any other day, any more than Robinson Crusoe did" (Boyd, 1929).

William Henry Foote, a minister and an historian of North Carolina, wrote about North Carolina's freethinkers. He discussed a debating society, a common institution in those days for debating political topics, to which the Alexander cousins belonged. A debate society was formed in the region of Mecklenburg County that included part of Sugar Creek, Steele Creek, and Providence. The society had a circulating library with what Foote (1846) called "infidel philosophy and infidel sentiments of religion and morality."

The late Charlotte, North Carolina historian, Harriet M. Irwin (1882), described the membership of the debate society as a "coterie of infidels" that included Ezekiel Polk, the grandfather of President James K. Polk, Charles Alexander and Ezra Alexander, two signers of the *Mecklenburg Declaration of Independence*.

The society studied and spread the philosophies and works of Deists such as Voltaire, Rousseau, Gibbon, Hume, and Paine. Dr. J. B. Alexander in his *History of Mecklenburg County from 1740-1900* (1902) stated that the society "called in question everything connected with the Bible." He further stated that the debating society "embraced men of wealth and talent" and that as a result of the society "part of Mecklenburg (Steele Creek) became so infested with intemperance, infidelity, and universalism that a large part of Steele Creek and the adjoining counties ceased to attend church."

The society continued to question authority until about 1802 when its membership declined. Human (n. d.) states that membership declined due to three factors: the death of Charles Alexander in 1798 and of Ezra Alexander in 1801, the conversion of many Deists during the Great Awakening revivals of 1802, and Ezekiel Polk's move to Tennessee. Human made this observation about the freethinkers: "They stand as an inspiration of all who are independent in thought, word, and deed."

The Presbyterians and the American Revolution

Our Alexander branch of the family was, with a few exceptions, staunch Presbyterians, and was active in the American Revolution. There were approximately three million colonists at the time of the American Revolution. Of that number, nine hundred thousand were of Scots-Irish descent, most of whom were Presbyterians, six hundred thousand were Puritans, and about four hundred thousand were German or Dutch Reformed (Boettner, n. d.).

An American historian, George Bancroft, (1842) stated, "The Revolution of 1776, so far as it was affected by religion, was a Presbyterian measure." The English sometimes referred to the war in America as the "Presbyterian Rebellion" (Breed, 1876). A colonial supporter of King George III of Great Britain wrote, "I fix all the blame for these extraordinary proceedings upon the Presbyterians. They have been the chief and principal instruments in all these flaming measures. They always do and ever will act against government from that restless and turbulent anti-monarchial spirit which has always distinguished them everywhere" (Breed, 1876).

The Presbyterian Church and its ministers in colonial America were solidly on the side of the Colonists. Bancroft (1876) gives credit to the Presbyterians as making the first bold move toward independence when the synod assembled in Philadelphia in 1775 had the distinction of being the first religious group to declare publicly their desire for a separation from England. Conversely, the Episcopalian Church was still tied to the Church of England and had deep Loyalist sympathies (Boettner, n. d.).

Alexanders in the War of 1812

Muster Roll of the Soldiers of the War of 1812 (1851) lists the following Alexanders from Mecklenburg County:

Alexander, Abdon, Second Regiment, 1814

Alexander, Albertes, Ensign, Second Regiment 1814

Alexander, David, First Regiment, Seventh Company, 1812

Alexander, Eli, First Regiment, Seventh Company, 1812

Alexander, Ezekiel, First Regiment, 1814

Alexander, James, First Regiment, 1814

Alexander, John, Second Regiment, Nineth Company, 1812

Alexander, John D., First Regiment, 1814

Alexander, Laid, Second Regiment, Nineth Company, 1812

Alexander, Palau, First Regiment, Seventh Company, 1812

Chapter 10
Notable Alexanders Not in Our
Direct Line of Descent

Reverend James Alexander and Mary Maxwell

Reverend James Alexander was born around 1634 in Bughall, Scotland, and died on November 17, 1704 in Ireland. He married Mary Maxwell, born in 1634 in Raphoe, Donegal, Ulster, Ireland. She died in Cecil County Maryland. Mary Maxwell Alexander immigrated to the colony of Maryland after her husband's death (*Descendants of James Alexander, Generation No. 1*, n. d.).

Reverend James Alexander was ordained a Presbyterian minister, December 12, 1677, in Raphoe, Donegal, Ulster, Ireland. He was imprisoned for eight months for holding a day of prayer and fasting (*Descendants of James Alexander, Generation No. 1*, n. d.). In Ireland, the king, in an effort to subjugate the Irish, divided the counties into parishes, appointed clergy of the Church of England, and gave them both civil and ecclesiastical authority over the people.

The Presbyterian ministers were persecuted, and in retaliation, persuaded their congregations to immigrate to America where they would be assured of religious freedom (Falley, 1981).

James Alexander was minister of Raphoe, Third Minister at Convoy, on the Montgomery Estate. His salary in 1691 was twenty-four pounds in currency and twenty-four barrels of corn. These facts are recorded in *The General Synod of Ulster*. There is a three-volume copy of these records in the library of the Presbyterian Historical Society located in the Witherspoon Building in Philadelphia, Pennsylvania. Reverend James Alexander and his wife, Mary Maxwell, had nine children, all born in Ireland: William, Andrew, James, Francis, Samuel, Jane, Joseph, John, and Elizabeth. The Alexanders were Presbyterians and did not get along well with the Irish Catholics. The Presbyterians of Scotland had a secret symbol, the fish, which signified their allegiance to the Presbyterian faith.

It is generally accepted through stories handed down through the generations that seven Alexander brothers immigrated to the British colony of Maryland in America, specifically to Somerset County, Maryland, then to Cecil County, Maryland. They sailed from Ireland on the *Good Ship Welcome*. It is generally believed these brothers were the sons of Reverend James Alexander and Mary Maxwell Alexander. The evening before their departure, they sent for their old minister to baptize their children and have a religious service. The minister came to the ship to meet with his congregants. Before he finished, armed authorities came on board the vessel, broke up the meeting, and arrested the old preacher. Legend states that as the evening progressed, an old woman of the clan whose word was law, told her kinsmen, "Men, gang ye away, tak' our minister out o' the jail, and tak' him, guide soule, wi' us till Ameriky." Before morning, the old preacher had been rescued from jail and was on board the ship. He had no family and cheerfully set out with the Alexander's for the American colonies (Foote, 1846); (Graham, 1905).

They landed safely at Manhattan Island, New York where some of them remained. Other members of the group settled in New Jersey and Pennsylvania, and others moved on to Cecil County, Maryland. Some of the family settled in an established Presbyterian settlement at New Castle, Delaware in 1714. This settlement is now known as Christianna Hundred (*First Generation of Joseph Alexander Line in America*, n. d.); (Graham, 1905).

The British King had granted several thousand acres of land in the Maryland colony to Lord Baltimore who invited Catholics and Protestants to settle in the New World. He wanted to make certain that Catholics and Protestants were treated fairly under the new government (*Cecil Calvert*, 2009). The English Lord Baltimore offered land grants in 1643 to settlers, and guaranteed complete freedom of religion. In 1648, five hundred people of British and Scots-Irish descent came to the colony of Maryland. Alexanders and other early settlers purchased parts of this land in the Maryland colony and formed the town of New Munster. They built homes of field stone and logs mortared with clay (*First Generation*, n. d.).

This was the beginning of Scots-Irish colonization in Maryland. Eventually the Scots-Irish followed the southern frontier to the western back country of North Carolina, partly out of their resistance to taxes (*Tax History Project*, 1998). Most were prosperous landowners from Pennsylvania and Maryland.

Winds of Change in Europe

The political and religious atmosphere in England was changing. William of Orange, a Calvinist, invaded the country and displaced the Roman Catholic ruler, James II. The *Toleration Act* was passed by Parliament, May 24, 1689, giving limited freedom to Nonconformists, that is to say, Baptists, Methodists, and Congregationalists; however, it did not apply to Unitarians or Roman Catholics. The Nonconformists could worship as they pleased in their own churches with their own preachers and teachers.

Most English churchmen accepted the *Act of Toleration*; however, six bishops and about four hundred clergymen refused to take the oath to William of Orange (*Toleration Act*, 2008).

In the colony of Maryland, in 1649, the *Maryland Toleration Act* was passed. Lord Baltimore, a Catholic, gave the colonial governor, William Stone, a Protestant who had been appointed by Baltimore, a new law to be voted on by the Maryland assembly. It gave colonists freedom to worship any Christian faith if they were loyal to Lord Baltimore and the civil government. This law became known as the *Maryland Toleration Act of 1649* (Calvert, 2009).

Chapter 11
The McCalls: More Scottish Roots

Direct Line of Descent for the McCalls

James McCall and Janet Harris were the parents of Agnes McCall.

Agnes McCall and Elias Alexander, Jr. were the parents of Anne Alexander.

Anne Alexander and Stephen Camp were the parents of George Crenshaw Camp.

George Crenshaw Camp and Julia Ann Virginia Gabbert were the parents of Martha Camp.

Martha Camp and William G. Griffin were the parents of Virginia Griffin.

Virginia Griffin and John Webb were the parents of Lewis French Webb.

Lewis French Webb and Louise Hawkins are the parents of Arnold Ray Webb, Donald Roy Webb, Jo Ann Webb, and Judy Carol Webb.

Judy Webb and Billy J. Hubbell are the parents of William Griffin Hubbell.

James McCall and Janet Harris

James McCall was born in County Donegal, Ulster, Northern Ireland, probably in 1721, and immigrated with his brothers, William and Thomas, his sister Elizabeth, and his cousins Francis and Thomas, to Philadelphia, Pennsylvania from Ulster, Northern Ireland around 1733. The McCall family was accompanied by the James Harris family and the James Calhoun family. The grandson of James McCall, Hugh McCall, was the first historian of Georgia. According to his account, these three families had emigrated from Argyll County, Scotland where the McCalls were engaged in commercial pursuits in Glasgow. As Presbyterians, they were involved in the religious troubles that brewed. From Scotland, they escaped to Ulster together and later went to America where they settled on the Conachcocheque Creek in Pennsylvania (Northern, 2007); (von Rintein, 2008). James McCall married Janet Harris, daughter of Colonel James Harris, in 1738 in Lancaster County, Pennsylvania. James McCall lived in three Pennsylvania counties: Chester, Lancaster, and Cumberland Counties. He migrated to Augusta County, Virginia around 1746 and later moved to New River or Little Kenhoway in the western part of Virginia.

James McCall was living in Wythe County, Virginia in 1756 when the French and Indian War erupted. Several members of the Calhoun family were killed by hostile Native Americans (Northern, 2007); (von Rintein, 2008).

Because of Indian attacks, James McCall removed his family to Anson County (now Mecklenburg County), North Carolina. There James McCall received a grant of land, and served in the North Carolina militia in 1766 in Captain Adam Alexander's Company. He became a Revolutionary War soldier, along with his four sons: James McCall, Jr., Hugh McCall, Thomas McCall, and William McCall (von Rintein, 2008).

On April 20, 1773, James McCall and Janet Harris McCall made a deed to the land they owned at New River, Virginia, while living in Mecklenburg County. James McCall held public office there. He was listed as the head of household in the 1790 census of Mecklenburg County. In 1794, James McCall wrote his will, which was witnessed by Francis McCall, John Harris, and James McCaule. His wife, Janet, and his son, William, were named executors of his estate. The will is recorded in the *Mecklenburg County Will Book B*, p. 49. James Harris died at the age of one hundred ten years, according to Ettie Augusta Tidwell McCall (Gowen, 1988); (McCall, 1931); (Northern, 2007). James McCall and Janet Harris McCall had seven children; all married in Mecklenburg, North Carolina. My family is directly descended from their daughter, Agnes McCall, who married Colonel Elias Alexander, Jr.

James McCall, Jr.

James McCall, Jr., brother of Agnes McCall, from whom we are directly descended, was born in Pennsylvania in 1741, and married his cousin, Elizabeth McCall, in 1763. In 1771, James and Elizabeth McCall removed to Calhoun Settlement, South

Carolina. James McCall, Jr. had a distinguished military record. In 1774, he held the rank of captain in the South Carolina Minute Men. In 1775, he was a captain in the South Carolina Rangers. He fought in the siege of Augusta, Georgia, serving under General Elijah Clarke (Crawley, 2008); (von Rintein, 2008).

James McCall, Jr. fought in seventeen battles, and was wounded in the Battle of Long Cane, South Carolina. He was promoted to the rank of lieutenant colonel in the Continental Army. He served under General Marion and fought in the Battle of Cowpens, Battle of Ninety-six, Battle of Guilford Courthouse, and the Battle of King's Mountain. He also fought in engagements at Cherokee Nation, the Third Florida Expedition, Kettle Creek, Georgia, Fort Thicketty, Old Iron Works, Musgrove's Mill, Fishdam Ford, Blackstock's, Augusta, Georgia, Rutledge Ford, Long Cane, Hammonds Store, Harts Mill, North Carolina, and Beattie's Mill (*Auditor General Account*, 1778-1780).

The Battle of Long Cane

The British Major James Dunlap ordered his troops to subdue the colonial countryside because of the American's constant harassment of British supply lines. Dunlap and his troops, in their efforts to terrorize the colonists into submission, marched to Long Cane and plundered the home of Major James McCall, and abused his wife and daughter (O'Kelley, 2005). Lipscomb (1976) summarizes the events of this historic battle:

> *"Some of the South Carolina and Georgia troops who had fought with Sumter at Blackstock's, joined Colonel Benjamin Few of Georgia during the early part of December. Their combined force of five hundred men marched to the Long Cane settlement...On December 11, he sent out a combined force of regulars and militia numbering over four hundred, under the command of Lieutenant Colonel Isaac Allen...The Americans*

discovered Allen's troops and decided to engage them with an advance party of one hundred men commanded by Colonel Elijah Clarke and Lieutenant Colonel James McCall...Clarke was seriously wounded, McCall received a wound and had his horse shot from under him...The Americans got the worse of the engagement..."

Matthew Morgan McCall quotes Ettie Augusta Tidwell McCall as she described the following about the British backing of the hostile Native American tribes:

"In the invasion of South Carolina by the British, the fierce Cherokees thought they saw a favorable opportunity to overwhelm the frontiers and sweep away the settlements in the hurricane of slaughter. The British plan and the Indian ambition were therefore in full accord. Captain John Stuart, His Majesty's superintendent of Indian affairs for the southern district which included North Carolina, South Carolina, Georgia, and Florida with the assistance of Alexander Cameron, the Cherokee Indian agent, was always the chief agency behind the uprising which was always threatening, and was in close cooperation with Gen. Gage, the British Commander-in-Chief in Boston."

Captain James McCall was entrusted to capture Alexander Cameron and remove him from the scene of his scheming with the Native Americans. Captain McCall encamped near a large town in the Cherokee Nation where he conducted a conference with the chiefs. While in the conference, Captain McCall's small party was surprised by a party of Cherokee warriors. Captain McCall was taken prisoner and remained a prisoner for several weeks. He was tortured and sentenced to be executed but managed to escape. He traveled eight hundred miles on horseback without a saddle and fell in with some troops when he reached the Virginia frontier. He was wounded during the battle at Rugeley's Mill, December 4, 1780. At

Long Cane, December II, 1780, McCall was shot in the arm and narrowly escaped death when he became entangled with the horse that was shot from under him. Shortly thereafter, the Americans broke the power of the Cherokee. The resulting treaty ceded lands to South Carolina between the Savannah River, which included the counties of Greenville, Oconee, Anderson, and Pickens. Lieutenan Colonel James McCall, Jr. died of smallpox on April 16, 1781 in Georgia. He was only forty years old (Lipscomb, 1976); (McCall, H., 1811); (McCall, M., n. d.); (von Rintein, 2008).

Some of the descendents of James McCall, Jr. believe the military exploits of the main character in the movie, *The Patriot*, played by Mel Gibson, are based on the military career of Lieutenant Colonel James McCall, Jr. The movie was filmed in the area of the Carolinas where the Camp and McCall families settled (*Battle of Cowpens*, 2005).

Thomas Harris McCall/McCaule

Thomas Harris McCall, brother to Agnes McCall, changed the spelling of his name to *McCaule* while in college. Around 1770, he married Jane Harris, tenth child of Virginia Revolutionary soldier Samuel Harris and Martha Harris. Thomas McCall served as a chaplain in the Revolutionary Army. He received a certificate as a "refugee soldier of Georgia" signed April 4, 1784 by Colonel Elijah Clarke. He received a grant of two hundred eighty-seven acres of land on Long Branch Town Creek as bounty for his service in the Revolution. He taught at Mt. Zion School in Winnsboro, South Carolina in 1791. He later founded a classical school in Savannah, Georgia. He was the pastor of the Independent Presbyterian Church in Savannah in 1794 (Crawley, 2008); (Knight, 1920); (von Rintein, 2008).

Hugh McCall

Hugh McCall, brother of Agnes McCall, was born in Pennsylvania, and was a colonel in the Revolutionary Army of

North Carolina, serving in a light horse brigade. He received a grant of land in Wilkes County, Georgia as bounty for his service in the Revolution (*McCall*, n. d.); (von Rintein, 2008).

William McCall

William McCall, brother of Agnes McCall, was born at Little River, Virginia around 1752 and was a Revolutionary War soldier. He was married about 1778 to Elizabeth Stewart, daughter of Matthew Stewart, a Revolutionary soldier. McCall served in the First Battalion Infantry under Colonel Otto H. Williams and was with the First Maryland Regiment at Hillsborough. He died in 1827 at Mecklenburg, North Carolina, and is listed with the Daughters of the American Revolution as a soldier in the Continental Army (*McCall*, n. d.); (von Rintein, 2008).

Jane McCall Harris

Jane McCall, sister of Agnes McCall, was married around 1777 to Robert Harris, a Revolutionary War soldier, son of John Harris, in my family's direct line of descent, and a signer of the *Mecklenburg Declaration of Independence* (*McCall*, n. d.); (von Rintein, 2008).

Rachael McCall McCall

Rachael McCall, sister of Agnes McCall, eloped with her second cousin, Thomas McCall, son of Francis McCall, in 1762, and was married at sixteen years old. They had thirteen children. Thomas McCall was a soldier in the American Revolution serving in South Carolina. Thomas McCall received an indent issued August 10, 1785 for three hundred ninety pounds (British currency) for three hundred eighteen days of duty in the militia. He was also compensated for a horse and saddle he lost while serving in the war. As bounty for his military service, he received two hundred eighty-seven acres of land in Washington County, Georgia (McCall, n. d.); (von Rintein, 2008).

This brings us back to Stephen Camp and Anne Alexander, daughter of Col. Elias Alexander, Jr. and Agnes McCall Alexander from whom my family is directly descended.

Stephen Camp and Anne Alexander

Stephen Camp and Anne Alexander had nine children: Lewis (for whom my father was named), Elias, George Crenshaw, Julia, Eliza, Miriam (there are two Miriams, one born around 1820 and the other born around 1821. The first Miriam probably died as an infant, and the next child was given the same name), Adam, and William Carney Camp. My family is descended from George Crenshaw Camp, and his wife Julia Ann Virginia Gabbert Camp.

Chapter 12
The Huskeys: From Normandy to Virginia, and Onward to Arkansas
A Southern Backcountry Clan

NOTE: My family grew up with the Roy Huskey family of the Green Hill/New Hope communities in Drew County, Arkansas. My parents, Lewis and Louise Webb, were friends of Roy and Reba Montgomery Huskey. Roy and Reba's children and the Webb children were schoolmates and friends. I want to thank Wayne Huskey of Scottsville, Virginia, and the late Jimmy D. Berry of Marion, Louisiana. They helped make this chapter happen, and generously shared research materials with me.

Direct Line of Descent for the Huskeys

William Huskey and Elizabeth Porch were the parents of James Huskey.

James Huskey and wife (Unknown) were the parents of Blake Huskey.

Blake Huskey and Tabitha (Unknown) were the parents of Lucy Tennessee Huskey.

Lucy Tennessee Huskey and George Stokes Griffin were the parents of William G. Griffin.

William G. Griffin and Martha Camp were the parents of Virginia Griffin.

Virginia Griffin and John Wesley Bell Webb were the parents of Lewis French Webb.

Lewis French Webb and Louise Hawkins are the parents of Arnold Ray Webb, Donald Roy Webb, Jo Ann Webb Morrison, and Judy Carol Webb Hubbell.

Judy Carol Webb and Billy James Hubbell are the parents of William Griffin Hubbell.

The Huskey family emerged from the Norman Conquest of 1066. They were granted lands in Kent County, England by Duke William of Normandy for distinguished military service at the Battle of Hastings in 1066. There are several variations of the name including *Hussey, Houssey, Huzzy,* and *Huzzey*. It is believed that David Hussey, who came to the Colony of Virginia in 1648, is the progenitor of the Huskeys of the southern United States (*Huskey Family Crest,* 2009); (Reagan, 1978). The earliest Huskey I found in my family's direct line of descent is William Huskey of Brunswick, Virginia.

William Huskey and Elizabeth Porch

What we know about William Huskey is derived from legal documents in Brunswick County, Virginia. According to land records, on July 20, 1768, William Huskey acquired two hundred fifteen acres of land on the lower side of Pea Hill Creek (*Virginia Patent Book 37*). Court house records further reveal that William Huskey bought another two hundred acres of land that joined Pea Hill Creek at the mouth of Lick Branch from William Cook in 1772, making him a substantial land owner (Bradley, n. d.). We know that Elizabeth Porch Huskey was the daughter of James Porch, Sr. because of her being named in the *Last Will and Testament* (1776) of her father (*Sussex County, Virginia Will Book C,* 1776).

William Huskey wrote his *Last Will and Testament,* March 19, 1799, and died on or before April 22, 1799 (*Brunswick County, Virginia Will Book*). It is likely that he knew his death was imminent. In his will, he mentions his wife, Elizabeth, sons James and Lewis, and daughter, Oney. Elizabeth Huskey died on or before January 9, 1809. William Huskey's will states:

> "... To my wife Elizabeth - lend to her for life the land & plantation where I now live, also 1 gray mare, 1 bed & furniture, etc; also negro wench Tiller. To my daughter Oney

Huskey - give to her 1 bed & furniture, negro girl Patsey. To my son James - after my wife's death I give to him the land & plantation where I now live. After my debts are paid, the rest of my estate to be divided among all of my children except my son James; what I have lent to my wife to be sold after her death & divided in the same manner. Ex. my sons Lewis & James Huskey Wit: Robert Read, Elizabeth Tolley, Peter Read. Probate indicates that the sd excrs qualified with Gray Washington & Asa Holloway their securities."

The will is signed by William Huskey with an "X," an indication that he was illiterate. Elizabeth Huskey's land was sold January 9, 1809. James Huskey, believed to be her son, was one of the buyers. It is believed that William and Elizabeth Huskey had four sons: John, Lewis, Frederick, and James. John Huskey gave Charles May power of attorney to sell eighty acres of his land in Brunswick County, Virginia that joined the land of his brother, James Huskey. In this document, John Huskey stated that his late father was William Huskey of Brunswick County (Baird, 1985).

An official court record of Brunswick County, Virginia, February 25, 1782, lists William Huskey as a certified "person who gave aid to the American Revolution." The purpose of this court date was to reimburse known patriots for supplies given to the Revolutionary Army (Burgess, 1927). My family is directly descended from William Huskey's son, James. James Huskey was named in the will of William Huskey as a son (*Brunswick County, Virginia Will Book 6: 215, 232, 246 FHL # 30635 Document #10*).

James Huskey and Wife (Unknown)

James Huskey was born around 1772 in Brunswick County, Virginia. Land records indicate that this family lived in the Pea Hill community located on the Brunswick, Virgina/Northhampton, North Carolina line. James Huskey married around 1799 in

Brunswick County and died there in October of 1844 (*Individual Record: James Huskey*, 2009). The 1810 federal census for Brunswick County, Virginia, Meherrin District enumerates only two members of the household of James Huskey, one male age twenty-five or twenty-six, and one male under ten years old, as well as nine slaves. Blake Huskey, the eldest child of James Huskey, was the male under ten years old (Huskey, 2009). Perhaps James Huskey was widowed at the time of the census report. It is possible that he was married more than once. No occupation is listed, but we can safely assume he was a plantation owner as evidenced by the court house records.

It is believed that James Huskey had at least four sons, James Jr., Blake, Thomas, and Labon (Baird, 1985) (Carpenter, 2001, 2002). His *Last Will and Testament* (1843) mentions two sons, James Jr. and Blake, two daughters, Nancy Baird and Martha Baird, and the men who were their husbands, James Baird and William Baird. He also mentions a granddaughter, Evaline Wesson. The three executors of the will were James P. Harrison, F. W. Harrison, and Blake Huskey, indicating that Blake may have been the eldest son. The will reads as follows:

BRUNSWICK COUNTY, VIRGINIA - WILL BOOK 14

P. 231-232
JAMES HUSKEY

In the name of God amen. I James Huskey of the county of Brunswick and state of Virginia being of sound mind but feeble in health and calling to mind the frailty of poor human nature and the certainty of death think proper to dispose of my worldly estate in mannor and form as follows , to wit:

First I desire all my just and lawful debts and funeral expenses to be paid out of my estate.

Second I loan to my daughter Nancy Baird during her natural life the tract of land on which I now reside and the tract called Dobbins to her and to the heirs of her body forever.

Third I loan to my daughter Martha Baird during her natural life the tract of land called Ward's and the Lynch tract to her and to the heirs of her body forever.

Fourth I loan to my son James Huskey the tract of land purchased of Willie Harison and the tract which he sold, to him and to his heirs of his body forever.

Fifth I give to my granddaughter Evaline Vespon the property which are (sic) already in her possession. I give the same to her and her heirs forever.

Sixth I give William Baird one dollar.

Seventh I give to James Baird one dollar.

Eighth All the remainder of my estate both real and personal, I wish to be equally divided among the following (viz), Blake Huskey, James Huskey, Nancy Baird, and Martha Baird to them during their natural life and then to the heirs of their body forever.

Ninth I desire that the debts which James Huskey, James Baird and Wm. Baird now owe to be paid out of my estate and the amount of each individually to be deducted from their portions.

Tenth I desire that the money which I have paid for James Huskey, James Baird and Wm. Baird be deducted from their wives respective shares so that it may be as equal as may be.

And I do appoint my friends James Lynch and Wm. C. Harrison executors to this my last will and testament revoking all others by me heretofore made. In witness whereof I hereunto set my hand and seal this 12th day of October in the year of Our Lord 1843.

Signed and acknowledged James Huskey
in the presence of
George G. Lynch
John H. Clary
Samuel W. Ried
Brunswick County Court October term 1844
This last will and testament of James Huskey decd was proved by the oaths of George G. Lynch and John H. Cary witnesses thereunto & ordered to be recorded
And on the motion of Jones C. Lynch one of the executors therein named, who made oath Thereto, and together with James P. Harrison, F.W. Harrison & Blake Huskey his executors entered into and acknowledg es a bond in the Penalty of twenty five thousand dollars conditioned as the law directs, certificate is granted him for obtaining a probat of said will in due form.
Teste E.R.
Turnbull clerk
Exam'd
James Huskey
Brunswick Co., Virginia Will book 14, Pg. 231-232

Nancy Huskey Baird

There is an interesting story about Nancy Huskey. It seems that Nancy bore an illegitimate daughter before she married James Baird. This daughter, Mary Ann Elizabeth Huskey, was wed December 23, 1852 to George Washington Clary, a Confederate soldier from Brunswick County, Virginia (Pritchett, 2000). Reverend Sterling C. Pearson officiated. Apparently, Mary Ann Elizabeth Huskey never carried the Baird name, indicating that she was not James Baird's biological child (*Family History*, n. d.).

James Huskey, Jr.

According to Confederate military records, James Huskey, Jr. enlisted in the Confederate army, February 1, 1862 in Brunswick County, Virginia, and served in the Brunswick Rebel Artillery. He was present through February 28, 1865. He died of typhoid fever in a Union prison camp at Point Lookout, Maryland, June 10, 1865, just after the Civil War had ended. He is buried at the prison camp as Prisoner-of-War # 2091.

Thomas Huskey

Thomas Huskey married Sarah Ward in Shelby County, Tennessee (Whitley, 1982). Thomas Huskey had acquired an estate consisting of five hundred fifty-seven acres of land in Arkansas near the Hot Springs area (*Arkansas Land Records*, 1838). Thomas Huskey died with no children, so his estate was passed to his siblings. James Huskey, Jr., along with his sisters, Nancy and Martha, sold to Edward B. Wesson and James Harrison their interest in the five hundred fifty-seven acres of land in Arkansas that had belonged to their brother, Thomas Huskey (Baird, 1985); (Carpenter, 2001, 2002). There is no mention of Blake Huskey in this land transaction.

Laban Huskey

Laban Huskey died late in 1830 when he was between twenty and thirty years old, leaving a young widow and a small child. Apparently, he left no will; perhaps his death was caused by an accident (Carpenter, 2001, 2002).

Blake Huskey and Tabitha (Unknown)

Blake Huskey was born around 1801–1806 in Brunswick County, Virginia, and died around 1871 in Drew County,

Arkansas. He married Tabitha (Unknown) around 1829 in Virginia. Tabitha was born around 1797 in Virginia (*Federal Census Report, Shelby County, Tennessee,* 1850); (*Individual Record: Blake Huskey,* 2008). Blake Huskey and Tabitha are believed to have migrated to Shelby County, Tennessee (Memphis) around 1835. In December of 1834, Blake and Tabitha Huskey sold three hundred seven acres of land Blake had inherited from his father in October of 1833 (*Brunswick County, Virginia Deed Book*). The reason for their removal to Shelby County, Tennessee is unknown. One Huskey researcher (Huskey, 2009) suggests that perhaps the attractions were jobs, trade, and a major river crossing that may have been the gateway to the west at that time. Also, Blake's brother, Thomas, had settled in Shelby County, Tennessee.

I made an odd discovery when I searched the federal census records of 1840 for Shelby County, Tennessee. Tabitha Huskey was enumerated as head of the household that consisted of herself and seven children: one male under five years old; two males over five and under ten years old; one male over ten years old and under twenty years old; one female over five years old and under ten years old; and two females over ten years old and under twenty years old. This census report begged the question, "Where was Blake Huskey?"

Blake Huskey was in the Tennessee State Penitentiary serving eight years for an arson conviction and was therefore not enumerated in the 1840 federal census report (Huskey, 2009); (Sherrill,1997). Huskey family researchers have attempted with no success to learn the details of the arson conviction.

Recall that Blake Huskey's brother, Thomas, had bought land in Arkansas, five hundred fifty-seven acres, from the federal government on July 28, 1838. It seems that Thomas Huskey was killed by a renegade slave in Arkansas. The *Arkansas Gazette,* November 1, 1836, page two, column two, reported the murder of Thomas Huskey that occurred in Hot Spring County, Arkansas. Thomas Huskey, William Wright, and seven slaves were travelling together on the old Southwest Trail from Shelby County, Tennessee, toward the Sabine River in the Texas/Louisiana area. The purpose of the trip is unknown.

Edward Calvert who was travelling in the same direction came upon the bodies of Thomas Huskey, William Wright, and all but one of the slaves near the small town of Rockport, Arkansas in Hot Spring County. According to the newspaper account, the bodies of Huskey and Wright were "shockingly mangled and burned." Evidence pointed to the slave who had, it was believed, staged a violent escape. His name was "William," and he was the property of Thomas Huskey.

I was amazed to find several accounts of this event in various scholarly publications. A recent publication, *Southern Society and Its Transformations, 1790–1860* (2011) commented on the murders and its subsequent events:

> "*The trauma of forced migration westward provided a similar context for the collective killing of a slave in 1836. William allegedly axed to death his master, another white man, and five slaves. Tennessee law officers apprehended William in his previous home of near Memphis and conveyed him to the locale of the crime, Hot Springs (sic) County, Arkansas, where whites seized the slave from the sheriff and burned him to death*" (p. 51).

Delfino et al. (2011) imply that the slave, William, was taken from his home and family, and that this forced separation was the motive for the murders of Huskey, Wright, and the other slaves. The slave, William, eventually returned to Shelby County, Tennessee and, when apprehended, told authorities that the Indians had attacked the party of travelers and that only he had escaped (*Arkansas Gazette*, 1836). Meanwhile, Blake Huskey had been actively searching for the slave believed to be his brother's murderer; he posted a notice in the newspaper describing the slave and seeking his whereabouts (Huskey, 2009). Apparently no one believed that the Indians committed the murders. The newspaper account (1836) stated that William was believed to have had an accomplice, another slave, in committing the murders.

Frazier (2009) describes the events and comments on a newspaper account that described the crime but condemned vigilante justice:

> "The sheriff of Hot Spring County, Arkansas brought a chained Negro through Memphis, Tennessee. He had murdered his master, another white man, and three Negroes, and had burned their homes. The paper referred to the culprit slave as the 'infuriated demon,' and its story concluded, 'The wretch will most assuredly expiate his diabolical fury in the flames. We raise our protest against such punishment, notwithstanding the monstrous crime.'"

A slave, William Wells Brown, wrote a narrative about the cruelty of slavery. In this document, Brown commented on the lynching of the slave, William, who was believed to have killed Huskey and Wright. The scanned version was placed online by the University of North Carolina at Chapel Hill. One obscure paragraph may tell the true story of what happened. In a discussion by Brown, in his book, *Narrative of William W. Brown, an American Slave,* he quotes the *Arkansas Gazette,* Oct. 29, 1836:

> "We have been informed that the slave William, who murdered his master (Huskey) some weeks since, was taken by a party a few days since from the sheriff of Hot Spring, and burned alive! yes, tied up to the limb of a tree and a fire built under him, and consumed in a slow lingering torture."

This quote from the *Gazette* is found in numerous publications. Blake Huskey may have taken his revenge as described in the newspaper account. I have been unable to find the details of the arson committed by Blake Huskey. If the lynching of the slave William was the crime that sent Blake Huskey to the Tennessee penitentiary, no doubt he was avenging his brother's grisly death. It seems obvious that the arson was "payback" for the burned bodies.

The lynching of William made national headlines. The *Arkansas Gazette* (1836) editorialized against the heinous murder of William by vigilantes:

> *"We have mentioned this disgraceful and barbarous outrage that the ministers of the law may take steps to bring those implicated in the guilt of so black a crime to punishment... The circumstances of this criminal outrage are aggravated by the fact that the evidence against the Negro was of such a character that there was no chance of his escape from a just expiation of his crime by law—his condemnation was next to certain."*

I spent many frustrating months trying to find information on Blake Huskey and the arson conviction that sent him to the penitentiary. Goodspeed's *History* (1974), commented on the case but gave no particulars. It only stated that "George W. Payne and B. Huskey were sentenced to the penitentiary, the former for five years and the latter for eight years for arson in January, 1837." Payne may have been Blake Huskey's accomplice, or their sentences may have been unrelated.

The arson conviction of Blake Huskey raises some questions: If Blake Huskey committed the crime in Arkansas, why was he sent to the Tennessee State Penitentiary? If he burned the slave, would the charge not have been murder rather than arson? Perhaps not, because slaves were regarded as property in 1836 and arson is a crime against property.

Three Huskey family genealogists, Wayne Huskey, the late Jimmy Berry, and I, feel strongly that Blake Huskey's penitentiary offense was somehow related to the murder of Thomas Huskey and the renegade slave, William. Whatever Blake Huskey burned cost him four years and five months at hard labor (Sherrill, 1997) and possibly caused him to lose his family.

Blake Huskey began serving his prison term on January 21, 1838. Prison records state that Blake Huskey was thirty-two years old (if this is correct, his year of birth would have been around 1806), five feet ten inches tall, weighed one hundred seventy-five pounds, with fair hair, blue eyes, heavy eyebrows, a sleepy look, had a small scar on his left knee cap, and that he had worked in the millwright business but was not a professional millwright. Prison records further state that Blake Huskey was born and raised in Brunswick County, Virginia and that he had a wife and seven children living near Morning Sun Post Office, Shelby County, Tennessee. Blake Huskey was released from prison on June 21, 1842 (Sherrill, 1997). Penitentiary records state Blake Huskey was paroled for good behavior after serving four and one-half years of an eight year sentence.

Blake Huskey was enumerated in the 1850 federal census for Shelby County, Tennessee, District Nine, as a forty-nine-year-old farmer born in Virginia. Also enumerated was Tabitha Huskey, fifty-three years old, and born in Virginia. This would make Tabitha Huskey's year of birth 1797 and Blake Huskey's year of birth 1801. Three of their children were enumerated: Lucy Huskey, eighteen years old, and born in Virginia; William Huskey, fifteen years old, and born in Virginia, and like his father, described as a farmer; and George Huskey, fourteen years old, and born in Tennessee. George Huskey's place of birth tells us that Blake and Tabitha Huskey had been in Tennessee at least since 1836, the year of George Huskey's birth.

Oddly, there is also a Blake Huskey enumerated in the 1850 federal census report for Brunswick County, Virginia, and was described as a forty-one-year-old farmer. The household is made up of him alone. Perhaps this is a different Blake Huskey, or maybe he went back to Virginia temporarily and was enumerated in both census reports; however, the age listed in the Virginia census is not the same as the age listed in the Tennessee census.

After Blake Huskey served his prison term, he removed to Drew County, Arkansas. Federal land records dated July 1, 1859, reveal that Blake Huskey purchased one hundred sixty acres of land in Drew County, Arkansas from the Bureau of Land Management (*United States Department of the Interior*, n. d.).

Blake Huskey found in:
Land Records: AL, Arkansas, FL, LA, MI, MN, OH, WI, 1790-1907
    Document number: 8594 Description number: 1
    Number of acres: 160.0000 Accession number: AR2230___.041
    Patentee Surname: Huskey Patentee given name: Blake
    State name: Arkansas
    Volume: 2230 Page number: 41
    Land office: Champagnolle Aliquot part reference: NW
    Section number: 20
    Township: 13 South Range: 7 West
    Meridian or special survey area: Fifth Principal Meridian
    Title transfer authority: Sale-Cash Entries
    Combined signature date: Jul. 1, 1859
    Multiple patentees: N Multiple warrantees: N

The 1860 federal census report for Marion Township, Drew County, Arkansas, gives us the following information about household 141. It consisted of only two members, raising more questions: Blake Huskey, fifty-two years old, and a farmer, born in Tennessee and Elizabeth Huskey, sixty-eight years old and, born in Virginia. Perhaps the ages are incorrect. Blake and Tabitha could have divorced, or Tabitha could have died and Blake married Elizabeth, an older woman. It is also possible that Tabitha was Tabitha Elizabeth. Perhaps Blake Huskey migrated to Arkansas ahead of his family, or perhaps they were estranged. It is likely that Tabitha Huskey suffered miserably trying to bring up seven children alone while her husband was in prison. She may have found it impossible to forgive Blake Huskey for putting his desire to avenge his brother's death ahead of the well-being of his family, and these hardships may have alienated some of Blake Huskey's children. I have found no definitive evidence that Tabitha Huskey ever came to Arkansas. Perhaps she died in Tennessee.

The fact that Elizabeth Huskey was born in Virginia leads me to believe that Elizabeth could have been the mother or stepmother of Blake Huskey (recall that only Blake and his father comprised a household in the 1810 federal census). Perhaps his mother (or stepmother) stood by him when no one else did, but this is mere conjecture.

The 1860 federal census report for Marion Township, Drew County, Arkansas, holds answers to some of these questions. Household 139 was comprised of a young couple: George W. Huskey, twenty-four years old and a farmer born in Tennessee, and Susan E. Huskey, twenty-three years old and born in Georgia. George W. Huskey was the son of Blake Huskey. The next clue can be found in the census data for household 140 that consisted of the following family members:

George Griffin, forty years old, and a farmer born in Georgia

Lucy Griffin, thirty years old and born in Virginia

William Griffin, seven years old, and born in Texas

Blake B. Griffin, six years old, and born in Texas

John Griffin, two years old, and born in Arkansas

Lucy Griffin was Lucy Tennessee Huskey Griffin, called "Tennie" as revealed in the 1880 federal census report for Drew County, Arkansas. She was the daughter of Blake Huskey and had named one of her sons Blake in honor of her father. "Tennie" was my great-great grandmother. The eldest son of George and Lucy T. "Tennie" Griffin, William George Griffin, was my great-grandfather. William George Griffin's daughter, Virginia, who married John B. Webb, was my grandmother and the mother of my father, Lewis French Webb.

Households 139, 140, and 141 were neighbors and family members. They most likely lived on and worked the one hundred sixty acres of land Blake Huskey had acquired from the federal government. In 1860, a farm consisting of one hundred sixty acres was considered to be fairly large, and before the advent of mechanized farming, it took a large family to work that much land, particularly if they grew cotton, a labor intensive crop.

At the time of the 1860 federal census report for Marion Township, Drew County, Arkansas, Blake Huskey had thirty thousand dollars worth of real estate and nine thousand dollars worth of personal property, making him something of a financial success. In the 1850 federal census report for Shelby County, Tennessee, Blake Huskey had a property valuation of three hundred dollars. Migrating to Arkansas seems to have been a good economic move for Blake Huskey.

Blake Huskey served during the Civil War in the Monticello Home Guard, commanded by Captain John S. Handly. Bryan Howerton (2001), a well-known civil war researcher, offers this description of the Monticello Home Guard:

> "The Monticello Home Guard was organized and enlisted on October 5, 1863, at Monticello, Drew County, Arkansas. With civil authority collapsing in many parts of the State, and Confederate troops being sent to faraway battlefields, local jurisdictions were encouraged to form companies of home guards to protect persons and property, enforce the Conscript Law, and support Confederate troops when requested. The home guards were generally composed of men too old or too young for regular military service. The Monticello Home Guard was composed of 47 men between

the ages of 38 and 62, with an average age of 50 years. For this reason, it was popularly known as the 'Old Man's Company.'"

Blake Huskey, fifty-five years old, held the rank of Private (Gerdes, 2001). After the war, Blake Huskey resumed his life as a farmer. He sold a piece of land to William T. Wells, February 14, 1871 (*Drew County, Arkansas Sale Bills of Personal Estates 1870-1899*). He would have been about seventy years old in 1871. Blake Huskey died in Drew County, Arkansas sometime after 1871 and is believed to have been buried in Green Hill Cemetery in Drew County, Arkansas. However, his grave has been lost over the years.

Henry Huskey and Robert Huskey—Slaves of Blake Huskey?

There were two interesting Huskey "enlistments" in the Confederate Army. Apparently Blake Huskey sent his slave, Henry, to serve. Henry "enlisted" June 16, 1862 in Hardy's Regiment, Arkansas Infantry. Henry was the chief cook for the regiment. He was accounted for as "present" in February, 1864. Confederate conscription laws allowed that, in some cases, a substitute could be sent by a potential draftee; however, Blake Huskey served his military duty in the "home guard" due to his age. Perhaps he sent Henry as a gesture of support of the Confederate cause. Henry is listed on the roster as "Henry, chief cook." Robert Huskey is listed on the roster as "Under Cook." I do not know if Robert Huskey was black or white, slave or free. I tend to believe he was also a slave because he was the assistant to Henry. No white man in the Confederate Army would have served as an assistant to a slave. Robert Huskey enlisted January 1, 1864 and was present in February, 1864 (Gerdes, 2001).

Children of Blake Huskey and Tabitha Huskey

George W. Huskey, William Huskey, James C. Huskey, and Lucy Tennessee "Tennie" Huskey Griffin, are only four of the seven children of Blake and Tabitha Huskey for whom I have been able to account, and all the information I have on William Huskey is that he was fifteen years old when he was enumerated in the 1850 census in Shelby County, Tennessee. I do not know what became of William Huskey. I would like to know what happened to Tabitha Huskey, William Huskey, and the other three children. Blake Huskey may have had as many as nine or ten children (Carpenter, 2002).

Blake Huskey's son, James C. Huskey, died in the Civil War. Private James C. Huskey enlisted in Company A, Chicot Rangers, First Arkansas Confederate Mounted Rifles, at Fort Smith, Arkansas, June 15, 1861, at age twenty-four, and was discharged in 1861. He then enrolled in the Desha County Militia at Laconia, Arkansas, November 18, 1861. He enlisted in Co. E, Twenty-sixth Arkansas Infantry, at Selma, Arkansas, May 12, 1862 (*Compiled Service Records of Confederate Soldiers Who Served in Organizations from the State of Arkansas*).

The Chicot Rangers fought at the Battle of Pea Ridge, Arkansas, March 7–8, 1862. Other major engagements were Murfreesboro, Chickamauga, Dalton, Resaca, New Hope Church, Kennesaw Mountain, Moore's Mill, Lovejoy Station, Peach Tree Creek, Atlanta, Ezra Church, Jonesboro, Moon Station, Franklin, Nashville, and Bentonville (Gerdes, 2001).

Private James C. Huskey died of disease at Camp Rust, Arkansas, July 29, 1862 (*Compiled Service Records*). The 1860 federal census report for Desha County, Arkansas states that James C. Huskey was born in Virginia around 1835, and lists his occupation as bricklayer.

Another son of Blake Huskey, George W. Huskey, mentioned earlier in this chapter, also served and died in the Confederate Army. He was one of the original volunteers who formed the Company B, Sixth Battalion, Arkansas Cavalry, known as the "Drew County Light Horse Company." He enlisted at Little Rock, Arkansas as a Private, August 11, 1861, when the battalion mustered into service. Less than one year later, on April 20, 1862, George W. Huskey and his comrades were consolidated into Company A, Monticello Cavalry. A short time later, on May 15, 1862, they become part of Company B, Seventh Regiment, Arkansas Cavalry, and, finally, a part of the Sixth Arkansas Cavalry Battalion (*Compiled Service Records*).As units sustained losses, it was a common practice to consolidate with other units. Unfortunately, few records survived for this battalion.

George W. Huskey served in the Civil War almost from start to finish; a dispatch rider, he died in the waning days of the war when, in the line of duty, he and his horse drowned in Flat Creek, located in Ashley County, Fountain Hill, Arkansas, during high water. He was carrying a military message from Vicksburg, Mississippi to Camden, Arkansas when he suffered this mishap. He is buried in Flat Creek Cemetery in Fountain Hill, Arkansas (DeArmond, 1980).

Sadly, his family did not find out what happened to him until approximately five years after his death. He was not quite thirty years old when he died. He left his young wife, Sarah E. Huskey (Susan) a widow with two young children, Joe (Joseph Thompson) and Mat (Martha Jane) to support (*Federal Census Report, Drew County, Arkansas Marion Township, 1870*).

The 1880 census of Drew County, Arkansas enumerates the mother of Sarah Huskey, seventy-five-year-old Sallie (Sarah) Brantly, as a member of the household. According to this census report, both Sarah and her mother, Sallie, were born in Georgia; Joe and Mat were born in Arkansas. This census report shows residing near Sarah Huskey, George and "Tennie" Griffin. In 1893, Sarah E. Huskey applied for a Confederate pension from Drew County, Arkansas. Her pension was approved August 3, 1893.

The 1880 federal census report for Marion Township, Drew County, Arkansas, enumerates Sarah E. Huskey as head of her household that included her two children, Joe (Joseph Thompson Huskey), Mat (Martha Jane Huskey), and her mother, Sallie (Sarah) Brantley, seventy-five years old, and born in Georgia. The next household in the 1880 census report is that of George S. Griffin and Lucy Tennessee "Tennie" Huskey Griffin, the sister of George W. Huskey, and the daughter of Blake Huskey. No doubt, after the death of George W. Huskey, Sarah E. Huskey and her family were able to survive with the help of her husband's extended family.

Joseph Thompson Huskey and Sarah Ellen Kissinger

Joseph Thompson Huskey, the son of George and Sarah Huskey, was enumerated in the 1880 federal census report for Drew County, Arkansas, and was described as nineteen years old and born in Arkansas. His occupation was working on the farm. Sarah E. Huskey's daughter, Mat (Martha Jane) Huskey, was also enumerated and described as fifteen years old and born in Arkansas. The 1920 federal census report for Veasey Township, Drew County, Arkansas, enumerated Sarah Huskey, and described her as eighty-four years old and living in the household of Henry C. and Kattie E. Wilson. The census report described Sarah Huskey as the great-aunt. Sarah Huskey's daughter, Martha Jane (Mat) married Tracy Wilson, and that probably explains why Sarah Huskey was living in the Wilson household.

Joe Huskey was thirty-eight years old in 1900, a bachelor, and lived in the same household as his mother, Sarah Brantley Huskey, sixty-three years old. Also living in the same household was Malinda Wilson, a second cousin, twenty years old (*Federal Census Report Drew County, Arkansas Marion Township*, 1900). Joe Huskey did not remain a bachelor, however.

My father, Lewis French Webb, often spoke fondly of his Aunt Sarah and Uncle Joe Huskey. Joseph Thompson Huskey was born, September 11, 1861 in Drew County, Arkansas, and died December 10, 1946. There is an interesting story about the courtship of Joseph Thompson "Joe" Huskey and his future bride, Sarah Ellen Kissinger (DeArmond, 1980).

A visiting friend of Joe's told him about Sarah who lived in Missouri. Joe and Sarah began corresponding, and Joe decided to go to Missouri and marry her. Joe Huskey and Sarah Kissinger were married February 20, 1901 in Missouri and returned home to the Green Hill/New Hope community in Drew County, Arkansas where they spent the rest of their lives and apparently had a long and happy marriage (DeArmond, 1980).

Sarah Ellen Kissinger was born around 1863 in West Plains, Missouri and was brought up in Howard County, Missouri. Sarah's mother's maiden name was Clark (DeArmond, 1980). Joseph Thompson Huskey and Sarah Ellen Kissinger were the parents of my father's cousin and great pal, Roy Thompson Huskey that I mentioned in the notation at the beginning of this chapter. I cannot begin to count the number of stories I have heard my father tell of his and Roy Huskey's antics and boyhood adventures. Roy T. Huskey married Reba Montgomery, the daughter of Mary Effie Mays Montgomery and J. B. Montgomery. The family of Joseph Thompson Huskey, including his mother, Sarah, are buried in Green Hill Cemetery, Drew County, Arkansas (DeArmond, 1980); (*Drew County Arkansas Cemetery Records, 2002*).

Roy Thompson Huskey and Reba Montgomery

In her book *Old Times Not Forgotten* (1980), Rebecca DeArmond, later to become the daughter-in-law of Roy and Reba Huskey, related a story about the courtship of Roy Huskey and Reba Montgomery. It seems that Roy was out running his traps when he stopped by Reba's home to get a drink of water. DeArmond quotes Roy as saying, "It tasted pretty good, so I started going back for more." DeArmond is married to Roy Wayne "Bimbo" Huskey. The children of Roy and Reba Huskey are Joe, Joy, Dona, Betty, Kathy, Roy Wayne "Bimbo," and Billy.

My parents and Roy and Reba Huskey remained friends throughout the years and raised their families together. Of the four, only my mother, Louise Hawkins Webb, survives at the present time. My father often told the story of how he received the news that World War II had officially ended. He told Reba Huskey, who had a radio, that he would be plowing all day, and if she heard that the war had come to an end, to signal him with a shotgun blast. Reba fired the shot that was heard around Green Hill and New Hope. My father knew the war had ended in an American victory and that his brother, Herman Webb, and my mother's brother, Howard Hawkins, would return home safely. It was a joyous day for all Americans.

Roy Huskey descended from Blake Huskey through Blake's son, George W. Huskey. My family descended from Blake Huskey through Blake's daughter, Lucy Tennesse "Tennie" Huskey Griffin, wife of George Stokes Griffin.

Chapter 13
The Griffins and the Stovalls: More English Roots

Direct Line of Descent for the Griffins

William Griffin I and Margaret Hatch were the parents of William Griffin II.

William Griffin II and Jane (Unknown) were the parents of William Griffin III.

William Griffin III and Rebecca (Unknown) were the parents of William Griffin IV.

William Griffin IV and Elizabeth Griffith were the parents of Richard Griffin.

Richard Griffin and Mary Green were the parents of Owen Griffin.

Owen Griffin and Anne Stovall were the parents of Drury Griffin.

Drury Griffin and Wife (Unknown) were the parents of George Stokes Griffin.

George Stokes Griffin and Lucy Tennessee Huskey were the parents of William G. Griffin.

William G. Griffin and Martha Camp were the parents of Virginia Griffin.

Virginia Griffin and John Wesley Bell Webb were the parents of Lewis French Webb.

Lewis French Webb and Louise Hawkins are the parents of Arnold Ray Webb, Donald Roy Webb, Jo Ann Webb, and Judy Carol Webb.

Judy Carol Webb and Billy J. Hubbell are the parents of William Griffin Hubbell

◆

The Griffin surname is among the top one hundred surnames in Ireland. The family may be of several origins including Irish, British, or Welsh. Settlers with the Griffin surname arrived from Wales in the wake of the Norman Invasion (O'Laughin, 1997).

Other spellings include *Griffen.* Several men with the surname *Griffin* served in the American Revolutionary War; we are direct descendants of several of these soldiers. Thomas Griffin was born around 1750 in Virginia and died around 1807 in Anson County, North Carolina. Today, this is Union County, North Carolina. Connie Thompson (2007) submitted this information about Griffin: "I have read from an undocumented source that he served under Captain John Gist's Company in Colonel Nathan Gist's First Virginia Regiment in 1777 and that he enlisted a second time and served in the Second Virginia Regiment under Captain John Smith's Company in Colonel Gregory Smith's Regiment" (Ganis, 2007).

The Virginia Magazine of History and Biography, Volume I, p. 254, states:

> *"The first of this Griffin family in Virginia was Thomas Griffin who receives various grants of land in Rappahannock county from 1651. Edward Bradshaw in his will Lancaster County, 1675 "makes bequest to my countryman Thos Griffin and to his ____T. ____G daughter Winifred Griffin....married Sarah and died on or before 1660. His widow married secondly Samuel Griffin of Northumberland county children: 1. Colonel Leroy of Rappahnhannock born 1646...."*

Another source, *Chronicles of the Boit Family and Their Descendants and of Other Allied Families* by Robert Apthorp Boit (n. d.) states the following:

> *"The Griffin family of Virginia was founded by Thomas Griffin who took up various grants of land, from 1651 on the Rappahannock River in Virginia. Thomas and his brother Samuel came to America from Wales. They left their eldest brother in Wales who possessed an estate of 600 pounds sterling annum. He died without issue and Samuel went back to Wales to look after the estate. He died before his business was finished. Thomas then sent over an agent to collect the revenue of the estate. Thomas Griffin*

never left Virginia. His wife's maiden name is not known. Her baptismal name is Sarah. Their eldest child was Colonel Leroy Griffin, Justice of Rappahannock County 1680–1695 married Winifred, daughter of Colonel Gawin Corbin. The oldest son of Colonel Leroy and Winifred Griffin was Thomas Griffin of Richmond County Virginia who was a member of the House of Burgess for Richmond County from 1718–1723."

The following information concerning land acquisition in Virginia by the Griffin family came from documents, chiefly unpublished, relating to the Huguenot emigration and the settlement at Manakin-Town (Brock, 1886):

"The tradition of the Griffin family is that it is of Welsh extraction. There are grants of 1,155 and 1,046 acres of land to Samuel Griffin in Rappahannock County, in 1660 and of 1,000 acres to William Griffin in Northhampton County in 1662, of record in the Virginia Land Registry."

The Lost Colony of Roanoke and Rowland Griffyn

Jamestown, Virginia was the first permanent English colony in America. However, there was an earlier unsuccessful effort to establish a permanent English colony on Roanoke Island in present-day North Carolina. In the spring of 1585, Sir Walter Raleigh sent a military expedition of one hundred eight men to establish a colony in the New World. The result of this effort became shrouded in mystery. When the colony was established, a ship was sent back to England for supplies. It was unable to return until 1590. When the supply ship returned to Roanoke, the colony was gone. It is believed the colonists moved to another location. Only one clue was left, the word "Croatan," the name of an island in the area occupied by friendly natives, was carved in a tree. One of the many theories concerning the disappearance of the colony was that the settlers left to live among the natives on the island of Croatan and carved the word in the tree to explain their absence. However, the settlers were never found. Among those settlers was Rowland Griffyn, one of the one hundred eight military men who established the colony and who mysteriously disappeared with the group (Estes, 2009); (Lost Colony 2008).

Miscellaneous Griffins in Virginia

Owen Griffin

Some believe that Owen Griffin, in 1605, was the earliest Griffin in Virginia, based on an entry from *The General Historie of Virginia, Vol. 1* by Captain John Smith. On page forty, Smith says, "we exchanged one Owen Griffin with them (the Indians) for a young fellow of theirs, that he might see if he could discover any treachery…." Owen Griffin, acting as a spy for Captain Smith, discovered treachery. The Native Americans had assembled two hundred eighty-three armed warriors and were not interested in trading as they had indicated. I do not know if this particular Owen Griffin is in our line of descent, but based on his name, I can make a strong guess that he is, because of the repetition of the Christian name *Owen* throughout the generations of our branch of the Griffin family.

Ambrose and Joyce Griffin

Ambrose Griffin, in 1619, arrived in America on the ship, *Bono Nova,* and settled on the James River. He was thirty years old, and from Gloucester, England. He worked as a sawyer-carpenter. Court records dated April 7, 1623 indicate that Griffin had been working on building an inn at Jamestown prior to the March 22 attack by Native Americans. Griffin had also helped build the palisade and court of guard in Jamestown. On December 8, 1623, Captain William Tucker of Elizabeth City ordered Ambrose Griffin to Warwicksqueake to assist Captain Roger Smith in building a fort there. Census records of February 16, 1624 indicate that Griffin was living at Buckroe on land that belonged to the Virginia Company. In early 1625, he was described as a resident of Elizabeth City where he and his wife, Joyce, lived in the home of Thomas Garnett, an ancient planter (see Dodson Chapter for discussion of ancient planters). Ambrose Griffin was then thirty-three years old, and Joyce Griffin was twenty years old. Both Ambrose and Joyce were free and were probably Virginia Company tenants. Joyce was an interesting character. She arrived in Virginia in 1624 on the ship *Jacob* and settled on the James River. On March 25, 1629, Joyce was identified as one of the women who examined Thomas Hall, a hermaphrodite, to determine his gender. Hall was a servant in the household of Edward Gordon (McCartney, 2007).

Rowland Griffin

Rowland Griffin, a vagrant in Farrington, Dorset, England, was ordered by the courts to be sent to Virginia. He arrived in 1624 (Coldham, 2009); (McCartney, 2007).

Leonard Griffin and the Reverend Charles Griffin

Leonard Griffin and the Reverend Charles Griffin were associated with the East India School established in colonial Virginia. The following is a brief description of the East India School (McCartney, 2007):

> "As early as 1617 King James had issued his letters patent throughout the kingdom for collecting funds for a college at Henrico in Virginia, and almost contemporaneously money was raised for a school at City Point (then called Charles City), which was named the East India School, in honor of its first benefactors. The first contribution came from some of the East India Company that came home in the ship Royal James, and the school as 'a collegiate

or free school' was to have dependence upon the college at Henrico, which should be made capable to receive scholars from the school into such scholarships and fellowships as should be endowed."

"The question of the college received discussion in 1619 in the assembly at Jamestown, the first ever convened on this continent. But though the college and the school were rapidly pushed, and a rector for the college, a master and usher for the school, and a manager for the college lands and tenants were selected, and all but the rector sent over to the colony, the Indian massacre of 1622, by destroying at one blow three hundred and fifty persons in the settlement, effectually crushed both the college and the school" (Tyler, 1897).

Tyler mentions, in a footnote, the school master, Reverend Charles Griffin. A school for teaching Native American boys was established by Alexander Spotswood at Christina, near the Meherrin River. After some years, Griffin was transferred to the college where another Indian school was in operation, established by the charity of Robert Boyle, Esquire.

Reginald Griffin and Rice Griffin

Reginald Griffin arrived in Virginia in 1621 on the ship, *Bona Nova*. Rice Griffin arrived in Virginia in 1621 on the ship, *Flying Hart*. A muster, dated February 7, 1625 identified Rice Griffin as a twenty-four-year-old servant at Daniel Gookin's plantation (*Daniel Gookin Muster*, 1912); (McCartney, 2007).

Richard Griffin

Richard Griffin arrived in Virginia in 1622 on the ship, *James*. He settled in Elizabeth City. He was listed as dead at Elizabeth City after April 1623 but before Feb. 16, 1624 (*Colonial Records of Virginia*, 1874); (McCartney, 2007).

John Griffin

John Griffin arrived in Virginia before 1622 and was reportedly killed at Warresqueake in the attack by Native Americans, March 22, 1622 (McCartney, 2007).

Thomas Griffin

Thomas Griffin set sail for Virginia, July 31, 1622 on the ship, *James,* accompanied by his master, Alexander Lake. Thomas died at Warresqueake after April 1623 but before Feb. 16, 1624 (Boyer, 2009).

John Griffin

John Griffin arrived in Virginia in 1624 on the ship *William & John.* On January 24, 1625, he was described as a twenty-six-year-old servant in the household of George Menefie in Jamestown (*Colonial Records of Virginia,* 1874); (Griffin, J. & Griffen, Z., 1912).

John Griffin

This particular John Griffin arrived in Virginia in 1626 and settled at Henrico, Virginia. He was a landowner identified as the patentee of fifty acres within the corporation of Henrico. His land was described in 1634 as lying north of Thomas Sheffield's acreage, but south of Christopher Branch's land (Griffin, J. & Griffen, Z., 1912).

John Sergeant Griffin

John Sergeant Griffin set sail from England, August 24, 1635, aboard the *Constance.* He was born around 1608–1609. In June of 1638, when Lord Baltimore of Maryland ordered an attack of the Viriginia Islands of Kent and Palmer, which were under the protection of Captain Claiborne, secretary of the Colony of Virginia,

John Sergeant Griffin escaped by ship and left Virginia. His name first appears on New Haven, Connecticut records in 1642, and he was enrolled in the militia. On January 4, 1643, he was fined a few pence for not having his weapons in shape. Griffin swore the *Oath of Fidelity* at New Haven, July 1, 1644. He removed to Windsor, marrying there and appearing in the Windsor records in August of 1659. John and Anna Griffin were among the first settlers from Windsor to remove to Simsbury, where he was a representative for some years. His estate inventory of August 23, 1681 included about three square miles of land, or about one thousand nine hundred twenty acres. He was a member of the Simsbury, Connecticut Train Band (Coldham, 2009); (Griffin, J. & Griffen, Z., 1912); (Nugent, 1987).

Ann Griffin

Ann Griffin arrived in Virginia in 1637 as an indentured servant. Her fare was paid by Joseph Harmon to whom she was indentured. Harmon was awarded land, May 21, 1638, for bringing Ann Griffin to Virginia (Greer, 1982); (Pledge & Foley, 2009).

Will Griffin

Will Griffin arrived in Virginia in 1637 as an indentured servant. He was transported to America by Theodore Moyses who received an award of land, May 23, 1637, for bringing a new settler to Virginia (Nugent, 1987).

Edward Griffin

Edward Griffin also arrived in Virginia as an indentured servant in 1638. He was transported by Joseph Harmon who received an award of land, May 21, 1638, for sponsoring Edward Griffin to Virginia (Nugent, 1987).

William Griffin I and Margaret Hatch

I was able to trace the Griffin branch of our family back to William Griffin I, born, May 26, 1596, in West Pennard, Somerset, England. He died, October 30, 1634, in Somerset, England. William married Margaret Hatch, born around 1600, and died in 1695 in Somerset, England. Her parents were William Hatch, born in 1574, died in 1661, and Margaret Hatch, born in 1577, and died in 1667 in Somerset, England. They had the following children (Griffin/Findeisen, n. d.):

Ann Griffin, born February 23, 1622 in West Pennard, Somerset, England

William Griffin II, born October 19, 1628 in West Pennard, Somerset, England

Edward Griffin, born December 18, 1631 in West Pennard, Somerset, England

There may have been other children as well. My family is descended from William Griffin II.

William Griffin II and Jane (Unknown)

Our first *Griffin* ancestor to cross the Atlantic Ocean and settle in the colony of Virginia was William Griffin II. Some family researchers believe he immigrated to Virginia when he was ten years old in 1638. His family probably came as part of the settlement of the Virginia Colony, and became successful tobacco farmers (Griffin/Findeisen, n. d.); (Nugent, 1987). He married Jane (Unknown) who was born in 1649 in Steeple, Wiltshire, England. Their children were as follows (*Griffin/Findeisen*, n. d.): William Griffin III, born 1665, and John Griffin, born 1667. There may have been other children. William Griffin II left a will dated January 1, 1683. The legal document describes him as "William Griffin of Cittingborne (sic) Parish in the County of Rappa, Planter." The will states the following (Sweeny, 1998):

> "To son William 225 acres of land I bought of Mr. Mott and to have it next to the river and the rest of that tract being 125 acres to son John. Also to son John 75 acres bought of James Jackson which makes the number given to my son John equal to that of William. If either of my sons die without issue, the survivor to enjoy the whole estate. To sons John and William two-thirds of my personal estate and the other third to my wife. My sons to remain with my wife until they are twenty one if she remains a widow but if she remarries my will is that they be free at the age of eighteen. Wife Jane, executrix. Wit. James Harrison, James Jackson."

My family is descended from the older son, William Griffin III.

William Griffin III and Rebecca (Unknown)

William Griffin III was born in 1665 and died in 1725 at Sittingbourne, Richmond, Virginia. He married Rebecca (Unknown). William Griffin III owned land on the other side of the Rappahannock River inherited from his father (*Griffin/Findeisen*, n. d.). By 1712, he was operating a business called Foxhall Mill. It seems that William Griffin III was dishonest in his business dealings. He was fined fifteen shillings for "not keeping lawful measures" at his mill. Richmond County records elaborate on the incident (*Richmond, Virginia County Records*, 1704–1724, 19):

> "William Griffin of Sittenbourne Parish having been presented by the Grand Jury for not keeping lawful measures in his mill, this day appeared in court to answer the said presentment but offering nothing material in barr thereof, it is therefore ordered that he be fined fifteen shillings to our Sovereign Lord and King."

William Griffin III and Rebecca (Unknown) had the following children: Joyce, Elizabeth, Anne, John, born in 1684 in Rappahannock Co, Virginia, and William IV, born in 1685 in Richmond, Virginia (*Griffin/Findeisen*, n. d.).

The *Last Will and Testament* of William Griffin III dated November 25, 1681 reads as follows:

> *"His land to his son William Griffin. To daughter Anne a cow named Rose with all her increase. To daughter Elizabeth one cow named Browning with all her increase. To daughter Joyce one cow named Blackface with all her increase. To son William one cow named Madam. To each child a horse or mare or either of them that shall the the (sic) produce of Two mares one called Bess the other two year old. To wife my horse with all her stock that belongs to my plantation. To son William a copper kettle and two guns when he is of age. To Mr. William Moss and Mr. Wm Seargent each one a pair of gloves each and he appoints them overseers of his will. Wit. Wm Lathoope, Thomas X James, aged 36 or thereabouts. Power of Atty 2 Aug 1692. Rebecca Griffin wife of Wm Griffin, planter, to Tho Parke of Essex Co to back sale of land to Edward Price of Richmond Co. "Tayler"* (Sweeny, 1998).

The older son, John, was not mentioned in the will, indicating that John Griffin may have

died young. The *Richmond County Deed Book (1692–1693)* recorded the following business transaction and gives us a glimpse into the everyday life of this family of planters; tobacco was a big cash crop for them:

> *"September 1691 William Griffin of Sittenburne Parish in Rappe County and 'Rebecca my wife' to Edward Price of same county for 2950 lb tobacco, 112 acreas in Rappa Co 'it being part of a dividend or parcel of land formerly bought by*

*Mr. John and Mr. George Motts by William Griffin Esqr.' This
land on the N. side of the river. Signed William Griffin, Rebecca
X Griffin. Wit. Tho Parke, Charles-illegible, George X Proctor,
Rec 22 Aug 1692."*

My family is descended from William Griffin IV, the younger
son of William Griffin III. His mother, Rebecca Griffin, may have
been illiterate due to the "X" used as her mark in signing the will.

William Griffin IV and Elizabeth Griffith

William Griffin IV was born in 1685 in Richmond, Virginia
and died in 1751 in Lunenburg, Virginia. He married Elizabeth
Griffith who was born in 1683 in Virginia and died May 14, 1728
in Prince George, Virginia. The surnames *Griffin* and *Griffith* cause
some confusion due to their similar spellings. They had the following children: Abigail, John, William Griffin V, Elizabeth Griffin,
and Richard Griffin, born in 1700 in Prince George County,
Virginia (*Griffin/Findeisen*, n. d.). There may have been other children. My family is descended from the third son, Richard Griffin.
The *Last Will and Testament* of William Griffin IV states:

"William Griffin (1680-1751) / Last Will and
Testament dded this on 28 Dec 2008.William
Griffin of Lunenburg, being sick and weak To my
wife – I lend her my plantation which I now live on,
with 300 acres of land appertaining thereto, during
her widowhood, after which I give the land to my son,
William Griffin. I also lend my wife 2 feather beds,
3 dishes, I basin, and 6 plates, 2 iron pots, I brass
kettle, and I frying pan, during her widowhood. I also
give her I feather bed, 2 rings, and I sheet, I cow and
calf, and I horse. Also, I give her all my hogs. To my
son William - I bed, bolster, bed quilt, blanket, and

sheet. Also I mare, 4(?) cows and calves, I bed that I have lent my wife. To my daughter Elizabeth - when she comes to the age of 18 years, I cow and calf. To Henry Green, son of John Green - 100 acres of land on Buffalo Creek, to be laid off at the upper end of my land. To Ralph Griffin, son to Richard Griffin - 100 acres of land adjoining the aforesaid Henry Gren [sic] on the lower side. To my son and daughter - the household goods that is not given, is to be equally divided between them. As for my debts, to be got to discharge mine and to the support of my family, I rifle, I smooth-bore gun, I black horse, to be sold to pay my debts and to support my family. My will is that no part of my estate shall be appraised."

Executors — Ralf (sic) Griffin and William Woodward. Executrix —my wife.
Signed Oct 17, 1750 - William Griffin (-o his mark)

Witnesses - William Jackson, William Sizmore, Charles Smith

The within will of the deceased was exhibited at Apr 2, 1751 Court, and was proved by the oaths of the witnesses.
The within will of the deceased was exhibited at Apr 2, 1751 Court, and was proved by the oaths of the witnesses (Lunenburg County, Virginia Will Book I, 31).

The will of William Griffin IV was signed by his mark, an "X," indicating that he was probably illiterate.

Richard Griffin and Mary Green

Richard Griffin was born in 1700 in Prince George County, Virginia and died September 23, 1766 in Halifax County, Virginia.

He married Mary Green in 1720. She was born in 1703. Richard Griffin was listed as a constable, June 10, 1749. Richard Griffin and Mary Green had the following children (*Griffin/Findeisen*, n. d.):

Richard Griffin, Jr., born around 1720 in Prince George County, Virginia

Ralph Griffin, born February 16, 1725 in Prince George County, Virginia

John Griffin, born June 22, 1727 in Prince George County, Virginia

James Griffin, born around 1733 in Prince George County, Virginia

Samuel Griffin, born around 1735 in Prince George County, Virginia

Mary Griffin, born 1738 in Prince George County, Virginia

Francis Griffin, born 1738 in Prince George County, Virginia

Anthony Griffin, born around 1740 in Halifax County, Virginia

William Griffin, born November 21, 1740 Prince George County, Virginia

Owen Griffin, born 1745 in Prince George County, Virginia

Griffith Griffin, born 1748 in Halifax County, Virginia

My family is descended from the tenth child of Richard and Mary Griffin, Owen Griffin.

Owen Griffin and Anne Stovall

Owen Griffin was born in 1745 in Prince George County, Virginia and died in 1789. He married Anne Stovall around 1770. Anne Stovall was born in 1750 in Granville, County, North Carolina, and died in 1822 in Wilkes County, Georgia (*Ancestors of Richard Landon Miller*, 2009). Her parents were John and Dorcas Stovall (*Griffin/Findeisen*, n. d.). Sometime later Owen Griffin moved south to Granville County, North Carolina. The first child of Owen and Anne Griffin, Mary, was born on January 29, 1771. The following is excerpted from chapter twenty-five of a family history book of the Harbour family (Adair, 1995); it is a discussion of the Griffin branch of the Harbour family, and gives some interesting information about Owen Griffin:

> *"The Griffins of Gabriella Harbour's mother's family can be traced back to Richard Griffin Sr. and his wife Mary Green. They lived near Lunenburg County, Virginia during the middle part of the 1700's. A son, Owen Griffin, was born there circa 1745.*
>
> *Owen at one time owned some land on Hico Creek in Halifax County, Virginia. This land was part of a 118 acre tract sold to his parents on 16 April 1764 by Ralph Griffin of Halifax for 50 pounds. Owen sold his share to his cousin John on 13 September 1767."*

By the middle of the 1780's, Owen and Anne Griffin had followed her family to Wilkes County, Georgia. Owen Griffin purchased land on Soap Creek in Eastern Wilkes County in what is now Lincoln County. His namesake, son Owen, was born in 1786 in Wilkes County. Owen Griffin, Sr. died sometime in 1789. His will was probated on April, 3 1790. Anne continued to live on the Soap Creek farm for the next thirty years, raising her children and paying taxes on the land. Owen Griffin's estate was not divided until Anne Griffin died. By 1820, Anne was very old, and was documented in the 1820 census as living with her son. They were still living on the farm; she paid taxes on it in 1822. In December of 1822 a deed was drawn up passing the farm to Owen Griffin, Jr.

John Stovall, Sr., father-in-law of Owen Griffin, in his will dated July 29, 1781, left a female slave and personal property to Owen Griffin (Thompson, 1993). The will reads, "To my son in law Owen GRIFFIN my Negro girl Patt and her increase, my bell mettle skillet, dutch oven, and looking glass" (*Stovall, John Will of, Granville County, North Carolina,* 29 July 1781).

Owen Griffin and his wife's family, the Stovalls, served in the American Revolutionary War.

Direct Line of Descent for the Stovalls

Bartholomew Stovall and Ann Burton were the parents of John Stovall, Sr.

John Stovall, Sr. and Dorcas Drury were the parents of Anne Stovall

Owen Griffin and Anne Stovall were the parents of Drury Griffin.

Drury Griffin and Wife (Unknown) were the parents of George Stokes Griffin.

George Stokes Griffin and Lucy Tennessee Huskey were the parents of William G. Griffin.

William G. Griffin and Martha Camp were the parents of Virginia Griffin.

Virginia Griffin and John Wesley Bell Webb were the parents of Lewis French Webb.

Lewis French Webb and Louise Hawkins are the parents of Arnold Ray Webb, Donald Roy Webb, Jo Ann Webb, and Judy Carol Webb.

Judy Carol Webb and Billy J. Hubbell are the parents of William Griffin Hubbell

Bartholomew Stovall and Ann Burton

Bartholomew Stovall was born August 24, 1665 in Surrey, England. Bartholomew Stovall married Ann Burton, born in 1670 in Henrico, Virginia. Bartholomew Stovall died around 1721 in Powhaten, Virginia (Bishop, 1999). They were the parents of John Stovall, Sr.

John Stovall, Sr. and Dorcas Drury

There is some dispute over Dorcas Stovall's maiden name; some say it is Drury; others believe she was a Poole. She was probably a Drury because she named one of her sons Drury; this name shows up repeatedly in future generations of the family as a Christian name. John Stovall, Sr. and Dorcas Drury were the parents of the following eleven children (Bishop, 1999):

Bartholomew, born 1733 in Powhaten, Virginia; died 1802, Orange, North Carolina

Delilah, born around 1735, Goochland, Virginia; died June 30, 1821, Granville, North Carolina

John, Jr., born 1737, Goochland, Virginia; died Granville, North Carolina

Elizabeth, born Feb. 10, 1739, Goochland, Virginia; died Spartanburg, South Carolina

William, born April 12, 1740, Goochland, Virginia; died 1802, Granville, North Carolina

Thomas, born 1744, Powhaten, Virginia; died Mecklenburg, Virginia

Josiah, born 1749, Lunnenburg, Virginia; died November 20, 1798 in Lincoln, Georgia

George, born 1750, Lunnenburg, Virginia; died Aug. 3, 1820, Franklin, Tennessee

Anne, born 1750, Lunnenburg, Virginia; died Wilkes, Georgia

Drury, born May 16, 1752, Granville, North Carolina; died May 12, 1826, Morgan, Alabama

Benjamin, born around 1755, Granville, North Carolina; died Oglethorpe, Georgia

John Stovall, Sr. was our first Stovall ancestor born in America. John Stovall, Sr. was a Revolutionary War veteran, having served as a Private in the North Carolina militia (Anderson, 2010). Patriot leaders, in an effort to discover who supported their cause, and who supported the Crown, required men who were of age to sign an oath of allegiance to the Patriot cause. If an individual refused to sign, he was subjected to ridicule and persecution, could be prosecuted, and have his land confiscated. Signing from Granville County, North Carolina, County Line District, were John Stovall and his sons (his name appears twice—probably John Sr. and John Jr.), Drury Stovall (name also appears twice), Bartholomew Stovall, Thomas Stovall, Josiah Stovall, William Stovall, and son-in-law, Owen Griffin. Benjamin Stovall, another son of John Stovall, Sr., either refused or neglected to sign (*State Records of North Carolina*, n. d.).

The name of Owen Griffin, son-in-law of John Stovall, Sr., appeared on the Muster Roll of the Grenadier Company in the 2nd Regiment, South Carolina Infantry, commanded by Colonel Isaac Motte. Owen Griffin enlisted, July 11, 1777 (*American Revolution*, 2002). Several of John Stovall, Sr.'s sons also fought for the Patriot cause in the war (Bishop, 1999). John Stovall, Jr. and Bartholomew Stovall were listed in Captain Daniel Harris's Company in 1754 and 1755. Drury Stovall, William Stovall, and Josiah Stovall were listed in Colonel Henderson's Regiment (Anderson, 2010). These were the brothers of Anne Stovall who married Owen Griffin (Bishop, 1999). The biography of former Louisiana Governor William Wright Heard makes mention of several of his ancestors who were Revolutionary War Patriots; John Stovall and Owen Griffin are among those ancestors listed (Davis, 2006).

In contrast to this family's deep-seated desire for freedom from the British government, John Stovall, Sr. was a slave owner. The following is a list of the names of his eleven slaves: Aggy, Anthony, Jacob, Jane, Hanner, Patt, Fanny, James, Philis, Dilsey, and Abraham. As mentioned earlier, Owen Griffin inherited the slave, Patt, from Anne's father (Anderson, 2010).

Owen Griffin and Anne Stovall, continued

Owen and Anne Stovall Griffin's children are as follows *(Griffin/Findeien, n.d.):*

Mary Griffin was born January 29, 1771; married Ansel Cunningham in 1806; died November 4, 1852 in Jackson County, Georgia.

Joseph Griffin, born 1773 in Granville County, North Carolina and died January 1824 in Montgomery County, Alabama. He married Mary Heard on September 18, 1806 in Wilkes County, Georgia.

Drusilla Griffin was born in 1776; she married John Wright.

Rachel Griffin was born in 1779 in Granville County, North Carolina or Virginia; married William Heard; died in 1866 in Cherokee County, Georgia.

Dorcas Griffin was born in 1783 in Granville County, North Carolina.

Drury Griffin was born in 1784 in Granville County, North Carolina; died in Montgomery County, Alabama.

Owen Griffin, Jr. was born in 1786 in Wilkes County, Georgia; married Elizabeth Heard

September 10, 1820 in Wilkes County, Georgia. She was born in 1795 in Wilkes County, Georgia.

Susannah Griffin was born in 1788 in Wilkes County, Georgia; married E. Lay.

My family is descended from Drury Griffin, sixth child of Owen Griffin and Anne Stovall Griffin.

Drury Griffin and Mary "Polly" Gullatt

Drury Griffin was born in 1784 in Granville County, North Carolina, and married Mary "Polly" Gullatt, born around 1780–1784. Drury Griffin and Polly Gullatt were married January 5, 1809 in Lincoln County, Georgia. Drury Griffin died in 1834/1835 in Montgomery County, Alabama. I was able to document the following children of Drury Griffin and Polly Gullatt Griffin through the *Last Will and Testament* of their son, John G. Griffin. They are as follows: John G. Griffin, Peter G. Griffin, Elizabeth Ann Griffin, Louisa S. Griffin, George Stokes Griffin, born around 1817-1819, and Tabitha D. Griffin, born around 1825.

Will of John G. Griffin, April 21, 1846

John G. Griffin names several of his siblings in his will, dated April 21, 1846, and probated in Montgomery County, Alabama. Apparently John G. Griffin was on his death bed when he made out his will. The will was probated six days later. It seems that John G. Griffin had no wife or children.

In his will, he left the bulk of his estate to his brother, George Griffin; he named his brothers and sisters as the recipients of one dollar each. He names Tabitha D. Strange, Elizabeth Halton, and Peter G. Griffin. John G. Griffin further states his desire to leave to the heirs of his deceased sister, Aury Williams, the sum of one dollar.

I have no explanation why Louisa Griffin is not mentioned by name; I suspect she went by some nickname. Her mother, Mary Gullatt Griffin went by "Polly." I also suspect that *Aury* is a misspelling of that nickname; however, that is merely conjecture. He mentions three sisters; Tabitha and Elizabeth are both named in the will, so it stands to reason that the third sister called *Aury* is Louisa. The will of John G. Griffin, dated April 21, 1846, probated April 27, 1846, states the following:

> *"Know all men by the presents that I, John G. Griffin, of the State of Alabama, Montgomery County, weak in body though strong in mind and conscious of the certainty of death, do make this my last will and testament.*

> *After payment of my just debts, I give and bequeath to my brother George L. Griffin: all goods and chattles, rights and credits, lands and linements, after paying to each of my brothers and sisters the sum of one dollar, that is to my sister Tabitha D. Strange one dollar; to Elizabeth Halton one dollar; and my brother Peter G. Griffin one dollar; also to the heirs of my deceased sister Aury Williams the sum of one dollar.*

> *Executor: I also make and constiute and appoint my brother George L. Griffin executor.*

> *Witnesses: William Judkins, James C Pullen, John H Griffin (Recorded in Will Book 3:30, Montgomery County, Alabama; Bishop, 1999).*

George Griffin's middle initial is incorrect in the document. He was George Stokes Griffin. My family is descended from the youngest son of Drury Griffin and Polly Gullatt, George Stokes Griffin. Drury Griffin died in 1834/1835 when his son, George Stokes Griffin, was about seventeen years old.

George Stokes Griffin and Lucy Tennessee "Tennie" Huskey

The 1880 federal census report for Marion Township, Drew County, Arkansas lists George Griffin's year of birth as 1819 and his place of birth as Alabama. It also states that both his parents were born in Georgia and that he was a farmer. I have seen his year of birth, listed in several documents, as anywhere from 1816 to 1820. If he was born in 1819, he was sixty-one years old at the time of the 1880 census. This census information tells us that Lucy Tennessee "Tennie" Griffin was forty-five years old, sixteen years younger than her husband.

The family of George Stokes Griffin immigrated to Alabama shortly before his birth, probably to settle on government land ceded from the Cherokee Native Americans. In my research, I have failed to learn much about George Stokes Griffin's early life. After his birth in Alabama, the next record of George Stokes Griffin is found in Victoria, Texas before his marriage to Lucy Tennessee Huskey.

The information I found about George Stokes Griffin came from the 1850 federal census report for Victoria County, Texas. According to this data, George Stokes Griffin's year of birth was about 1820, and his place of birth was Georgia, but I believe the place of birth is incorrect. His parents made a settlement in Montgomery County, Alabama shortly before his birth and remained there until their deaths, so it stands to reason he was born in Alabama. He was listed as a member of the household of C. D. (Chesley) Strange, thirty-nine years old, and his wife, T. D. Strange, twenty-five years old. T. D. Strange was George Stokes Griffin's younger sister, Tabitha D. Griffin Strange, and she was fourteen years younger than her husband. The Strange household had five children. The youngest child, Allace E. Strange was described as being ten months of age and born in Alabama, so from this information, we know that the Strange family were newcomers to Victoria, Texas. Both George Stokes Griffin and C. D. Strange are described as farmers in the census information.

Chesley D. Strange was the first postmaster of Woodport, a community in Victoria County, Texas. Woodport was a small community located near the confluence of Garcitas and Arenosa Creeks (Hand, 2001); (Wheat, n. d.). This is probably an indication that Chesley D. Strange could read and write, an advantage he had over most of his neighbors. The position of postmaster may have carried with it a small measure of prestige.

I do not know what brought George Stokes Griffin and the Strange family from Alabama to the wild, lawless Texas-Mexico borderland. Raids by plains tribes of Native Americans were common during the 1800s. Larry Griffin (2011) of Midlothian, Texas, a descendent of George Stokes Griffin, was able to answer some of my questions about George Stokes Griffin's settlement in Victoria, Texas.

Larry Griffin states that Chesley D. Strange was married to George S. Griffin's sister, Tabitha D. Griffin, and that George S. Griffin had a cousin, John W. Griffin, who fought in the Mexican-American War in Veracruz, Mexico, and was wounded and hospitalized at Port Isabel, Texas. Larry Griffin believes that George S. Griffin may have come to Victoria, Texas to take his injured cousin home to Kemper County, Mississippi. John W. Griffin's wife, Barbara A. Harbour Griffin, had family in Kemper County.

One of the Strange children was named *Druory* according to the census data. This name is probably misspelled and should be *Drury*. The name Drury is significant because George Stokes Griffin named one of his sons Drury (1880 Federal census report for Marion Township, Drew County, Arkansas), and the father of George Stokes Griffin was Drury Griffin.

I do not know how or where George Stokes Griffin met his wife, Lucy Tennessee Huskey. I had always assumed they were married in Drew County before they migrated to Caldwell County (Lockhart), Texas, but that is incorrect. They were married in Caldwell County, Texas. The Huskeys migrated from Shelby County, Tennessee down to Drew County, Arkansas. Therefore, I believe it is possible that George Griffin came to Drew County before his removal to Caldwell County, Texas. Larry Griffin hypothesizes that George Griffin may have met Lucy Tennessee Huskey while visiting or living with his Uncle Owen Griffin, went back to Caldwell County, Texas, and waited until she came of age to marry. It may also be possible that the Huskeys migrated to Caldwell County, Texas before their settlement in Drew County, Arkansas, but I have found no evidence to support this theory.

In spite of the fact that the Griffins and the Huskeys were probably unrefined, rough, hard-scrabble people, I find it unlikely that the Huskeys would have allowed their unmarried daughter to travel to south Texas with a man who was not yet her husband. This leads me to conclude that the couple must have met in Shelby County, Tennessee or Drew County, Arkansas, but that still does not explain why they married in Caldwell County, Texas.

I discovered an interesting bit of information about the marriage of George Stokes Griffin and Lucy Tennessee Huskey. They were married on September 22, 1853 in Caldwell County (Lockhart) Texas; however, their marriage was not recorded until 1995. A box of unrecorded marriage certificates dating from 1852–1856 was discovered in 1995 when the Caldwell County, Texas Court House was evacuated so it could be restored (*Caldwell County Texas Genweb Project*, 2011). According to the certificate, George and "Tennie" Griffin were married by W. Addison Smith, VDM (*Caldwell County, Texas Marriage Book B, Vol. 31*). VDM is derived from the Latin for *preacher of God's word* (*The Free Dictionary*, 2008).

This information intrigues me for a number of reasons. Lucy Tennessee Griffin was forty-five years old at the time of the 1880 federal census, making her year of birth around 1835. This being the case, she was about eighteen years old in 1852 when she married George Stokes Griffin who was at least thirty-four years old, perhaps several years older, at the time of their marriage. It is likely George Griffin was a widower when he met Lucy Tennessee Huskey, and may have had other children.

Lucy Tennessee Huskey Griffin gave birth to her first child, William George Griffin on June 25, 1854, nine months and three days after her wedding day and proceeded to produce a house full of boys. Five of the six sons of George Stokes Griffin and Lucy Tennessee Griffin were enumerated as part of their household in 1880. The eldest, William G. Griffin, was on his own by 1880; he married Martha Ann "Mattie" Camp, February 10, 1874 in Drew County, Arkansas (*Drew County, Arkansas Marriage Book C*). The following are the children of George Stokes Griffin and Lucy Tennessee "Tennie" Huskey Griffin (*Family Group Record*, 2008); (*Federal Census Veasey Township, Drew County, Arkansas*, 1870):

William George Griffin was born June 25, 1854 in Lockhart, Texas (Caldwell County). Caldwell County is in the area of Austin, Texas; he died May 8, 1941 in Drew County, Arkansas, and is buried in Union Ridge Cemetery. My family is directly descended from William George Griffin.

Blake B. Griffin, born June 1856 in Lockhart, Texas; died in Drew County, Arkansas; buried in Union Ridge Cemetery. His grave has been lost.

John Lucas Griffin, born June 21, 1858 in Drew County, Arkansas; died August 26, 1939 in Elk City, Oklahoma

Drury Pickney, "Toss" Griffin, born 1859 in Drew County, Arkansas; died 1930 in Drew County, Arkansas; buried in Union Ridge Cemetery, but his grave has been lost.

Philip Stokes Griffin, born February 2, 1861 in Drew County; died in Drew County, Arkansas,

February 21, 1942; married Flora Chambers around 1889 in Drew County; buried in Green Hill Cemetery

James Floy (Jamie) Griffin, born March 1870 in Drew County, Arkansas

I so not know the reason this family settled in Lockhart, Texas, and then migrated to Arkansas. Migration patterns were usually toward the west. My father, Lewis French Webb, quoted family lore that George and Lucy "Tennie" Griffin had moved to Texas out of a belief that their slaves would not be freed in Texas. However, the census data do not support this theory, nor does the marriage data.

Chances are that their migration to Texas was part of the westward movement to the frontier prevalent at that time. They likely returned to Arkansas to be near family, or perhaps Texas was too dangerous during the time (1854–1858) they resided there. South Texas was a wild, rough, lawless place during these years. The Comanche Native American tribe under Chief Buffalo Hump was not on friendly terms with the white settlers of south Texas. The Battle of Plum Creek was fought at Lockhart, Texas, on August 12, 1840. The Comanche Great Raid of 1840 was the largest raid ever mounted by Native Americans on white settlements in this country. The Texas Revolution was fought in 1835–1836 (Brice, 1987); (Wallace & Hoebel, 1952).

During the 1850s, the Comanche and the Mexicans were still not on good terms with the white settlers, and there were frequent raids on pioneer settlers into the early twentieth century. George Stokes Griffin and Lucy Tennessee Huskey Griffin may have removed from Texas to Arkansas to work the farm land her father purchased in Drew County, well north of the Comanche and Apache raids.

When Lucy Tennessee Huskey Griffin's father, Blake Huskey, was released from the Tennessee penitentiary, he removed to Drew County, Arkansas where he purchased one hundred sixty acres of land. This may have been the motivation for George and Tennie Huskey's removal to Drew County, Arkansas. They may have been given the opportunity to farm some of the acreage owned by her father, Blake Huskey.

John Lucas Griffin was born in Arkansas in 1857/1858 according to the 1860 census, so we know the family had relocated to Arkansas by 1857/1858, the year of his birth and before the beginning of the Civil War (1861–1865). The war commenced April 12, 1861 when Confederate forces fired on Fort Sumter, South Carolina. George Stokes Griffin joined the Confederate Army, December 18, 1861. It is appropriate at this point to discuss the Civil War. It had a huge and still lingering impact on Arkansas and the other Confederate states.

Rich Man's War, Poor Man's Fight

The Civil War greatly impacted the lives of George and Tennie Griffin. Using the census data (1860), George Griffin was born around 1819, and was about forty-two years old when he went marching to war in 1861, leaving behind a wife and four young boys ranging in age from eight years to ten months.

One can only imagine the hardships Tennie Griffin endured during the approximately fourteen months of George Griffin's military service. She ran the small farm in the southwestern part of Drew County with the help of a few slaves and raised four little boys, one of whom was an infant. She had to produce all their food and construct their clothing. Wild game was in relative abundance; root and grain crops provided vegetables, and corn meal was ground locally. Only coffee and sugar were purchased, and these commodities became scarce as the war progressed, as well as during the period of Radical Reconstruction that followed the war. Tennie Griffin no doubt performed hard labor each day to put food on the table during her husband's absence. It is important to remember that Arkansas was part of the American frontier at this time, and Tennie was probably a typical frontier woman, hard-scrabble tough and a survivor. She had probably endured hardship while her father, Blake Huskey, was in prison, and life was hard in frontier Arkansas.

The 1860 federal census revealed that for the twelve months ending June 1, 1860, eight thousand eight hundred fifty-six persons died in Arkansas—one in every forty-eight persons, about two percent of the population, giving Arkansas the dubious distinction of having the highest death rate in the nation.

Drew County was a somewhat untamed region of the frontier. Willis (1998) quotes George J. Vinning, a native of England, and a drifter, who came to Drew County in 1853 at age sixteen. Vinning was shocked by the rowdiness of the people he encountered in Drew County. He stated in his diary:

> *"Those people were certainly worse than heathens in some things—the women were companions for the men; Sunday was the time for all kinds of doings but worshipping God; shooting matches, horse-racing, drinking, gambling, fighting— anything else thrown in to fill the day."*

Vinning also observed that Drew County men "were jealous of the walk and character of their wives and daughters." Vinning became a Lieutenant in the Ninth Arkansas Infantry, Confederate States of America, in which George Stokes Griffin served.

According to the 1860 census report, there were 111,115 slaves and 324,335 whites in Arkansas in 1860, the year prior to the outbreak of the Civil War. South and east Arkansas were the slave-holding regions of the state where cotton was king. So diverse were north and south Arkansas that there was a movement for the secession of certain counties from the state. The 1860 federal census further revealed that among the white population, only thirty-eight percent were native to Arkansas: 66,609 were from Tennessee (the Webbs, the Dodsons, the Hawkins; some of the Gabberts, and some of the Huskeys came to Arkansas from Tennessee), 24,433 from Alabama, (the Griffins), 18,030 from Georgia, 17,747 from North Carolina, 16,351 from

Mississippi (the Camps), 11,803 from Kentucky, 10,704 from South Carolina, and 6,484 from Virginia (Lucy Tennessee Huskey Griffin). Ten percent of the white population was foreign born, mostly from Ireland, followed by the German states. George Griffin, born in Alabama, was of English descent, as was his wife.

Tennie Griffin tried to do right by her slaves, and I realize that having slaves and "doing right" are contradictory terms. According to my father, his grandfather, William G. Griffin, told the story of his mother, Tennie Griffin, feeding her children and the slave children at the same table. All the metal had been melted down for bullets during the war years, and the family had one "bob-tailed" wooden spoon. The Griffin children and the slave children took turns with the spoon to eat their meals.

One must wonder why a man in his forties with a wife and four young children, one of whom was an infant, and only a few slaves, would volunteer to fight in a war. In *Arkansas Confederates in the Western Theater* (1998) James Willis, a Drew County native, offers some reasons for George Griffin's enlistment. Passions ran high when President Lincoln called for a blockade of the Confederate states. War was glorified, and the desire for "honor" and "glory" was a motivating force. Lincoln was despised by most Arkansans, especially those in south Arkansas. Patriotism for the South was at a fever pitch, and men were expected to enlist, especially by women. Women gave impassioned speeches, almost taunting men to go to war. Willis quotes a Drew County newspaper, *The Sage of Monticello* that contained a transcript of one of these lofty speeches delivered by Mollie Quindley. Willis includes the transcript of another eloquent speech delivered on horseback by another young lady, Rocky T. Howard, invoking an ancient Spartan directive to its fighting men to come home with their shields or upon their shields. Men who did not enlist were sent packages of women's underclothing, petticoats in particular, as a barbed suggestion of their lack of manly qualities.

Confederate conscription (draft) laws were stringent. Men between eighteen and forty-five years old were required to serve.

The federal census of 1860 enumerated sixty-five thousand two hundred thirty-one white males, age eighteen to forty-five, living in Arkansas; at least sixty-five thousand white men from Arkansas served in the Confederate army, a staggering number that nearly depleted Arkansas of its adult male population. During the war, Arkansas had seven hundred seventy-one military actions. Women were left in charge of slaves, crops, children, home, and hearth. It is safe to say that these women had what is called "true grit." The old men and the young boys belonged to the Home Guard, a military unit whose purpose was something like law enforcement.

On July 2, 1861, Arkansas Governor Henry Rector issued a proclamation calling for ten regiments of volunteer infantry to be raised. One such infantry was the Arkansas Ninth Infantry in which George Stokes Griffin would serve. Willis (1998) chronicles the history of the Arkansas Ninth in his book; information about George S. Griffin is listed on p. 766. I dreaded reading Willis's nine hundred three-page tome, thinking it would be tedious and boring, but I was pleasantly surprised. It is readable and has been an excellent source of research.

George Griffin did not enlist until December 18, 1861. One can only speculate as to why he delayed joining. Perhaps he wanted to get his crops harvested. The previous year's crop had been lost to drought in many parts of Arkansas. No doubt this caused much hardship for the family. Ironically, the next year, there was too much rain, damaging the cotton and fodder, and doubling the price of beef, pork, flour, and grain (Willis, 1998). Perhaps, at his age, George Griffin had a more mature view of war and did not have visions of glory; he may have been somewhat reluctant to jump into the fray.

Conscription Act of 1862

Confederate President Jefferson Davis signed the *Conscription Act* into law on April 16, 1862. Prior to this legislation, the

Confederate Army consisted of volunteers. This law added two more years to a Confederate soldier's tour of duty for all men between the ages of eighteen and thirty-five (Shaw, 1962).

During the first year of the war, volunteers were considered to have done their duty after an enlistment of one year. There were some unpopular provisions in the *Conscription Act*; preachers, teachers, and owners of more than twenty slaves were exempt from the draft. A draftee could send a substitute to perform his military duty, if he could afford a substitute. The *Conscription Act* became a hot subject of discussion. To the small farmers, the provision exempting owners of more than twenty slaves was unfair; they complained that a man with a wife and twelve children to support was not exempt, while the rich slave owner was exempt. Out of this debate, the slogan "Rich Man's War, Poor Man's Fight" was popularized. Some provisions of the *Conscription Act* were repealed. In December 1863, the substitution provision was repealed, and the conscription age was extended to include men of seventeen to fifty years old. The law continued to be unpopular throughout the war years (Gallagher, 1997); (Moore, 1924); (*Rich Man's War*, 2008); (Willis, 1998).

Confederate war records document that Private George S. Griffin served in Company B, Drew County Cut-Off Guards, Ninth Arkansas Infantry. Cut-Off Creek was a well-known stream in Drew County. George S. Griffin was later transferred to Company F, Drew County Dixie Guards, Ninth Arkansas Infantry. The Ninth Arkansas was organized in Pine Bluff, Arkansas, and recruited in Jefferson, Union, Drew, Bradley, and Ashley counties. It was nicknamed the "Parson's Regiment" by the *Helena Shield* newspaper because it contained more than forty ministers from various denominations (Gerdes, 2003); (Willis, 1998). The paper erroneously reported that the regiment had in its membership a preacher seventy years old. In a footnote, Willis states that Private John Law was not a preacher but was eighty-four years old and served until June 29, 1862 when he was discharged because of his age. A monument memorializing the Ninth Arkansas was erected at the White Sulphur Springs Confederate Cemetery, a few miles east of Pine Bluff.

Military Actions of the Arkansas Ninth

The Arkansas Ninth, in which George Stokes Griffin enlisted, served east of the Mississippi River throughout the war. The regiment fought in the following battles: Belmont, Missouri, Nov. 7, 1861; Battle of Shiloh, Tennessee, April 6–7, 1862; Siege of Corinth, Mississippi, April 29–May 30, 1862; Battle of Vicksburg, Mississippi, May 18–July 27, 1862; Grand Gulf, Mississippi, May 26, 1862; Grand Gulf, Mississippi, June 9, 1862; Battle of Corinth, Mississippi, Oct. 3–4, 1862; Hatchie Bridge (Davis Bridge); Big Hatchie, Tennessee, Oct. 5, 1862; Water Valley Station, Mississippi, Dec. 4, 1862; Coffeeville, Mississippi, Dec. 5, 1862; Hernando, Mississippi, April 18, 1863; Perry's Ferry, Coldwater River, Mississippi, April 19, 1863; Champion's Hill, Baker's Creek; Edwards Depot, Mississippi, May 16, 1863; Big Black River Bridge, Mississippi, May 17, 1863; Siege of Jackson, Mississippi, July 10–16, 1863; Assault on Jackson, Mississippi, July 12, 1863; Evacuation of Jackson, Mississippi, July 16, 1863; Sherman's Meridian Campaign, Feb.3–March 2, 1864; Assault Kennesaw, Georgia, June 27, 1864; Battle of Atlanta, Georgia, July 22, 1864; Siege of Atlanta, Georgia, July 23–August 25, 1864; Battle of Ezra Chapel, Georgia, July 28, 1864; Siege of Decatur, Alabama, Oct. 26–29, 1864; Battle of Franklin, Tennessee, Nov. 30, 1864; Battle of Nashville, Tennessee, Dec. 15-16, 1864; Battle of Averysborough (Taylor's Hole Creek), North Carolina, March 16, 1865; Battle of Bentonville, North Carolina, March 19–21, 1865. On April 26, 1865, the few remaining members of the Arkansas Ninth surrendered at Bennett's Place, North Carolina (Gerdes, 2003); (Willis, 2002). Several of these battles were major, including the Battle of Shiloh, the costliest in human lives in American history up to that time.

The Battle of Shiloh

The Yankees called this battle Pittsburg Landing. The Rebels called it Shiloh. Ironically, *shiloh* means "place of peace" in Hebrew.

Shiloh was the name of a church at the battle site in southwestern Tennessee. George Griffin and his comrades were part of a plan to attack Union General Ulysses S. Grant and his army at dawn, April 4, 1862. The Confederates had been slowed down by rain and mud and by disorganization due to young and inexperienced officers. They did not begin their march to Shiloh until Saturday, April 5.

On Thursday April 3, the night before they were to begin their march to Shiloh, the Arkansas troops were awakened and ordered on a fourteen-mile march to Iuka, Mississippi where the enemy was believed to be. The rebels marched double time through the rain and mud. The black sky was periodically illuminated by brilliant, severe lightening. The men brought only what they could carry and had no tents to escape the elements. They did not find the enemy at Iuka and returned to camp at Burnsville where they were ordered to prepare five days rations in the torrential rain.

The Arkansas soldiers fell out the next morning, Saturday April 5, before dawn and ate a hasty breakfast of wet biscuits and raw bacon. Cold and exhausted, they set out for Pittsburg Landing with little to eat and very little sleep. They marched through deep mud in a heavy drizzle. One of the officers of the Dixie Guards of the Arkansas Ninth, Captain William J. Haislip of Monticello, resigned his commission and went home, basically deserting. He was thereafter sarcastically referred to as "the great warrior" by many of the Arkansas Ninth (Willis, 2002).

In the late afternoon of Saturday April 5, the weary Arkansas Ninth arrived at Pittsburg Landing, going into camp in line of battle, resting on their arms. Thick brown mud was everywhere, but the rebels could build no fires because of the nearness of the enemy. Within two miles of their camp, there were eighty thousand men, both Union and Confederate. The Yankees were unaware of the impending battle, and thought the next day would be a beautiful, quiet Sunday.

Before dawn on April 6, the Arkansas Ninth again had to eat a hasty breakfast of wet biscuits and raw bacon. They suffered from exposure as a result of two days and two nights of rain. When the fighting started, men questioned why they were there. War no longer seemed a noble undertaking to many of the Union and Confederate soldiers (Willis, 2002).

The Arkansas Ninth suffered heavy casualties, losing one hundred thirty-two men at Shiloh on April 6 and 7, 1862 during its attack of the "hornet's nest." A total of twenty-three thousand seven hundred forty-six soldiers from both the Union and the Confederacy died in what was the bloodiest battle in United States history (McPherson, 2005); (Scott, 1880); (Willis, 2002), and George Stokes Griffin survived. The bloody Battle of Shiloh was considered a Union victory. The Union lost thirteen thousand forty-seven men, and the Confederates lost ten thousand six hundred ninety-four (McPherson, 2005); (Scott, 1880).

Siege of Corinth

The Confederate Army retreated to Corinth, Mississippi, and the Siege of Corinth lasted from April 29, 1862 to June 10, 1862. The Confederates ran out of drinking water and resorted to digging holes and drinking muddy seepage; rations ran desperately low. Dysentery, typhoid, and measles broke out, resulting in an estimated eighteen thousand men becoming ill at Corinth. Many died from these diseases.

After the battle, Union soldiers burying the dead discovered parched acorns in the Confederate knapsacks. Many Rebels had survived on acorns and muddy water, a fact that gave the Unions soldiers a respect for the dedication of the Confederates (Willis, 1998).

George Stokes Griffin Returns Home

I believe that George and Tennie Griffin were illiterate, but in spite of that, they communicated during his absence; according to the 1860 federal census, one in every ten white adults in Arkansas was illiterate, twice the national average. However, Tennie had somehow gotten word of his discharge and the date he would be returning home. Perhaps George Griffin sent word to his wife by another soldier. I obtained George Griffin's pension records from the Arkansas History Commission, and it reveals Lucy T. Griffin's signature as an "X," indicating that she was illiterate.

My father's sister, the late Julia Webb Barnette, related the story of her grandfather, William G. Griffin, as a child, riding a mule and leading another mule to Ozment's Bluff or Gee's Landing on the Saline River to meet his father returning home from the war. Ozment's Bluff and Gee's Landing were, at that time, steamboat landings and located within a few miles of the old home place in the Green Hill community of Drew County. It is plausible that a boy of William's age (about ten years old in 1863) would be given the job of meeting his father upon his return from the war. George Griffin resumed his life with Tennie and the boys. The 1870 census report for Veasey Township, Drew County, Arkansas reveals that two more sons, Philip Stokes Griffin and James Floy Griffin, were born to the couple, and possibly one other child.

Lucy Tennessee Huskey Griffin was a plain-spoken woman with a fierce demeanor. I have seen a picture of her copied from an old tintype. Her eyes were very expressive. Apparently she had a "falling out" with her adult son, John Luther Griffin. Family members have an old, undated letter she wrote to John Luther Griffin. There seems to have been a family squabble about Tennie's spinning wheel, and who was to use it. The tone of the letter is harsh and straight forward:

> *"Well John I will write you a few lines though I reckon you don't want to hear from me. I am well and getting along very well better than common. We are still at mother's but will get us a place soon as we gather our crop and then move to ourselves. I have lived in peace this year only when I have a fussy frame....I suppose that you have forsaken mother and brothers all the friends you had on earth. I have seen buzzards fly high before they had to come to the ground for food and water. I can say John that you were once a...child to*

me but for the last three years past you have been like a stranger and gets worse every year. I understand you say Fanny (John Luther Griffin's wife) is not to blame about Sis not getting my wheel you are both to blame. If Fanny was sick and not able to spin you ought to let Sis have the wheel to spin her knitting thread. I positively tell you to let them have the wheel without another word about it. I suppose you was all highly insulted at the last letter. I shant make no apologies for I meant what I said. I am not this today that tomorrow. What I am I am all the time and that is the way for everyone to be always the same. I will close by asking you all to be good to yourselves. You can write to us if you wish to."

I do not know if Lucy Tennessee wrote this letter, or dictated it to someone. Other documents suggest she was illiterate.

Confederate pension records show that George S. Griffin's widow, Lucy T. Griffin, applied for a Confederate widow's pension in Drew County, Arkansas in 1901, when she was seventy-one years old.

I ordered George Griffin's pension records from the Arkansas History Commission for a fifteen dollar fee. I received a copy of the widow's application that showed the date of the application, August 16, 1901, and that the application was approved for a widow's pension of fifty dollars per year. The notarized document states that Lucy Griffin was in "indigent circumstances." The notarized signatures of A. L. Oslin, W. T. Wells, and R. C. Knox follow. Knox served in the First Arkansas Infantry. Oslin, Wells, and Knox were the officials who approved or rejected pensions (*Arkansas Confederate Pension Records*, 2007).

I also received the "Proof of Service for Widow" form that revealed some interesting information. A war comrade, F. M. Shewmake, attested that he had known George Griffin for six or eight months during the war; he was also a member of Company B, Ninth Arkansas Infantry. William G. Griffin, son of George and Lucy T. Griffin, also served as a witness. This document was dated July 6, 1901.

WIDOW'S APPLICATION FOR PENSION.

STATE OF ARKANSAS,

COUNTY OF *Drew*

I, *Lucy T Griffin* do solemnly swear that I

am the widow of *George S. Griffin* who

served as a soldier in the army (or sailor in the navy) of the Confederate States, being a member of *9th Arkansas* Regiment of *Infantry*

from the State of *Arkansas* or a member of the crew of the ship

called , that he was honorably discharged (paroled or released)

from such service on or about the day of *February* 186*5*

and did not desert the same; that I am now, and for the past twelve months have been, a bona fide resident of this State; that I do not own property, real or personal, or both, or money or choses in action, in excess of the value of $400.00 (exclusive of household goods and wearing apparel), nor have I conveyed title to any property to enable me to draw a pension, and that I am not in receipt of any income, annuity, pension or wages for any services, the emoluments of an office, in excess of $150.00 per year; that my said husband died *on July 1881*

after the close of the war

and that I have not since remarried, so help me God

Attest J H O Kimbro (Signature) *Lucy × T. Griffin*

Subscribed and sworn to before me, this *29* day of *June* 190*1*

J H O Kimbro

STATE OF ARKANSAS,
County of Drew } ss.

We, the undersigned, sitting as a Pension Board for Drew County, do certify that we have examined the application of the within named Lucy J. Griffin for pension, under Act of the General Assembly of the State of Arkansas, as approved March 11, 1901, and the proof in support of same, and find that said applicant is the widow of a Confederate soldier, is in indigent circumstances, and that her claim is just, and that she should be allowed $50.00 pension.

A. L. Ozlin [SEAL]
W. J. Wills [SEAL]
R. C. Knox [SEAL]

The form states that George Griffin was:

"honorably discharged (paroled or released) from such service and did not desert the same. That he is now dead and that his widow has been for the past twelve months a bona fide resident of Arkansas. That to the best of our knowledge, all property now owned by the widow is not worth exceeding $400 (exclusive of household goods and wearing apparel). That his widow is not in receipt of any income, annuity, pension or wages for any services, or the emoluments of an office, in excess of $150 per year, and that she has not since remarried. That we have no interest in the claim."

The signatures of F. M. Shewmake and W. G. Griffin follow. Inadequate funding often prevented pensioners or their widows from receiving their full yearly payment.

I do not know if George Griffin spoke of the horrors he undoubtedly witnessed in battle, particularly in the Battles of Shiloh, Corinth, and Vicksburg. My father, Lewis French Webb, never passed on stories about his great-grandfather. If his grandfather, with whom my father lived until 1940, ever told those stories about George Griffin's war experiences, I am certain my father would have passed them on because he always loved to tell family stories. I have to wonder if, when George Griffin returned home from the war to his small, dirt farm at Green Hill in Drew County, Arkansas, he thought all the bloodshed was worth it. George Stokes Griffin and Lucy Tennessee Huskey Griffin are buried in Mount Tabor Cemetery, Drew County, Arkansas.

My family is descended from George and Lucy T. "Tennie" Griffin's eldest son, William, for whom my son, William Griffin Hubbell, is named. According to my mother, Louise Hawkins Webb, William Griffin was an extremely kind, good person. My son is very compassionate and kind-hearted as well.

William Griffin served as an elder in the Church of Christ that was established in the Bowser community of Drew County in July of 1870. Earnest Camp of the Camp branch of our family was another elder in the congregation. William Thomas Breedlove of Tyro came once a month in a horse-drawn buggy to preach the sermon. Breedlove served the congregation for many years until he became too weak to stand and had to sit in a chair to preach. The congregation met in a schoolhouse that was heated with a pot-bellied stove with lighting provided by coal-oil lamps hung on the wall. Nearby ponds were used for baptisms, and frequently, the ice had to be broken in the winter months. The church often had "all-day singing and dinner on the grounds." The congregation moved to its present location on South Gabbert Street in Monticello on February 8, 1959 (Allen, 1984).

Another Notable Griffin: James R. Griffin and the Arkansas First Infantry

Private James R. Griffin enlisted in Company I, Monticello Guards, I[st] Arkansas Infantry, Confederate States of America, on May 8, 1861 at Monticello, Arkansas. He was awarded the Medal of Honor for valor at the Battle of Chickamauga, Georgia, August 10, 1864. The Battle of Chickamauga took place September 18–20, 1863 and was the largest battle fought in the state of Georgia. The North suffered about sixteen thousand casualties, and the South around eighteen thousand. It is generally regarded as the greatest Confederate victory of the war. Although the Union lost the battle, it achieved its objective of capturing the city of Chattanooga, Tennessee (*New Georgia Encyclopedia*, 2002).

James R. Griffin was wounded and captured at Franklin, Tennessee on December 17, 1864 and sent to the United States Military Prison at Camp Chase, Ohio. He experienced the horrors of a prisoner-of-war camp for about three months before he was exchanged at City Point, Virginia in March of 1865. James R. Griffin was born around 1840 and was described as a farmer (Gerdes, 1999). I have been unable to determine the relationship of James R. Griffin and George Stokes Griffin. Perhaps they were cousins, and it is also possible they were not related. James R. Griffin was a true hero and did Drew County, the Arkansas First Infantry, the gray uniform, and the Griffin name proud in the Civil War.

The Confederacy had only one medal for valor, the Confederate Medal of Honor known as the <u>Southern Cross of Honor</u>. Twenty-seven soldiers of the First Arkansas Infantry were awarded the medal, although the Confederacy lacked the funds to manufacture the actual medals.

There were two other Griffin soldiers in Company I, First Arkansas Infantry. John D. W. Griffin enlisted as a private on the same date as James R. Griffin, May 8, 1861. He was born around 1836, and like James R. Griffin, was a farmer. By July 23, 1862, John D. W. Griffin was detailed to duty with a supply train. There is no record of his military service after August 31, 1864 (Gerdes, 1999).

Christopher Columbus Griffin enlisted at Monticello, Arkansas on February 22, 1862, and was wounded at Murfreesboro, Tennessee on December 31, 1862. He served to the end of the war when he surrendered at Greensboro, North Carolina on April 26, 1865 (Gerdes, 1999).

James R. Griffin and John D. W. Griffin were probably brothers, enlisting on the same date and in the same unit, and they were both farmers. Apparently, they were somewhat atypical of soldiers in Company I, First Arkansas Infantry, in that they were farmers and not professional men. Gerdes (1999) describes Company I, First Arkansas Infantry:

> *"The 'Monticello Guards' was organized at Monticello, Drew County Arkansas, on May 8, 1861, with 105 officers and men. James A. Jackson was elected captain; Lawrence W. Livingston, first lieutenant; Stinson Little, second lieutenant; and John W. Colquitt, third lieutenant. The company was composed mostly of men from Monticello, with some men from the surrounding countryside, and a handful from neighboring counties. This was an unusually well-educated and literate company of men. Its ranks included lawyers, physicians, clerks, merchants, and skilled artisans of all trades. Unlike most Arkansas companies, farmers were a distinct minority in the Monticello Guards. Interestingly enough, men whose skills and professions, such as the many physicians who enlisted in the company, could have easily been used to secure commissions or staff appointments; instead chose to serve in the ranks as privates. Very few desertions occurred in the Monticello Guards. They served from Manassas to Bentonville, in some of the bloodiest battles of the war, sustaining appalling casualties (especially at Shiloh), yet remained true to the colors to the end. This appears to have been a highly-motivated group of men."*

I do not know the relationship of the three Griffin men in Company I, First Arkansas Infantry, nor do I know their relationship, if any, to George Griffin, but I suspect they were all related in some way. It is also interesting that all four Griffins from Drew County survived the Battle of Shiloh.

My family is descended from William George Griffin, eldest son of George Stokes Griffin and Lucy Tennessee Huskey Griffin.

William George Griffin and Martha Ann "Mattie" Camp

Martha Ann Camp was the oldest daughter of George Crenshaw Camp and Julia Ann Virginia Gabbert Camp and was born in 1848 in Mississippi according to the 1850 federal census report for DeSoto County, Mississippi. She died in 1928 in Drew County, Arkansas, and is buried in Union Ridge Cemetery. She married William G. Griffin, February 10, 1874 in Drew County, Arkansas (*Drew County, Arkansas Marriage Book C: 168 FHL# 986551 Document #6*).

William G. Griffin and Martha Ann "Mattie" Camp had nine children that I can document (*Drew County, Arkansas Cemetery Records, 2002*):

> **Lucy Griffin was born around 1875 in Drew County Arkansas, and was named for William G. Griffin's mother, Lucy Tennessee Huskey Griffin.**

> **Virginia "Virgie" Griffin was born April 19, 1876 in Drew County, Arkansas, and died October 4, 1956 in Drew County. She married John Wesley Bell Webb in Drew County, and is buried in Union Ridge Cemetery, Drew County. My family is directly descended from Virginia Griffin.**

> **George C. Griffin was born December 12, 1877 in Drew County, Arkansas, and died November 12,**

1878 in Drew County, Arkansas. He is buried in Union Ridge Cemetery, Drew County, Arkansas.

Susan Jane "Susie" Griffin was born March 19, 1879 in Drew County, Arkansas. She married William Tom Gill. She died September 20, 1958, and is buried in Union Ridge Cemetery, Drew County, Arkansas.

Mary E. Griffin was born October 2, 1880 in Drew County, Arkansas, and died August 22, 1895 when he was about fifteen years old, in Drew County. She is buried in Union Ridge Cemetery, Drew County.

Ina P. Griffin was born May 19, 1882 in Drew County, Arkansas, and married H. E. Webb. She died May 5, 1916, and is buried in Union Ridge Cemetery, Drew County.

Fred Griffin was born in December of 1883 in Arkansas, and died February 1, 1948. He is buried Union Ridge Cemetery, Drew County, Arkansas.

Frank Griffin was born in May of 1885 in Arkansas, and died in 1940. He is buried in Union Ridge Cemetery, Drew County, Arkansas.

Infant, born and died same day in Drew County, Arkansas, 1887; buried in Union Ridge Cemetery, Drew County.

William G. Griffin and Martha Camp Griffin knew the horror of death claiming their children. Only five or possibly six of their nine children lived to adulthood. I do not know how long their firstborn child, Lucy, lived, and I do not know where she is buried. She may be buried in Union Ridge Cemetery, and the grave has been lost over the years. I believe she lived to adulthood because I have often heard my father, Lewis French Webb, speak of his "Aunt Lucy." Virginia Griffin, born in 1876, was my father's mother and the younger sister of Lucy Griffin.

William and Martha Griffin lost a son, George C. Griffin, at eleven months old. They also lost an infant. There are no dates on the headstone, nor is the gender of the child noted. Both are buried under the big cedar tree at Union Ridge Cemetery in Drew County. They lost a fifteen-year-old daughter, Mary E. Griffin. She is buried in the family plot beneath the big cedar tree (*Drew County, Arkansas Cemetery Records*, 2002).

William George Griffin and Martha Camp Griffin. Photo courtesty of Larry Griffin.

Left to right, Obie Mae Sanders Young, Lela Griffin, Helen Beatrice Griffin Burton. This picture was taken at the old home place in Green Hill, Drew County, Arkansas. This is where I lived until I was three years old. At one time, four generations lived together in this house: William Griffin; his daughter, Virginia (Virgie), and her husband, John Wesley Bell Webb; their son, Lewis, and his wife, Louise, and their son, Ray. This photo was taken around 1920. Photo courtesy of Larry Griffin.

Martha Camp Griffin was about eight years older than her husband, William G. Griffin, which was somewhat unusual. My theory is that many of the eligible young men were killed during the Civil War, depleting the pool of potential suitors. The dates on William G. Griffin's headstone are incorrect, his surname, Griffin, is misspelled (*Griffen*) on the headstone. According to my parents and other family members, William Griffin was a kind soul. In the Drew County history, *Old Times Not Forgotten* (1980), the author relates a story that illustrates his compassion. She quotes Marietta Webb's account of how the Block family of Drew County received their name:

> "When Uncle Billy Griffin (William) was on his way from Mississippi, he came upon a colored man in a ditch limping. He began to ask him questions and found that he was free, but that he had previously been mistreated by his master, who tied him with a block and tackle. The man had no name, so Uncle Billy called him 'Block' and brought him to Drew County."

The Blocks of Drew County are now a large African-American family, many of whom are prominent in the community.

The Frank Griffin family, seated, left to right: Chester Wood Griffin, William Frank Griffin, Lela Griffin, Lettie May Barnes Griffin, Helen Beatrice Griffin Burton. Standing, left to right: Claud Barnes, Howard "Bunt" Barnes, Luther Drury Griffin, Obie May Sanders Young. This appeared in the Advance Monticellonian between 1976 and 1983. Image Courtesy of Larry Griffin.

Ida Sue Gilliam, Ellis Gilliam, Perry Webb, Howard
(Bunt) Barnes, Grandpa Griffin, Chester Griffin, Obie
Young, Helen Griffin Burton, Grandma (Martha)
Griffin Frank Griffin, Lettie Griffin, Christine Griffin.
Velma Webb
Behind. Ed Barnes, Ray Webb, Claud Barnes. Albert
Gilliam, Hazel Griffin, Luther Griffin & Morris Webb

Photo courtesy of Larry Griffin.

William Griffin died of skin cancer in 1940 and is buried in Union Ridge Cemetery under the big cedar tree next to his wife, Martha. My mother said that Grandpa Griffin loved to hold and rock my brother, Ray, when he was little, and that he had awful skin cancers on his face that broke open and bled. At that time, four generations lived together in his house in the Green Hill community of Drew County: William Griffin; his daughter, Virginia Griffin Webb, and her husband, John Webb; his grandson, Lewis Webb, and his wife Louise; and Lewis and Louise Webb's oldest son, Ray Webb.

My mother often tells of William Griffin's work ethic. She says that Grandpa Griffin believed in physical labor and that everyone should work at least enough to break a sweat each day. Mother said that even into his last years he would work each day until his shirt was damp with sweat.

William Griffin's daughter, Virginia Griffin Webb, lived to a ripe old age (born April 19, 1876, died October 4, 1956). She, too, was doomed to the horror of losing children to death. She bore twelve children and lost six of them from birth to three years old.

Chapter 14
The Webb Family: Noble Roots

Parent to Child Line of Descent for the Webbs

Sir Henry Webb and Wife (Unknown) were the parents of Geoffrey Webb.

Geoffrey Webb and Wife (Unknown) were the parents of John Webb.

John Webb and Wife (Unknown) were the parents of William Webb.

William Webb and Joan Stone were the parents of John Alexander Webb.

John Alexander Webb and Wife (Unknown) were the parents of Henry Alexander Webb, Sr.

Sir Henry Alexander Webb, Sr. and Grace Arden were the parents of Henry Alexander Webb, Jr.

Sir Henry Alexander Webb, Jr. and Mary Wilson were the parents of William Micajah Webb.

William Micajah Webb and Wife (Unknown) were the parents of Richard Webb.

Richard Webb and Wife (Unknown) were the parents of John Webb.

John Webb and Jane (Unknown) were the parents of John Webb.

John Webb and Sarah Cocke were the parents of William Webb.

William Webb and Jane Martin were the parents of John Webb.

John Webb and Sarah Byars were the parents of John Byars Webb.

John Byars Webb and Mary Webb were *probably* the parents of William Morris Webb, Sr.

William Morris Webb, Sr. and Mary Ann Ward were the parents of William Morris Webb, Jr.

William Webb, Jr. and Georgia Harris were the parents of John Wesley Bell Webb.

John Wesley Bell Webb and Virginia Griffin were the parents of Julia Webb Barnette, Alvin Chance Webb, Lewis French Webb, Maywood Webb Young, Herman D. Webb, and Gertrude Webb Berryman.

Lewis French Webb and Louise Hawkins are the parents of Arnold Ray Webb, Donald Roy Webb, Jo Ann Webb Morrison, and Judy Carol Webb Hubbell.

Billy James Hubbell and Judy Carol Webb are the parents of William Griffin Hubbell.

Note: There is some dispute about the reliability of this line of descent. I am fairly satisfied that it is correct from the present day back to John Webb and Sarah Cocke Webb.

The surname *Webb* means "weaver of fabric" and is from the Old English word *webba*, meaning a "woven cloth" (Hanks, 2010). The famous medieval poem, *Piers Plowman* (Langland, 2006), contains the line, "My wife was a webbe and woolen cloth made." The oldest known record that contains this family name is the *Olde English Byname Register*. Recorded in this document is the name Alger se Webba, of the County of Devon (*Webb Coat of Arms*, 2010) and dates to about 1100 during the reign of King William II (*Internet Surname Database*, 2009). The Webb(e) surname can be found throughout English history. *The Yorkshire Poll Tax of 1379* contains the name of Johannes Wybbe (*Webb Coat of Arms*, 2010); (*Webb Surname DNA Project*, 2006). The English *Pipe Rolls* contain numerous references to the *Webb(e)* surname. Osbert Webbe in the County of Suffolk is listed in the pipe rolls. These medieval records are described in the following passage (*Some Notes on Medieval English Genealogy*, n. d.):

> "The pipe rolls of the Exchequer contain accounts of the royal income, arranged by county, for each financial year. They represent the earliest surviving series of public records, and are essentially continuous from 1155 onwards until the 19th century; one roll from 1129-30 also survives. A copy of each pipe roll - known as the Chancellor's Roll - was also sent to the Chancery. (The unusual name - officially it started out as the 'Great Roll of the Exchequer' - comes from the distinctive way in which the membranes were sewn together, which made them look like pieces of piping when rolled up). The sheriffs' accounts form the core of the early pipe rolls. The sheriff was the king's representative in the county, and was responsible for collecting revenues from the royal estates and other sources."

The *Webb Surname DNA Project* (2006) lists several references to Webbs, with various spellings, in English documents. In 1299/1300 Simon le Webbe de Purtepoll was elected Bailiff of the Guild of Weavers of London, and in 1301, Simon le Webbe was a witness to an agreement between two couples in the parish of St. Andrew de Holebourne (Sharpe, 1901).

One particular Webb suffered in the religious controversies of England. John Web/Webbe, gentleman, was burned at the stake at Canterbury in 1555 (*Webb Surname DNA Project*, 2006). The name Thomas Webbe of Suffolk, son of Roger Webb, was inserted into a list of forfeited lands for treason (*Journal of the House of Commons*, 1802). In 1591, William Webbe was the Lord Mayor of London (*List of Lord Mayors*, n. d.).

Many Webbs migrated to the American colonies where those with weaving skills were offered good wages. George Washington, in 1790, authorized the first federal census, and three hundred ninety-five Webb families were listed with an average of 5.7 members per family. The United States Census Bureau (1990) reported that the Webb surname was the 125th most common surname in America.

The Webb family was originally from Dorset, one of the shires of England on the southern coast of Wales, where Webb is a common surname. The Webb name is concentrated in the English shires (counties) of Essex, Somerset, Wiltshire, Hants, Suffolk, Norhampton, and Worchestershire (*Descendents of Sir Henry Webb,* 2008); (*Webb Coat of Arms,* 2010); (Webb, 1894).

Sir John Alexander Webb, Sr. of Oldstock was an officer in the army of King Henry VII and King Henry VIII of England. On June 17, 1577, he was granted the Webb Coat of Arms at Hampton Court during the reign of Queen Elizabeth I (*Descendents of Sir Henry Webb,* 2008). The New Nobility earned its rank of nobility or gentry by meritorious service to the Crown. The British peerage system is still important today. You may recall that during the bitter divorce of Prince Charles and Princess Diana, Diana fought unsuccessfully to retain her title "Her Royal Highness." A family's coat of arms was a sign of prestige because it defined the noble class throughout Europe. In 1894, a letter from Hiram Webb of New Bedford, Massachusetts to Dr. Robert Dickins Webb of Yazoo City, Mississippi, explains the meaning of the heraldic ensignia:

> *"The family coat of arms is a cross gule before four eagle falcons and border scroll, red with gilt letters, brown shadows on all, or crest out of a ducal coronet, and a device eagle displayed. A Crown has 2 red and 3 blue shots of gold, with red hollows, scarlet shield, and eagles light yellow. The cross shows that our ancestor was a crusader. The hawks denote swiftness and courage. The coronet that he was fighting under one of the confederate ducal sovereigns of France, and that he was an officer."*

The *Webb Family Genealogy* (2005) offers a slightly different interpretation:

> "...the cross in the arms shows that the ancestor was with King Richard Cour de Leon in the 3rd Crusade or Holy War. And the falcons are the birds of Palestine and denote swiftness and courage, and they show that the ancestor was at one time employed in Palestine. The ducal crown in the crest was given to those who had been in the service of one of the sovereign dukes of The French Confederation, and the eagle shows that the ancestor had won a battle at sea while in command of the vessel in which it was fought."

It is generally accepted that Sir Henry Webb of Dorsetshire was the founder of the Webb lineage in the New World with his emigration to America with his four sons. The family members became wealthy when they sold their estate in England prior to their departure for the New World in 1629. Three of the sons settled in Boston, Massachusetts, and in Connecticut. A fourth son, William Micajah Webb of Warwickshire, settled in the Isle of Wight, Virginia, and was the progenitor of the southern branch of the Webb family (*Descendants of Sir Henry Webb*, 2008); (*Webb Surname DNA Project*, 2004).

Miscellaneous Webbs

Stephen Webb, eighteen years old, is recorded in Hotten's *List* (1874) as being transported to the colony of Virginia on the ship *Transport* in 1635. It appears that he travelled alone to the New World. He had taken the required *Oath of Allegiance and Supremacy* before embarking on his journey from the Port of London, as recorded by Hotten.

Richard Webb, thirty-six years old, is recorded in Hotten's *List* (1874) as being transported to the colony of Virginia on the ship *Primrose* in 1635. He was administered the *Oath of Allegiance and Supremacy*, necessary to demonstrate his allegiance to the Church of England. He too departed from the Port of London. He was one of two hundred twenty-one passengers, all men. Like Stephen Webb, he appears to have travelled alone.

Seventy-seven patriots are listed in the Index of Revolutionary War Pensions with the Webb surname (White, 1995). A book by Henry F. Waters entitled *Genealogical Gleanings in England, Vol. 1* (2010) that originally came out in 1907 contains interesting information about several Webbs. Wills and other legal documents make up most of its contents. The Webb name is frequently found in these documents. I selected a few that I found most interesting:

> *William Taylor, a citizen and haberdasher (men's outfitter of clothing) of London, in his Last Will and Testament, July 19, 1651, left to his daughter, Margaret Webb, wife of William Webb, a grocer, forty shillings for a ring (probably a mourning ring, a popular item to commemorate the death of a loved one).*

> *Daniel Williams of Hoxton, near London, a Doctor of Divinity, in his Last Will and Testament of June 26, 1716 leaves much of his estate to religious work; it included a gift of four pounds apiece to several ministers' widows, among them a Mrs. Webb of Fromley. It can be concluded from his Will that Dr. Williams was a Presbyterian minister, regarded by the Church of England, the official religion of the realm, as a group of radical dissenters, and that Mrs. Webb was the widow of a Presbyterian minister.*

> *John Aldworth of the city of Bristol, a merchant, in his Last Will and Testament of December 18, 1615, requests that John Webbe, Mayor, and his good friend, to be one of the overseers of his will, and that he leaves to him a gown to solemnize his funeral.*

Thomas Callowhill of the city of Bristol, a linen draper, in his Last Will and Testament of November 28, 1711, left parcels of land to his kinsman, Brice Webb of Bristol, a linen draper (a dry goods merchant). Callowhill stated in his will that he was a partner in a packett boat business headquartered in Bristol that regularly sailed to New York and other places in America. Brice Webb was one of the partners. Callowhill, in his will, named Brice Webb as one of the overseers of his will.

Nathaniel Webb of Mountserratt, a merchant, had his Last Will and Testament proven by his son, Robert Webb, Esquire, March 26, 1741. In his will, he discusses the leasing of his Negro slaves belonging to his plantation in the parish of St. Anthonyon the island of St. Christopher, commonly called Carroll's Plantation, in the Caribbean, to his "beloved wife Jane." To his eldest son, Robert Webb, Esquire, he leaves an estate in the County of Somerset (Taunton, England). To his son, Nathaniel Webb, he leaves plantations in Mountserratt and a house in Bassterre on the island of St. Christopher's. His son, John Webb, inherited "all my lands in the county (colony?) of Connecticut in New England near the town of Seabrook, they containing about five hundred acres." Nathaniel Webb mentions his brother, John Webb, of Abington, and leaves to him one hundred pounds sterling, and forgives him of debts owed to him. To his brother, in Antigua and was one of the executors. Nathaniel Webb appointed his brother, Harry Webb, and his eldest son, Robert Webb, to be the guardians of his minor children. He left his "honored mother" one hundred pounds sterling.

Margery Cox of Debtford in the County of Kent, a widow, in her Last Will and Testament of May 30, 1656, proven

June 11, 1656, mentions her brother, Giles Webb, living in the colony of Virginia. She leaves him twenty pounds. There was a Captain Giles Webb who commanded a company of rangers in Henrico County, Virginia in 1692.

Waters (1907) states that the name, Webb, was prominent in Virginia. John Webb, a "mariner," was granted fifty acres of land in Accomac County, Virginia, December 13, 1627. Stephen Webb (perhaps this is the Stephen Webb who came to Virginia in 1635 at eighteen years old) was a Burgess from James City in October 1644. George Webb was elected, December 17, 1776, by the Virginia Assembly as Treasurer of Virginia.

Thomas Dumer, gentleman, of the County of Southhampton, in his Last Will and Testament of April 12, 1650, and proven November 9, 1650, names his brother-in-law, Erasmus Webb, one of the Canons of St. George's Chapel, as one of the overseers of his will.

In or near Mecklenburg County, North Carolina, there was a John Webb who met a bad end in 1789. Abstracts From State Gazette of North Carolina (1787-1791) relates the following account: "Wednesday last Patrick Cassady and John Webb, having returned from exile, contrary. . .to their late pardon for capital offences, and been convicted of felony since their return. . .were executed on the gallows, near this town. . ."

The September 20, 1879 edition of the Monroe Enquirer of Union County, North Carolina reported that Miss Mary Ann Webb who lived with her brother near the Beaver Dam community committed suicide in the woods near her home by hanging herself.

> *Lewis Webb is listed in the 1814 muster roll of the Mecklenburg County, North Carolina Militia, Second Regiment, during the War of 1812 (Muster Roll, 1861).*

> *The first Webb to arrive in America was Thomas Webbe, gentleman, one of the Jamestown, Virginia settlers (Original Settlers, 2007).*

Sir Henry Webb and Wife (Unknown)

I was able to trace my family's direct line of descent back to Sir Henry Webb, born May 15, 1350, at Stratford, Warwickshire, England. He was a member of the English nobility. He had a son, Geoffrey Webb, born April 12, 1372 in Warwickshire, England (*Descendents of Sir Henry Webb 2008*) ;(*Individual Record: Henry Webb*, 2008).

Sir Geoffrey Webb and Wife (Unknown)

Sir Geoffrey Webb and Wife (Unknown) had a son, John Webb, born January 5, 1404/05 at Stratford, Warwickshire, England. Geoffrey and Wife (Unknown) were married before 1404. They had two children, John and Alice (*Descendents of Sir Henry Webb*, n. d.); (*Individual Record: Geoffrey Webb*, 2008).

Sir John Webb and Wife (Unknown)

Sir John Webb and wife (Unknown) had a son, William Webb, born March 16, 1423/24 at Stratford, Warwickshire, England (*Descendents of Sir Henry Webb*, n. d.); (*Individual Record: John Webb*, 2008).

Sir William Webb and Joan Stone

Sir William Webb married Joan Stone, a widow. William Webb and Joan Stone had a son, John Alexander Webb, born July 9, 1450 at Stratford, Warwickshire, England (*Individual Record: William Webb,* 2008).

Sir John Alexander Webb, Sr. and Wife (Unknown)

Sir John Alexander Webb, Sr. and Wife (Unknown) were the parents of John Alexander Webb, Jr., born January 16, 1482/1483 at Stratford, Warwickshire, England (*Descendents of Sir Henry Webb,* n. d.).

Sir John Alexander Webb, Jr. and Wife (Unknown)

Sir John Alexander Webb, Jr. was an Officer of Rank in the army of King Henry VIII of England. He was a Knight Baron. John Alexander Webb, Jr. and wife (unknown) had a son, Henry Alexander Webb, born May 11, 1510 in Stratford, Warwickshire, England. He had three other children, Henry, Mary, and Abigail (*Family Group Record, John Alexander Webb,* 2008). Mary Webb married Robert Arden and was the grandmother of William Shakespeare (Web-Lucas, 2002).

Sir Henry Alexander Webb, Sr. and Grace Arden

Sir Henry Alexander Webb, Baronet, married Grace Arden, daughter of Thomas Arden, in 1533 in Stratford, Warwickshire, England. Grace Arden was born in 1514 in Warwickshire, England. She died, December 3, 1639 in Warwickshire (*Family Group Record: Henry Alexander Webb,* 2008). One source credits Sir Henry Alexander Webb with establishing the Webb family for all future times because the crown granted him a crest or heraldic insignia rank in the New Nobility (*Webb Family Genealogy,* n. d.).

The New Nobility was based on meritorious service performed for the king. The hereditary coat of armor had grown out of the twelth century. It was a major factor in defining the European nobility and was passed on to the eldest son. This was granted due

239

to personal service that Sir Henry Alexander Webb had rendered to the Crown (*Webb Family Genealogy*, n. d.).

Sir Henry Alexander Webb, Sr. and Grace Arden had a son, Henry Alexander Webb, Jr., born December 24, 1534 at Stratford, Warwickshire, England. They had three other children: Abigail Webb, Henry Webb, and Mary Webb. Mary Webb and Abigail Webb were the grandmothers of the famous playwright and poet, William Shakespeare. Mary and Abigail Webb were daughters of Sir Alexander Webb and sisters of Sir Henry Webb of Hampton Court (*Webb Family Genealogy*, n. d.).

Sir Henry Alexander Webb, Jr. and Mary Wilson

Sir Henry "Alexander" Webb, Jr. married Mary Wilson around 1579 in Warwickshire, England. Sir Alexander Webb, Jr. and Mary Wilson had five sons and a daughter: Christopher, Richard, Henry, John, William Micajah, and Elizabeth. The family immigrated to America in 1629. Some sources believe this was the beginning of the Webb family in America. Anne Webb Nelson (2006) disputes this claim based on DNA research (*Webb Family Genealogy*, n. d.).

The brothers had amassed a great deal of wealth. They sold their inherited estate in England for a large amount of money to stake their future in America. The lands had originally been confiscated by the king at the suppression of the monasteries and were located in Dorsetshire, England. Sir Henry Alexander Webb was close to Catherine Parr, sixth wife of King Henry VIII of England (*Webb Family Genealogy*, n. d.).

Robin Webb-Lucas (2002) refers to the fact that Sir Henry Alexander Webb was Usher to the Privy Council of Catherine Parr. She quotes from one of the few existing documents connected with the regency of Catherine Parr, a letter to the Council of Catherine Parr executed while Henry VIII was conducting the siege of Boulogne in 1544. Its purpose was to request that Sir

Henry Alexander Webb receive a grant of land he had been promised as well as privileges earned in service to the Crown. Webb-Lucas (2002) quotes from the letter from Catherine Parr to her council in which she refers to Sir Henry Alexander Webb as her "trusty, well-beloved servant." Her letter concludes, "We most heartily desire and pray you to be favourable to him at this our earnest request." The letter is dated July 23 of the thirty-sixth year of the reign of King Henry VIII.

Sir William Micajah Webb and Wife (Unknown)

Sir William Micajah Webb, born January 9, 1583, at Stratford, Warwickshire, England, and died in Norfolk County, Virginia, is said to be the common ancestor of the southern branch of the Webb family. He came to America with his father and brothers around 1629 (*Descendents of Sir Henry Webb*, n. d.).

Some researchers believe William Micajah Webb settled in Connecticut where he died in 1656. Others believe William Micajah Webb may have come to Virginia and settled south of the Potomac River. His son, Richard, came to Virginia around 1622, leading some researchers to believe that two older sons, Giles and James, may have been born in England and other children were born in Virginia. William Micajah Webb may have first settled at Isle of Pines, then at Smithfield, Isle of Wight, and then at Norfolk, Virginia (*Ancestors of Edward A. Pereira*, n. d.).

Nonie Webb of Tennessee has published several books on Webb family genealogy (2001) and states that "almost invariably, all the Webb families prior to 1800 in the southern states are of William Micajah Webb, known as a skilled ship builder and designer and was referred to as the "merchant of Norfolk." He is believed to have died in Norfolk, Virginia. Some researchers believe that William Micajah Webb had the following children: Richard, James, Jane, Isaac, John, and William. My family is descended from Richard Webb (*Descendents of Sir Henry Webb*, n. d.).

Richard Webb and Wife (Unknown)

Richard Webb and Wife (Unknown) were the parents of the following:

> Giles Webb was born in 1620, in Gloucestershire, England, and died in 1692, in Richmond County, Virginia. Giles Webb served as as member of the Virginia House of Burgesses, the first elected lower house in the legislative assembly in the New World established in the colony of Virginia. On March 20, 1660, the Assembly of James City, Virginia assumed the full power of the government and appointed officers. Giles Webb was among the Burgesses of Upper Norfolk (Turner, 2007).

> Richard Webb was born in 1629 in Essex County, Virginia, and died in 1760 (*Descendents of Sir Henry Webb*, n. d.).

> John Webb was born in 1631 in Essex County, Virginia. My family is descended from John Webb (*Descendents of Sir Henry Webb*, n. d.).

> Alexander Webb was born around 1635 (*Descendents of Sir Henry Webb*, n. d.).

> William Webb was born in the 1630s (*Family Group Record: Richard Webb*, 2008).

> Berry Webb was born in 1637 (*Family Group Record: Richard Webb*, 2008); (Webb-Lucas, n. d.).

John Webb, Sr. and Jane (Unknown)

This John Webb has the distinction of being our first Webb ancestor born in America. John Webb, Sr. and Jane (Unknown) were the parents of John Webb, Jr. (*Our Family Tree*, 2004).

John Webb, Jr. and Sarah Cocke

John Webb, Jr. was born April 20, 1664 in New Kent County, Virginia. However, there is some dispute about the place of his birth. One source (*Webb Family Genealogy*, 2005) states John Webb was transported from England to Henrico County, Virginia in 1678. He died in 1726 in Henrico County, Virginia. He married Sarah Cocke(s); Sarah's surname was possibly Smith (Webb, 1998). Sarah Cocke was born around 1673 in New Kent County, Virginia (*Family Group Record: John Webb and Sarah Cocke*, 2008). They were the parents of the following:

> **Elizabeth Webb was born in 1688 in New Kent County, Virginia, and was baptized April 8, 1688.**
>
> **James Webb was born June 25, 1690 in New Kent County, Virginia, and was baptized Oct. 19, 1690, and died as an infant.**
>
> **John Webb, III was born April 20, 1694 in Henrico County, Virginia, and married Mary Martin on February 2, 1712.**
>
> **William Webb was baptized on September 9, 1694 (*Book #1682 St. Peter's Parish*) New Kent County, Virginia, and married Jane Martin at St. Peter's Church. Jane Webb was baptized on June 11, 1697, in New Kent County, Virginia.**

Abraham Webb was born in 1702.

Wentworth Webb was born on May 5, 1702, New Kent Count, Virginia, and died in 1747 in Albemarle County, Virginia.

Mary Webb was born on March 19, 1703/04 in New Kent County, Virginia.

Henry Webb was born in 1705.

The children of John Webb and Sarah Cocke are listed in *The Parish Register of Saint Peter's, New Kent County Virginia 1680–1787* (Vestry Book 1905). St. Peter's Church is rich in history, and much can be learned about the Webb family from the records of the parish. The colonial records of New Kent County were destroyed by a fire in 1787, a result of arson. John Price Posey was convicted and hanged for the act. The records for New Kent County between 1787 and 1864 were destroyed by another unfortunate fire (*New Kent County, Virginia Genealogy Project*, 2010).

St. Peter's Church

St. Peter's Church, built in 1701, is one of the oldest churches in the Commonwealth of Virginia. The site was purchased for one hundred forty-six thousand pounds of tobacco. The original portion of the church that remains is one of the few examples of Jacobean Baroque architecture in America. J. Esten Cooke (1874) called it "southern ecclesiastical architecture." The bricks used to build the church were imported from England. The stump tower built in the 1740s is somewhat unusual (*St. Peter's Episcopal Church*, 2007). The vestry books of the parish go back to 1682. Virginia's General Court confirmed the establishment of St. Peter's Parish in 1679. At present, it is the oldest parish church in the Diocese of

Virginia and the third oldest in the Commonwealth of Virginia. Episcopalians and Presbyterians worshipped as one congregation until 1856 by alternating services from Sunday to Sunday (*The First Church of the First First-Lady*, n. d.).

George and Martha Washington were among the congregants. Reverend David Mossom baptized Martha Washington and presided over both her weddings; he is buried in the northeast corner of the church's interior (Gerena, 1998). It is believed that the wife of President John Tyler, Letitia Christian, was baptized in the parish church in 1790 (*St. Peter's Episcopal Church*, 2007).

Sadly, in 1862, Union soldiers desecrated the church by using the historic structure as a stable. The wife of Confederate General Robert E. Lee, Martha Washington's great-granddaughter, was instrumental in restoring the structure (Chamberlayne, n. d.); (*St. Peter's Episcopal Church*, 2007).

William Webb and Jane Martin

William Webb and Jane Martin were married at St. Peter's Church, Henrico County, Virginia. The couple moved to Goochland, Virginia. They had the following children (Webb, 1998):

> Samuel Webb, born February 6, 1735, St. Peter's Parish, married Rebecca Smith.

> Martin Webb, born December 29, 1737 in St. Peter's Parish; was in Surry County, North Carolina in 1771, Smith County, Tennessee in 1778, Rutherford County, North Carolina in 1783 and 1789–1800, and White County, Tennessee in 1811–1814; died in1814 in either Warren or White County, Tennessee; appeared on 1790 tax list with Townsend Webb, grandson of

Reverend John Webb. Martin Webb had a son, also named Martin, who served in the Civil War.

Merry Webb was born around 1745, and married Elizabeth White (Buckingham County, Virginia). Merry Webb's daughter, Mary, married her first cousin, John Byars Webb, son of Reverend John Webb and Sarah Byars, making for a confusing family tree.

William Webb was born in 1741, and married Rachel Smith, May 5, 1760.

Mary Webb was born around 1739, and died in Buckingham County, Virginia.

John Webb was born around 1740/42, and married Sarah Byars. He passed through Buckingham, Amhurst, and Franklin Counties, Virginia on the way to Surry County, North Carolina (Loiselle, L., 2001). John Webb's son, John Byars Webb married his first cousin, Mary Webb, daughter of Merry Webb. This John Webb is probably the Reverend John Webb who married Sarah Byars.

Our family *probably* descended from John Webb and Sarah Byars, as well as Merry Webb and Elizabeth White as a result of the marriage of first cousins, Mary Webb and John Byars Webb. A copy of Merry Webb's *Last Will and Testament* gives us a great deal of insight into the lives of these Webbs:

> *Last Will & Testament of Merry Webb*
> *February 6, 1774*
> *Last Will and Testament of Merry Webb—*

-I lend to my dear-and loving wife, Elizabeth, during her naturlife (sic) or widowhood, three Negroes, to wit: Robin, Peter and Jane, with the increase of the saed (sic) Jane, together with all my stock of horses, cattle and hogs. And after the decease of my said wife, Elizabeth, my will and desire is that the Negroes Robin, Peter and Jane, together with the increase of the said Negro Jane, and the stocks of all kinds be equally divided between Merry Webb, John Webb, Mary Burns, Elizabeth Sams and Lucy Webb. And, in case, my said daughter, Elizabeth Sams should die without issure, (sic) then her part to be equally divided between the said Merry, John, Mary Burns and Lucy Webb to them-and their heirs forever.

Item: I give unto my son, Martin Webb, one shilling and no more.

Item: I give unto my daughter, Martha Dillard, one shilling and no more.

Item: I give unto my daughter Million Hall, one shilling and no more.

I given (sic) unto my daughter Million Hall, the tract of land she now lives on to her and her heirs forever.

Item: I give unto my daughter, Lucy Webb, two Negro girls named Sara and Aggy, with their increase to her- and to her heirs, lawfully begotten, and in case my daughter Lucy dies without issue, then I give the sameunto my sons and daugh-ters—namely, Merry Webb, John Webb, Mary Burns, Elizabeth Sams. I give sameto my daughter Elizabeth Sams., to wit: as a proportionate part of my other children, provided she have issue.

Item: I give unto my, son Merry Webb, one Negro girl named Hannah, to him and his heirs forever.

Item: I give unto my son, John Webb, one Negro boy called Joe, to him and his heirs forever.

Item: I give unto my daughter, Mary Burns, one Negro boy called Lewis, to her and her heirs forever.

Item: I give unto my daughter, Elizabeth Sams, one Negro boy called Ben, to her and her heirs of her body, lawfully begotten.

Item: My will and desire is that all my lands should be sold, together with my mill, and the money arising here from, shall be equally divided between my sons, Merry Webb, John Webb and between my three daughters, Mary Burns, Elizabeth Sams and Lucy Webb; in case my daughter Elizabeth Sams shoul (sic) die without issue, then her part to be equally divided between the survivors.

Item: I give unto my daughter, Lucy Webb, one feather bed to her and her heirs forever.

Item: I give unto my dear and loving wife, Elizabeth Webb, during her natural life, all my estate not beforedisposed of, and after her deceases, I give it to be equally divided between my two sons, Merry and JohnWebb, my daughters, Mary Burns, Elizabeth Sams and Lucy Webb-and in case, my daughter Elizabeth Sams should die without issue, then I give the same to the survivors to be equally divided, between them.

Lastly, I do appoint my wife, Elizabeth, Executrix and my two sons, Merry Webb and John Webb, Executors. Revoking all other wills by me hertofore made, in witness wherof, I have here unto set hand and affixed my seal, the sixth day of February, One Thousand Seven Hunderd (sic) and Seventy-Four.

/s/ Merry Webb

Witnesses:

Will Tunstall

George Elliott

John (x) Ray

At a Court held for Henry County, Virginia, on the 15th day of February, 1779, the within Executrix, Elizabeth Webb, and Merry Webb, the Executor, presented the within Last Will and Testament of Merry Webb, Deceased, and with Waters, Dunn, John Alexander and Phillip Ryan, their securities, entered into bond. /s/ John Cox, Clerk, Henry Co.

Will Book 1, pages 17-18
Henry County Circuit Court
Martinsville, Virginia 24112

Reverend John Webb and Sarah Byars

We are *probably* directly descended from Reverend John Webb, a primitive Baptist minister and planter, who was born in Rutherford, North Carolina or possibly Virginia, around 1742–1745, and died around 1800–1803 in Rutherford County, North Carolina. It is believed that he married Sarah Byars, born in 1742 in Granville County, North Carolina. John Webb is listed in the 1782 tax list and the 1790 federal census report for Rutherford County, North Carolina (Webb, 1998).

There is no documentation that John Webb was a preacher or verification that Sarah's maiden name was Byars; this information has been passed down through the generations. However, there is documentation that John Webb, planter, and his wife, Sarah, sold land in North Carolina in 1769; in fact, there were several land transactions by John and Sarah Webb in Orange County, North Carolina.

John Webb was also listed as a Tory (on the side of the British) in court records, and as a result, his land was confiscated by the American government. John Webb, William Webb, Sr., and Benjamin Webb were summoned before a grand jury in the Morgan District, Rutherford County, North Carolina, on the second Monday in July of 1782 to answer the charge of treason (*Morgan District, North Carolina*, 1782). The grand jurors returned a true bill to indict. The grand jury indictment stated that on October 1,

1780, the defendants "knowingly and willfully did aid & assist the said King by joining his army commanded by Major Ferguson and by bearing arms in the service of said King" (*Morgan District, North Carolina*, 1782). The Battle of King's Mountain was fought October 1, 1780 on the border of North and South Carolina; it was a decisive Patriot victory in the southern campaign of the American Revolutionary War (Alderman, 1986).

We know Reverend John Webb avoided hanging because he is found in the 1800 federal census report for Rutherford County, North Carolina. Interestingly, four of our Camp ancestors were listed as Tories in this same court case: Thomas Camp, James Camp, and two men named John Camp (*Morgan District, North Carolina*, 1782).

Reverend John Webb married Sarah Byars, born 1751 in Granville, North Carolina (*Gard's: James Webb*, 2001); (*Gard's: Webb Family*, 2001). Sarah was the sister of John/James Henry Byars. Some documents refer to him as *James Henry Byars*, others *John Henry Byars*; various documents spell the surname as *Byars* or *Byers*. James Henry Byars (1734–1781) served as a captain in the American Revolutionary War (*Descendants Chart*, 2001); (Parkes, 1979).

On September 29, 1832, at seventy-one years old, James Henry Byars appeared in open court before the Court of Common Pleas and Sessions to claim a military pension to which he was entitled for his Revolutionary War service. He stated that he had entered the service of the United States in September 1780 in the Spartanburg district of South Carolina and that he was born October 22, 1761 in Granville County, South Carolina. Reverend Joshua Richards and Jesse Tate provided affidavits attesting to the character and moral deportment of Byars/Byers. His signature was an "X," indicating that he was illiterate. He was awarded a pension of $23.33 per year for his service in the South Carolina militia. However, this document says he served as a private, not a captain (*Southern Campaign*, 2009). This may be a case of his military rank becoming embellished through the years of family lore.

The father of James/John Henry Byars and Sarah Byars was James Henry Byars, born in 1713 in Orange County, Virginia, and died in 1792 in Louisa County, Virginia. James Henry Byars first married Margaret "Peggy" Gentry who died in 1734. After Peggy's death, James Henry Byars married Rachel Matthews.

Reverend John and Sarah Byars Webb lived on the Broad River and were members of the Sandy Run Primitive Baptist Church. Later, Reverend John and Sarah Webb were on the membership list from 1812–1816 of Old Bildad Baptist Church located in Warren County, North Carolina (now DeKalb County) on Sink Creek. The church held strong beliefs about predestination. The church did not have a Sunday school or musical instruments, and preaching was held once a month, lasting for several hours. The singing was slow and very controlled (Webb, 1994). They had the following children, eight sons and three daughters (*Webb-L Archives*, 2000):

John Byars Webb, born 1762, Orange, North Carolina, married Mary Webb, daughter of Merry Webb, around 1782 in Rutherford County, North Carolina. John Byars Webb and Mary Webb were first cousins. John Byars Webb died around 1835 in Warren County, Tennessee.

Jesse Webb was born around 1760–64 in North Carolina, and died June 10, 1835 in Tennessee; he married Didama Townsend.

Joel Webb, born 1765

Jacob Webb, born 1768

Joshua Webb, born 1770

Chesley Webb, bor n 1772, married Henrietta Blackwell

Rebecca Webb, born 1774

Julias Webb, born 1776, married Polly (Unknown)

James Webb, born 1782

Webb Firsts

The young adventurer mentioned earlier in this chapter, eighteen-year-old Stephen Webb, was probably the first Webb to come to this country when he came to Virginia in 1635 on the ship *Transport* (Dorman, 1987).

Referring back to the list of children of Reverend John Webb and his wife, Sarah, you will find Jesse Webb who married Didama Townsend. Jesse Webb was born around 1760–1762 in North Carolina and died June 10, 1835 in Warren County, Tennessee. He married Didama Townsend around 1785–1791 in Pittsylvania County, Virginia. Didama Townsend was born November 18, 1765 in Pittsylvania County, Virginia, and died around 1855 at ninety years old in McMinnville, Tennessee. She was the fourth child and daughter of Thomas and Anaphileda Watson Townsend (*Descendants of John Webb*, 2009); (*Didama Townsend*, n. d.).

Jesse Webb bought land on Horse Creek, Greenville County, South Carolina from Shadrack Chandler on October 29, 1788. Jesse Webb is listed in the 1790 federal census report for the ninety-sixth district, Greenville County, South Carolina. Jesse and Didama Townsend Webb journeyed to Kentucky with Anaphilda Townsend and purchased land in Logan County, Kentucky on the south side of the Red River. They bought three parcels of land, eighty-seven acres, sixty acres, and twenty-seven acres in the early 1800s. The children of Jesse and Didama Townsend Webb are as follows: Townsend Webb, Celia Webb Bailey, Didama Webb Womack, Sally Webb Clark, Elizabeth Webb Hooper, Lucinda Webb Nowlin, Nancy Webb Burks, John Webb, Jesse Webb, James Webb, Ira Webb.

A copy of the will of Jesse Webb gives us a great deal of insight into the lives of this frontier family. The will was filed around January–April 1835 in Warren County, Tennessee. It was signed January 10, 1835 and can be found in Will Book I, p. 101.

> "...after all my just debts is (sic) paid the balance I give to my beloved wife Didama for her fully to possess and enjoy during her life time or widowhood and at her death or marriage the remainder part to be divided as follows: I bequeath unto my son Townsend Webb ten dollars also unto my daughter Celia Bailey one hundred dollars also unto my daughter Nancy Burks one hundred dollars and also unto my daughter Didama Womack one hundred dollars and also unto my daughter Sally Clark one hundred dollars and also unto my daughter Elizabeth Hopper and her heirs one hundred dollars and also unto my daughter Lucinda Nowlin one hundred dollars and for my four sons (to wit) John Webb, Jesse Webb, James Webb, and Ira Webb have received a recompence each to that amount in land except John him to have fifty dollars then and I also bequeath unto my grandson Austin Webb the son of Townsend Webb deceased one horse saddle and bridle to be worth seventy five dollars in trade to be paid to him when he is nineteen years old then the balance to be equally divided between all the lawful heirs of my body and I do also appoint my sons Jesse and Ira Webb my true and lawful executors for my testimony whereof I have set my hand and affixed my seal as my last will and testament signed sealed and acknowledged in the presence of this being the 10th of January 1835.

George H. Ballard, Jonas Webb, John Ellis, and Absolom Clark (Clark signed with an "X") served as witnesses.

State of Tennessee Warren Co. April Sessions AD 1835 of the Court of pleas and quarter Sessions in and for Warren County aforesaid and sixth day of said month this the last will and testament of Jesse Webb deceased was produced in open court by Jesse Webb and Ira Webb appointed therein as executors and offered the same for probate whereupon Jonas Webb, John Ellis, and Absolom Clark came into open Court and made oath they saw him sign and seal and publish the same as his last will and testament and that he was in sound mind and disposing memory at the time of doing the same and that they attested the same at his request and in his presence whereupon the court ordered letters of testimony to issue and that the same be certified for registration. Given under my hand at office in McMinnville this 6th day of April AD 1835.

Jesse Webb died within a few months of drawing up his will; he apparently had enjoyed some material wealth as evidenced by the details of his will. One hundred dollars was a great deal of money in 1835. It seems that he provided well for his ten living children.

Major Townsend Webb, son of Jesse Webb, was probably our first Webb ancestor to settle in the wilderness what would become the Arkansas Territory; he was listed in the 1814 Tax List of what would soon become the Arkansas Territory. He was one of the first white men to venture to that untamed region. In 1814, there were only one hundred thirty inhabitants on the tax list for the region, and Townsend Webb was on that list. He died in Phillips, Arkansas on April 2, 1826 at about thirty-six years old. Major Townsend Webb was elected to a four-year term as Justice of the Peace of Arkansas County on August 3, 1819 (Arkansas Circuit Court Clerk's Office Index, Bk C, p. 412).

The Arkansas Territory was formed in 1819, and by 1836, Arkansas had a population of sixty thousand and was eligible for statehood. Arkansas became the twenty-fifth state on June 15,

1836 (*Encyclopedia of Arkansas History & Culture*, 2009). Two million acres between the Arkansas and St. Francis Rivers were offered as bounty land for veterans of the War of 1812; each veteran was given a warrant for one hundred sixty acres, allocated through a land lottery system. Much of this land had been taken from Native American tribes such as the Quapaw, Caddo, and Osage (Dollarhide, 2004). Major Townsend Webb acquired land in the Arkansas Territory as bounty for his service in the War of 1812.

Townsend Webb and Nancy Kendrick

Townsend Webb was married to Nancy Kendrick who was said to be a full-blooded Cherokee Native American. Native American women who married white men usually took an English name, as was the case with Nancy. Townsend Webb and Nancy Kendrick were married on October 25, 1804 in Lincoln County, Kentucky (Davis, 2004). Their children were as follows: Nancy L. Webb, Austin Webb, Mary D. Webb, Riley Caldonia Webb, Sarah S. Webb, James Webb, William Webb, and John Webb.

Austin Webb, son of Townsend Webb, mentioned in his grandfather's will, was born in Phillips, Arkansas. Apparently he returned to Tennessee after the deaths of his parents. The obituary of Major Townsend Webb appeared in the *Arkansas Gazette* on April 11, 1826:

> DIED - In Phillips County, on Sunday night, the 2d inst. Maj. Townsend Webb.
>
> Few have departed this life so much respected and so dearly beloved by their acquaintances and associates. A kind husband, an affectionate father, and a generous friend, there are few who do not deeply regret his loss. Benevolent and useful to his neighbors, his death has spread a gloom in the circle where he resided. He has left, to deplore his loss a numerous family. Can any thing add one ray of consolation to the deeply wounded bosoms of his friends and relations; it must be universal sympathy with

which they meet. Can any thing cheer them for a moment; it must be the recollection of the rectitude of his course in life, and the good name which has left him.

Julius Webb and Hannah Watkins

Julius Webb, son of Reverend John Webb, was born in 1791 in Rutherford County, North Carolina and died June 15, 1834. It seems that Julius Webb created some scandal in his life. He married Hannah Watkins around 1812 in Tennessee. Hannah, born July 15, 1796 in Rutherford County, North Carolina and died August 10, 1867 in Sink Creek, DeKalb County, Tennessee, was the daughter of Daniel Watkins and Elizabeth Byars (Webb, 2002).

Julius and Hannah Webb had several children; among them was an illegitimate daughter fathered by Julius. The child's mother was seventeen-year-old Nancy Roberts, a crippled girl and youngest daughter of Revolutionary War veteran, Reuben Roberts and his wife, Millie Asher Roberts. The child was conceived during the marriage of Julius and Hannah Webb (Webb, 2002).

Family lore states that Hannah allowed Julius to bring his illegitimate child, Nancy, into their household where Hannah raised her as her own. It is not known what became of Nancy's mother, Nancy Roberts. In the Revolutionary War Pension application of Reuben Roberts, he stated that his daughter, Nancy Roberts, suffered from a prolonged leg injury that prevented her from working (*Southern Campaign Revolutionary War Pension Statements*, 2009). Perhaps her mother was unable to care for her child and asked Julius Webb to take her into his home. Maybe she had an opportunity to marry but did not want the emotional baggage of an illegitimate child.

Family lore does not state how old Nancy was when she became part of the household of Julius and Hannah Webb. We do not know if Hannah knew of Nancy's paternity immediately or if it took several years to come to light. The 1820 federal census does not indicate that Nancy was a member of the household at that time. However, the 1830 census enumerates Nancy as one of the children. Nancy received an equal share of Julius's estate when he died.

Apparently, Hannah Webb was good to her husband's illegitimate child conceived during their marriage. Chloe Cope Ford, a great-granddaughter of Julius Webb, stated in a 1961 interview what a good Christian woman Hannah was to take Nancy into her home. Sadly, their church disapproved of the living arrangement and excommunicated Julius and Hannah Webb (Webb, 2002). It seems that Hannah Webb could offer forgiveness, but the church could not. Nancy Webb married John Cantrell and had nine children, one of whom was named for her father, Julius. Nancy Webb Cantrell and her husband, John Cantrell, are buried in Old Bildad Two Seed Baptist Cemetery, DeKalb County, Tennessee (Webb, 2002).

John Byars Webb and Mary Webb Webb

My family is directly descended from John Byars Webb, second son of Reverend John Webb and Sarah Byars Webb. He married his first cousin, Mary Webb, daughter of Merry Webb, brother of Reverend John Webb, making for some twisted roots in the family tree.

Thomas Gray Webb, a DeKalb County historian, wrote *The Webb Families of DeKalb County, Tennessee and 23 Related Families* (2002). In this book, he states that his ancestors came from England to Virginia to North Carolina to Tennessee. He says that it has been impossible to determine the father of John Byars Webb and that some have thought he might be a son of Reverend John Webb, the pastor of the Old Bildad Primitive Baptist Church located in Warren County on Sink Creek (now DeKalb County).

The membership list of the church from 1812 to 1816 (*Old Bildad Church*), shows several Webbs and their wives: John B. and Mary; Julias and Hannah; Jeremiah and Sarah; James and Nancy; Joshua and Rebecca; Jesse and Didama; Jonus and Carolina; and

Julias and Polly. According to Thomas Gray Webb, the only relationship that is certain is that Julias Webb is the son of John B. Webb.

The 1812 tax list of Warren County, Tennessee lists the following Webbs: Elisha, John B., Jesse, Chesley, Joshua, John, Julias, Jesse, Sr., John Webb, Sr. *(Warren County, Tennessee, 2011)*. It is assumed they were all related, but that is not a certainty. John Byars Webb was born about 1762 in North Carolina. He married Mary Webb around 1782 and is believed to have died between 1835 and 1840.

The Southern Backcountry

Most of the Webb's migrated from Pennsylvania and Virginia to the Carolinas, then to Tennessee and Kentucky before moving on to Mississippi, Arkansas, and Texas. Our family followed the southern frontier. Our background is mostly English and Scots-Irish; it was, and probably still is, the dominant cultural influence in our family. We have some Native American, Irish, and German ancestors, but the English and Scots-Irish dominate.

It is appropriate to discuss the culture of the Carolina, Tennessee, and Arkansas backcountry, and the Scots-Irish influence that is embedded in the culture and heritage of our family. I learned much on this subject from David Fischer's book, *Albion's Seed* (1989).

The naming tradition of the Scots-Irish backcountry can be of great benefit to family historians. The rule of thumb was that the firstborn son was named for the paternal grandfather, the second son for the maternal grandfather, and the third son for his father. If older cousins already bore these names, the sons were named for uncles in order of age. This was not an ironclad rule but was widely used (Anderson, 2009).

The names William, John, and James are repeated through the Webb generations. *John* was the most popular Scots-Irish name for boys (Fischer, 1989). It could be argued that these names were simply popular during this time and that the naming pattern is a coincidence.

The Carolina, Tennessee, and Arkansas backcountry culture was barely civilized. Recall from an earlier chapter the attitude of young CSA Lieutenant George J. Vinning about the people of Drew County during the years of the Civil War. Fischer (1989) points out that the people of the back country were not as obsessed about sexual sin as the Puritans were. Perhaps this played a role in Hannah Webb's acceptance of her husband's illegitimate child by a seventeen-year-old crippled girl.

The Anglican Church was the official religion of the Carolina colonies; church officials became alarmed at the mounting numbers of Presbyterians in the backcountry. Anglican ministers were sent to convert the unruly Presbyterians to the "correct religion." Charles Woodmason was an Anglican missionary sent to the backcountry in 1760. He did not disguise his disdain for the people of the region and their Presbyterian religion, referring to them as "ignorant, mean, worthless, beggarly Irish Presbyterians, the Scum of the Earth, and Refuse of Mankind" (Hooker, 1953). His diary drips with contempt for the Scots-Irish.

Fischer (1989) quotes extensively from Woodmason's diary and correctly points out that Woodmason tended to exaggerate in his portrayal of the backcountry people. Woodmason calculated that ninety-four percent of backcountry brides whom he had married in the past year were pregnant on their wedding day, some of them "very big" with child. Fischer points out that a scarcity of clergy to perform marriages factored into the high percentage of pregnant brides. Woodmason was stunned by the open sexuality of the Scots-Irish backcountry settlers. He wrote the following in his diary:

> "The young women have a most uncommon practice, which I cannot break them of. They draw their shift as tight as possible round their breasts, and slender waists (for they are generally very finely shaped) and draw their petticoat close to their

> *hips to show the fineness of their limbs...indeed nakedness in not censurable or indecent here, and they expose themselves often quite naked, without ceremony—rubbing themselves and their hair with bears' oil and tying it up behind in a bunch like the Indians—being hardly one degree removed from them. In a few years I hope to bring about a reformation."*

Woodmason was unsuccessful in his reformation efforts. The backcountry settlers sensed his contempt for them, and gave him a hard time. Fischer (1989) describes a couple of these incidents:

> *"When Woodmason tried to conduct an Anglican sermon in the back settlements, Presbyterians disrupted his services, rioted while he preached, started a pack of dogs fighting outside the church, loosed his horse, stole his church key, refused him food and shelter, and gave two barrels of whiskey to his congregation before a service of communion. One Baptist tried to discredit the Anglican missionary by stealing a clerical dressing gown, climbing into bed with a woman in the dark, and 'making her give out next day the Parson came to bed with her.'"*

Commenting on the incident outlined above, Woodmason claims to have counted fifty-seven dogs that had been brought to disrupt his services (Hooker, 1953). He wrote in his diary in disgust, "They delight in their present low, lazy, sluttish, heathenish, hellish life, and seem not desirous of changing it." Fischer relates an incident in which Woodmason encountered a family of Scottish Presbyterians. The family flatly told Woodmason they wanted "no damned black gown sons of bitches among them" and threatened to use him as the back log in their fireplace.

Woodmason felt that it would be futile to bring charges against them because "as all the Magistrates are Presbyterians, [and] I could not get a Warrant–if I got Warrants as the Constables are Presbyterians likewise, I could not get them serv'd–If serv'd, the

Guard would let them escape" (Hooker, 1953). Many of the back-country people resented the Church of England and joined more evangelical Protestant sects. Methodist and Baptist missionaries fared well with the backcountry people and gained many converts.

The backcountry people were lukewarm on the political issue of independence from the rule of Great Britain. Because of their isolation, they were content to be neutral if they were left alone. From their frontier perspective, the conflict was between the British Crown and the coastal aristocrats who had rich farm land. They despised the colonial aristocrats as much as they did the British officials (Thomas, 1999).

In 1778, an unknown Hessian officer entered the following statement into his records, "Call this war by whatever name you may, only call it not an American rebellion: it is nothing more or less than a Scotch-Irish Presbyterian Rebellion" (Thomas, 1999). General George Washington highly valued the Scots-Irish rebels; he declared, "If defeated everywhere else, I will make my last stand for liberty among the Scotch-Irish..." (Thomas, 1999).

Fischer makes an amusing observation about the backcoun-try settlers and their earthy language. He points out that, "before the Victorians erased them from the maps of this region...in Lunenberg County, Virginia, two small streams were named Tickle Cunt Branch and Fucking Creek."

Fischer discusses the values of fearlessness, pride, and inde-pendence displayed by the Scots-Irish settlers of the southern backcountry. He quotes a description of one Scots-Irishman, "... his looks spoke out that he would not fear the devil, should he meet him face to face..." Fischer goes on to point out that these people "demanded to be treated with respect even when dressed in rags. Their humble origins did not create the spirit of subordination which others expected of lower ranks." Fischer lists two branches of our family, the Alexanders and the Hawkinses, as being two of the leading southern backcountry clans. Andrew Jackson, seventh president of the United States, was one the most successful and famous members of the southern backcountry culture. He displayed many of the character traits and values of these Scots-Irish people.

Fischer further discusses the attitudes of the southern backcountry people. It seems that stubbornness is a hallmark of the culture. The Scots-Irish prayer embodies this spirit, "Lord grant that I may always be right, for Thou knowest I am hard to turn." One Scots-Irish woman of the southern backcountry declared, "We never let go of a belief once fixed in our minds."

I became amused at myself after my study of Fischer's book. In the psychobabble terms of our modern society, I admit that I "own" the sentiment of the Scots-Irish prayer. I refuse to let go of a belief to the point that it becomes a character flaw. I use many elements of Scots-Irish speech and pronunciation, use "fixin' to" liberally, speak in the southern dialect, and apologize to no one for it. I carry pride to a fault, as well. I am independent and function best in a situation when I can work independently, going against the conventional wisdom that embraces the "teaming" concept in the workplace. I am suspicious of "foreigners" and harbor a great deal of skepticism toward clergy of all denominations.

When I read the passage in which Charles Woodmason rants about the women's seductive dress, I could hear my late father's comments. One of his pet peeves was preachers who carried on about women's dress. He laughed and commented that those preachers had their minds on "what was under those dresses." I think my father was right. There is no doubt in my mind that these Scots-Irish attitudes have been passed through the generations to the present.

The Arkansas Frontier

Arkansas was part of the historic Louisiana Purchase of 1803 in which President Thomas Jefferson doubled the physical size of the United States. It had fewer than five hundred white inhabitants, and Townsend Webb was one of them. Most of them were of French descent, living along the Mississippi River and the lower portions of the White and Arkansas Rivers. Hunting, fishing, and trapping attracted these rugged settlers.

On March 23, 1804, Lieutenant Andrew Many arrived at Arkansas Post in Arkansas County, established by French traders in 1686, to take control of the fort and the settlement in the name of the United States government. Arkansas Post was the first permanent European colony in the Mississippi Valley. Shortly thereafter, Congress established the official boundaries of the newly acquired territory (*Louisiana Purchase*, 2009).

A few American citizens had begun to trickle into Arkansas in the 1790s, but it was not until after the War of 1812 that settlement began in earnest; war veterans were able to draw from a lottery of seized tribal lands of Native Americans (*Louisiana Purchase*, 2009). After the War of 1812, Congress enacted legislation to reward military service by entitling veterans to claim land in the northwest and western territories. This so-called "bounty land" was not granted outright to the veterans but was awarded to them through a multistep process beginning with a bounty land warrant. McFarland (2010) describes this process:

> "Bounty land warrants weren't automatically issued to every veteran who served. The veteran first had to apply for a warrant, and then, if the warrant was granted, he could use the warrant to apply for a land patent. The land patent is the document which granted him ownership of the land. Basically, the warrant is a piece of paper which states that, based on his service, the veteran is entitled to X number of acres in one of the bounty land districts set up for veterans of the War of 1812. These land districts were located on public domain lands in Arkansas, Illinois and Missouri. The warrants, themselves, were not delivered to the veterans; all the veteran actually received was a notification telling him that Warrant #XXX had been issued in his name and was on file in the General Land Office. Prior to 1842, if a veteran chose to redeem his warrant for land, he was required to

choose land in one of the three states listed above. (After 1842, he could redeem his warrant for public lands in other states.) Warrants could be assigned or sold to other individuals."

Sarasen, Chief of the Quapaw's, was friendly and helpful to the white people who stripped the Native Americans of their lands and livelihoods. He is buried in St. Joseph's Catholic Cemetery in Pine Bluff, having died in 1832 at ninety-seven years old (*History of Pine Bluff*, n. d.). The federal census of 1810 showed the total white population of Arkansas, along with a few slaves, numbered 1,062 inhabitants. The census of 1820 found 14,273 inhabitants, but it did not include the Native American Cherokee tribe; in 1830 there were 30,388 inhabitants; this jumped to 97,974 in the 1840 census. The 1850 census enumerated 209,987, and in 1860, the census enumerated 435,450 inhabitants, an average of eight people per square mile. Today, Arkansas has nearly three million inhabitants.

Among the early immigrants to Arkansas were large numbers of people from Tennessee and Kentucky. The Webbs and the Hawkinses came to Arkansas via Tennessee and Mississippi. However, as cotton, sometimes referred to as "white gold," evolved as the most lucrative cash crop, many new settlers came from the Deep South as did the Griffin and Camp branches of our family. By 1860, around sixty percent of the inhabitants of Arkansas lived in the cotton growing region in the southern and eastern parts of Arkansas (*Louisiana Purchase*, 2009). The most numerous European-born people who migrated to Arkansas were the Germans (*Louisiana Purchase*, 2009), as our Gabbert ancestors were.

Land Acquisition in Arkansas

There were several ways for early settlers to acquire land in Arkansas. At first, titles grew out of Spanish grants in the eastern part of the state. These Spanish grants gave approximately one hundred square miles of land to private owners (*Louisiana Purchase*, 2009).

Land sales offices were in Little Rock and Batesville in 1822 and later in Fayetteville, Helena and Washington in Hempstead County. Congress provided land to settlers who had lost their land in the New Madrid earthquakes of 1811–1812. These settlers were allowed to select land in other regions of the state and take title to their new land free of charge. The federal government also gave Cherokee lands to settlers who had fought in the War of 1812 (*Louisiana Purchase*, 2009).

Congress passed the *Swamp Lands Act of 1850*, which provided several million acres of Arkansas land, at very low prices, to settlers who would agree to carry out drainage programs and construct levees. Many settlers in Arkansas "squatted" on federal land, thus avoiding purchasing the land and paying taxes on it; by 1840 the majority of settlers in Arkansas were "squatters." Hunting and subsistence farming provided the economic basis for the earliest white settlers in what would become the Arkansas Territory. By 1819, settlers were being drawn to the Territory by the potential for farming on a larger scale (*Louisiana Purchase*, 2009).

By 1840, a plantation economy had emerged in southern and eastern Arkansas bottom lands of the Arkansas, Mississippi, Ouachita, and Red Rivers. Cotton became the most important cash crop. Smaller farms in other regions of the state produced wheat, oats, corn, tobacco, and livestock (*Louisiana Purchase*, 2009). Slavery was practiced throughout Arkansas, but was more concentrated in the southern and eastern parts of Arkansas where cotton was grown. Bolton (2009) explains:

> "From 1840 to 1860, the per capita production of cotton rose from fourteen bales to eighty-four bales, a sixfold increase compared to the fourfold growth in population. Even in 1860, planters were only three percent of all taxpayers, and the owners of fewer than twenty slaves, most of whom had only one or two, were only seventeen percent. Nonetheless, southern and eastern Arkansas became the frontier of the cotton kingdom of the South."

It was against this historical backdrop that the Webb family migrated to Arkansas. William Morris Webb, Sr. first immigrated to Mississippi from Tennessee and then to Arkansas.

A Leap of Faith: William Morris Webb, Sr.

I must take a leap of faith, and the DNA zealots will probably flog me for it, but there is a problem. Webb family historians do not know with certainty the paternity of William Morris Webb, Sr. My cousin, Allen Webb, of Baton Rouge, Louisiana, has helped me tremendously with this chapter. He and I share some common beliefs about the paternity of William Morris Webb, Sr., but we can offer no definitive proof. We believe that William Morris Webb, Sr. was a son of John Byars Webb and Mary Webb, and we base this on three tenets. When William Morris Webb, Sr. was captured by the Yankees during the Civil War, he declared to them that he was from Davidson County, Tennessee (Nashville). John Byars Webb and his wife, Mary Webb, owned property that became incorporated from Warren County, Tennessee to Davidson County, Tennessee. The children of John Byars Webb and his wife, Mary, have never been officially documented. It is common knowledge that many of our Webb family historians have identified Davidson County, Tennessee, as a region settled by many of the descendants of John Byars Webb and his wife, Mary Webb, as indicated by the 1860 federal census of Davidson County, Tennessee. The federal census of Collin County, Texas, indicates that a massive enlistment effort by former Confederate General James Webb Throckmorton was successful with nearly three hundred Webb families from Georgia, Alabama, Tennessee, Missouri, and Mississippi settling there. All these families have been identified as descended from Merry Webb, III of Essex County, Virginia. This is my leap of faith, so I am going to proceed under this assumption, and that brings us to the elusive William Morris Webb.

Chapter 15
The Webb Family: Tennessee Roots

NOTE: When I started this chapter, I could not trace my Webb lineage back further than my grandfather, John Wesley Bell Webb. I did not know his father's name. I vaguely recalled my father stating that his grandfather's name was William. I had hit a brick wall in my efforts to find William (Bill) Webb, Jr. On October 10, 2008, I received a call from a distant cousin, Allen Webb, of Baton Rouge, Louisiana. Though Allen and I have never met, we talked for about an hour. I had posted a query on a genealogy message board; Allen responded, and he was a treasure trove of information about the Webb family. I want to thank Allen for his help with this difficult chapter. He and I talk frequently, and he continues to be a great resource. One of the greatest difficulties encountered in researching this chapter is the confusion generated by repetition of the names *William, James,* and *John* throughout generations of Webbs.

William Morris Webb, Sr. and Mary Ann Ward Carmichael

The aforementioned Allen Webb told me that William Morris Webb, Sr. was enumerated in the 1850 federal census report for Marion County, Tennessee. Marion County is located in southeastern Tennessee and shares borders with Dade County, Georgia and Jackson County, Alabama. The County seat of Marion County is Jasper, located about twenty-five miles west of Chattanooga, Tennessee. Marion County was named for the Revolutionary War hero, Brigadier General Francis Marion, known in history books as the "Swamp Fox." Prior to the Revolutionary War, Francis Marion had led successful attacks on the Cherokee (*Marion County History*, 2000).

Tennessee was admitted to the Union on July 1, 1796 as the sixteenth state. Marion County was formed in 1817 from lands seized from Native Americans; it had once been considered "Indian territory." In my conversation with Allen Webb, he commented that the Webb family has some Cherokee lineage. Recall that Townsend Webb's wife, Nancy Kendrick, was believed to be Cherokee.

William Morris Webb, Sr. was known to his family as "Will." He was married to Mary Ann Ward Carmichael from Walton County, Georgia. Mary Ann brought with her to the marriage a son from a former marriage, George W. Carmichael. According to Allen Webb, Mary Ann had been married to a Thomas Carmichael about thirty years her senior who died, leaving her a young widow. Marriage records in Walton County, Georgia document the marriage of Mary Ann Ward and Thomas Carmichael, December 27, 1833 (*Walton County Marriages*, 1833). If Mary Ann Ward was born in 1820, as the 1850 census indicates, she married Thomas Carmichael when she was thirteen years old, a practice not uncommon at the time. Thomas Carmichael would have been about forty-three years old when he married Mary Ann. If her son, George Carmichael, was born in 1843, she was married to Thomas Carmichael for at least ten years.

The 1850 federal census report for Marion County, Tennessee, seventh district, enumerates William Webb as a twenty-seven-year-old farmer, born in Tennessee, making his year of birth around 1823. I am uncertain about the accuracy of this information. The Prisoner of War Record for William Morris Webb described him as twenty-six years old in 1864, making the year of his birth 1838.

William Morris Webb was illiterate, a fact recorded in the census. Mary Ann Webb was enumerated as a thirty-year-old female born in Tennessee. Apparently, she could read and write. According to Allen Webb, Mary Ann conducted many of the family's business affairs. Allen bases this on the oral history tradition of his family. George W. is listed as a seven-year-old male born in Tennessee, and apparently he did not attend school, another fact recorded in the Tennessee federal census. I suspect that George W. Carmichael, stepson of Will Webb, was expected to work on the farm.

Allen Webb communicated to me that George was a stepson of William Morris Webb, Sr., and that he was a Carmichael, though the Marion County, Tennessee census did not record his surname, only that *William, Mary A,* and *George W.* comprised one household. William Morris Webb, Sr. and Mary Ann Carmichael were enumerated as Methodists, a preference of many backcountry settlers.

The William M. Webb family shows up next in the 1860 federal census report for Kemper County, Mississippi. The family consisted of William Webb, his wife Mary Ann, and sons William Webb, Jr. (listed as *Will* on the census) six years old, John Webb, four years old, James Webb, two years old, and George Carmichael, sixteen years old, and attending school. The Kemper County census confirms that George W. was a Carmichael. According to this census report, both George Carmichael and Will Webb, Jr. attended school.

The 1860 federal census report for Davidson County, Tennessee, contains an interesting item. Jenny Webb, twenty years old, was enumerated in the Fourth Ward, City of Nashville, as a prostitute. Virginia Webb, thirty-eight years old, was enumerated in the Tenth district of Nashville as a prostitute. Prostitution was legal in Nashville, and there are many "ladies of the evening" in the census. Allen Webb believes that Virginia Webb may have been the mother of Jenny Webb and that Virginia Webb is either a sister or a first cousin of William Morris Webb, Sr., and if that is the case, Virginia Webb's grandfather was Reverend John Webb.

The Civil War

When the Civil War began, Will Webb, thirty-eight years old, and his stepson George W. Carmichael, enlisted in Company A, Thirty-fifth Mississippi Infantry, known as Barry's Guards, having been recruited by Colonel W. S. Barry. Confederate military records show that Will Webb joined the Confederate Army, February 26, 1862, and that his term of enlistment was for three years. Allen Webb believes Will Webb joined this regiment because of a close friend, Enoch Spinks, who was an officer in the Thirty-fifth. During his service in the Thirty-fifth, Will Webb fought in the Battle of Vicksburg, Mississippi. Union General Ulysses S. Grant had laid siege to this strategic Confederate city perched on a bluff above the Mississippi River from May 25–July 4, 1863. The Confederate Order of Battle showed the Thirty-fifth Mississippi under the command of Lieutenant Colonel C. R. Jordan, as part of General John C. Moore's Brigade (*Order of Battle*, 2010).

The Confederate Army and the civilian population of Vicksburg suffered greatly during this time. Food was in short supply; flour sold for one thousand dollars per barrel if it could be found. The meat from dead horses and mules was consumed along with rats and mice. Shoe leather was even consumed by the starving rebels. The Confederate Army ran out of drinking water and hauled barrels of muddy water from the Mississippi River, teeming with all kinds of disease-causing organisms. On July 3, 1863, the Confederates raised the white flag to discuss the terms of surrender (*Battle of Vicksburg*, 2008).

On July 4, 1863, it was over. Vicksburg was lost. Confederate losses totaled

31,227. Will Webb survived and was captured, but his incarceration was short lived. The paroling of the men was done quickly and in duplicate. Union clerks filled in names and commands of Confederate soldiers and officers; one was kept by the prisoner and the other by the United States government (*Battle of Vicksburg*, 2008); (Foote, 1974); (Smith, 2002).

Grant did not want the expense of feeding thirty thousand Confederates in Union prisoner-of-war camps. He expected these starving, destitute rebels would not fight again; he had hoped their stigma of defeat would demoralize the rest of the Confederacy. General Grant was a magnanimous victor. He issued full rations to all the Confederates both sick and well, a total of about thirty-one thousand starving people. Grant had the Confederate prisoners of war sign an oath to lay down their arms (*Battle of Vicksburg*, 2008); (Foote, 1974); (Smith, 2002). Will Webb's oath reads as follows:

> "*Vicksburg, Mississippi. July 8, 1863. To All Whom it May Concern, Know Ye That: I, William M. Webb, a Private(?) of Co. (?) 35th Regiment, Mississippi(?) Vols. C. S. A. being a Prisoner of War, in the hands of the United States Forces, in virtue of the capitulation of the City of Vicksburg and its garrison, by Lieut. Gen. John C. Pemberton, C. S. A., Commanding, on the 4th day of July, 1863, do in pursuance of the terms of said capitulation, give this my solemn parole under oath—That I will not take up arms again against the United States, nor serve in any military police, or constabulary force in any Fort, Garrison or field work,, held by Confederate States of America, against the United States of America, nor as guard of prisons, depots or stores, nor discharge any duties usually performed by Officers or soldiers, against the United States of America, until duly exchanged by the proper authorities.*"

This document was signed "William M. Webb" by a military official. It also has the notation "his mark" with an "X" placed beside it, indicating that William M. Webb was illiterate. After the signature, it reads "Sworn to and subscribed before me at Vicksburg, Miss, this 8th day of July 1863." The signature of the paroling officer is illegible (*Military Records of William Morris Webb, 1862–1864*).

Will Webb did not go home as he had agreed to do upon his release at Vicksburg. He got back in the fray as soon as possible and was again captured at the Battle of Allatoona Pass in North Georgia on October 5, 1864, after the defeat of the city of Atlanta, Georgia, July 22, 1864, by Union General William T. Sherman (Golden, 2006).

The Confederates lost about eight hundred men at Allatoona Pass, and the Union about seven hundred. John Bell Hood assumed command of the Confederate Army during the fall of Atlanta, and ached to avenge the staggering loss for the Confederacy. Hood and his troops decided to attack General Sherman's supply line, the Western and Atlantic Railroad. They tore up track, and planned to attack the railway pass at Allatoona. The stores at Allatoona were well stocked with rations that the rebels desperately needed. Sherman had left the pass minimally guarded because he knew it would be easy to hold (Golden, 2006). The battle was bloody, but the Union prevailed, and William M. Webb was once again taken as a prisoner-of-war on October 5, 1864.

Will Webb was received as a POW at a military prison in Louisville, Kentucky, October 21, 1864 and was sent to Camp Chase, Ohio, where he arrived, October 24, 1864. Prisoner-of-war records described Will Webb as having a dark complexion, dark hair, and gray eyes, and was five feet seven and one-half inches tall.

At Camp Chase, Will Webb was again forced to sign an *Oath of Amnesty and Allegiance* to the United States government on June 11, 1865. Signing the oath was a prerequisite to his release on June 11,

1865. Will Webb was discharged after serving nearly eight months at Camp Chase.

One can only imagine the horrors Will Webb endured as a POW. The Union often maltreated captured Confederates in retaliation for the infamous Andersonville POW camp operated by the Confederates. The horrors of Andersonville are well documented. I highly recommend the books by Knauss (1906) and Speer (1997) that relate conditions in Union and Confederate POW camps.

It has always disturbed me that my great-grandfather, William Morris Webb, Jr., son of William Morris Webb, Sr. who was captured and imprisoned at Camp Chase, was by all accounts a wicked, cruel, person. Learning of his father's POW experience at Camp Chase gave me insight into the possible cause of his brutal behavior. I suspect William Morris Webb, Jr. was treated cruelly by his father, who likely suffered from what today is called post-traumatic stress disorder. His war experiences must have had a profound impact on him.

Will Webb went back to Kemper, County Mississippi, and showed up next in the Collin County, Texas, federal census. Allen Webb believes that the migration to Texas was because of Confederate General James Webb Throckmorton, a future governor of Texas and a member of Congress. Allen Webb believes that Throckmorton may have been a cousin to William Morris Webb, Sr.

Perhaps William Morris Webb, Sr. was trying to escape the punishment of Radical Reconstruction in Mississippi after the war. Allen Webb believes William Morris Webb, Sr. died in Collin County, Texas by 1890. Allen also shared with me that Will Webb and his brother Jim, at one time, had a goldmine in Oklahoma. Family members kept a gold nugget as a kind of souvenir.

James Webb Throckmorton

James Webb Throckmorton was a native of Sparta, Tennessee (White County), where his father was a physician. Dr.

Throckmorton moved his practice to Fayetteville, Arkansas in 1836 where his wife died. In 1840, he moved on to Texas, purchasing land in Collin County (McKinney). About a year later, Dr. Throckmorton died, and young James Webb Throckmorton became the man of the family. He later went to Kentucky to study medicine with his uncle (Minor, 2011); *(Portraits of Texas Governors,* 2011).

At the outbreak of the Mexican War, Throckmorton returned to Texas and volunteered for military service. He served fewer than three months in the field because of a kidney disease that plagued him throughout his life. He was reassigned as a surgeon's assistant in the Texas Rangers. He received a medical discharge in 1847 and left Texas in 1848 to marry Annie Rattan of Illinois. The couple returned to McKinney, Texas, where Throckmorton practiced medicine. He did not enjoy the practice of medicine but turned his interests to education and law, and became prominent in the community. He was elected to the Texas House of Representatives where he served from 1851–1857. Throckmorton helped negotiate a settlement of disputed land titles of early Texas settlers involving the Peters Colony (Minor, 2011); *(Portraits of Texas Governors,* 2011).

Peters Colony

The Peters Colony was probably what brought William Morris Webb, Sr. and William Morris Webb, Jr. to Collin County, Texas. The colony was a botched land investment scheme by twenty American and English investors. Peters Colony was the name given to this north Texas empresario grant made in 1841. William Smalling Peters was responsible for promoting the colony. The company purchased eight hundred sections of land in east Texas for the venture (Connor, 2006); (Wade, 2008). Wade (2008) discusses the terms of this venture:

"According to the terms of the contract the empresarios had to recruit settlers from outside the republic at the rate of 200 families in three years. In return the colonists were granted 320 acres per single man and a maximum of 640 acres per family. The empresarios were allowed to retain up to one-half of a colonist's grant as payment for services rendered, including land surveys and title applications. The empresarios provided powder, shot, and seed and in some cases built settlers' cabins. The empresarios also received 10 sections of premium land from the republic for each 100 families."

Later, the contract was extended and increased the number of the required colonists to eight hundred. They recruited heavily in Mississippi, Tennessee, and Arkansas. According to Allen Webb, nearly three hundred Webb families from Georgia, Alabama, Arkansas, Tennessee, Missouri, and Mississippi came to Texas as a result of the recruitment of James Webb Throckmorton. More than twenty counties in Texas made up the Peters Colony settlement. Three of those counties, Cooke, Denton, and Tarrant were within the colony; most of Dallas and Grayson Counties were part of the settlement (Connor, 2006); (Wade, 2008).

In the fall of 1842, a wagon train of settlers came to Peters Colony from Kentucky. By September 1842, fifty-four families made up the colony. According to the 1850 census, sixty-six percent of Collin County inhabitants were part of Peters Colony. The census indicated that a little over twenty-seven percent of the settlers came from Arkansas, and close to thirteen percent came from Tennessee; a little over eighty-seven percent of the settlers were farmers by occupation (Connor, 2006); (Wade, 2008).

Titles to the settlers' land were botched, and the settlers felt that it was unfair for the empresarios to claim up to one-half of their land. A controversy brewed, and it culminated on July 16, 1852 when an armed contingent of settlers attacked the empresarios' office and drove the agent of the company, Henry Hedgcoxe, out of the county. The encounter became known as the Hedgcoxe War. James Webb Throckmorton was a leader in this protest movement through his efforts for the colonists in the Texas legislature. It gained him much grassroots support. James Webb Throckmorton was instrumental in settling the land titles; it took nearly twenty years to straighten out the legal mess made by the company (Connor, 2006); (Elliott, 1938); (Wade, 2008).

As the Civil War brewed, Throckmorton was a delegate to the 1861 Secession Convention; he was one of eight delegates who voted against Texas withdrawing from the Union. He feared that Texas could not withstand a war, but he was one of the first men in Collin County to volunteer in the Confederate army (Elliott, 1938); (Howell, 2008).

Throckmorton helped organize the Company of Mounted Riflemen from Collin County in May 1861. He saw combat in Mississippi and Louisiana but was given a medical discharge for his recurring kidney problems on September 12, 1863. In December 1864, he was commissioned as a Brigadier General of the state's first Frontier District. He negotiated a number of treaties with Native American tribes on the frontier; they called him "Old Leathercoat" (Elliott, 1938); (Howell, 2008).

Throckmorton later successfully ran for Governor of Texas and was inaugurated on August 9, 1866. The *Military Reconstruction Act of 1867* placed post-war Texas under military command. Throckmorton openly opposed harsh measures of Radical Reconstruction advocated by Union General Charles Griffin and refused to implement many of the measures. Griffin appealed to Major General Phillip H. Sheridan to remove Throckmorton from office. Sheridan ordered the removal of Throckmorton from the governor's office on July 30, 1867 and prohibited Throckmorton from holding political office (Elliott, 1938); (Howell, 2008).

Throckmorton returned to his law practice in McKinney and was vocal in his criticism of the policies of Radical Reconstruction. In 1870, he and two other former governors attacked the policies of Radical Republicans as dangerous threats to the civil liberties of Texans. In 1872, the *Amnesty Act* was passed, allowing Throckmorton to return to elected office. He was elected to Congress in 1874 and was reelected in 1876. He made an unsuccessful bid for the governor's office in 1878. He returned to Congress in 1882 and was reelected in 1884 and 1886. He declined to seek reelection in 1888 because of health problems. He died April 21, 1894 after receiving serious injuries from a fall, compounded by his kidney problems (Elliott, 1938); (Howell, 2008).

What Kind of Person Was William M. Webb, Sr.?

Some Webb family researchers suspect that Will Webb had Ku Klux Klan connections. One of his relatives in Miller County, Arkansas, had both Klan and Masonic rituals at his funeral. This particular relative had bragged about taking part in a raid on a black settlement in East Texas and participating in the killing of several blacks who lived there.

Drew County was the scene of some unwelcome KKK activities. The October 4, 1892 edition of the *Advance Monticellonian* editorialized against the vigilantes:

> "Monticello - The good people of Drew county, this State, have been terrorized for some time past by the depredations of white caps. These lawless desperadoes have been taking good men from their homes at night, tying them to the nearest tree and whipping them unmercifully, going so far as to kill three men. The Grand Jury of Drew County is now in session and up to Saturday had returned sixty indictments, a large number of them being against the white cappers, of whom there is a well organized band of forty-nine. One of them was for one A. L. Hammell, who lives fiften miles south of Monticello, who was arrested Saturday evening for murder, as one of the white caps who had took Dan Baker, colored, from the jail at Monticello

and killed him. Baker had been 'white-capped' in Ashley County, and killed one of his assailants, and was lodged in the jail at Monticello for safe keeping. A desperate effort will be made by the Drew County authorities to rid the county of this lawless gang. Seven of the gang have already left the county and many more will probably make their escape since the arrest of their pal."

The next day, Oct 5, 1892, the *Advance* reported the following:

"The Grand Jury returned sixty-five true bills. Two white-cappers, Bud Goodwin and George Hammill, were placed in jail without bond, charged with complicity in the mob who killed Calvin Reed, an account of which was published in the Gazette a few months since, and also in the mob who took the negro from Sheriff Morgan and shot him to death in July. This will effectually break up the lawlessness that has prevailed in the southern portion of the county for some time: their accomplices having become alarmed at this capture, have fled the county."

Donald Holley, a history professor at the University of Arkansas at Monticello, wrote an interesting account of Klan activity in Monticello entitled *"A Look behind the Masks: The 1920s Ku Klux Klan in Monticello, Arkansas."* It was published in the *Arkansas Historical Quarterly*.

William Morris Webb, Jr.

My family is descended from Will Webb's eldest son, William Morris Webb, Jr., known as "Bill." William Morris Webb, Jr. was born November 21, 1851 in Mississippi and died April 12, 1932 in Monticello, Arkansas. The 1880 federal census report for Collin County, Texas contains the following information about William M. Webb, Jr. and his family. William Webb, was enumerated as head of household, and was described as twenty-nine years old, and a farmer born in Tennessee. It stated his father's birthplace was Tennessee. Georgia Webb was enumerated as the wife of William Webb; she was described as twenty-six years old, and keeping house was her occupation. She was born in Alabama, and her father's birthplace was Georgia, and her mother's birthplace was South Carolina. Amanda Webb was enumerated as the daughter of William and Georgia Webb. She was described as nine years old, and born in Mississippi. Amanda Webb married a Barnes man according to my mother, Louise Hawkins Webb. James Webb was enumerated as the son of William and Georgia Webb, and was described as seven years old, and born in Mississippi. John Webb was enumerated as the son of William and Georgia Webb, and was four years old, and born in Mississippi. Eugene Webb was enumerated as the son of William and Georgia Webb, and was nine months old, and born in Texas.

My family is descended from John Wesley Bell Webb, known throughout his adult life as J. B. Webb, the third child of William and Georgia Harris Webb. J. B. Webb was the father of Lewis French Webb, my father. Why would someone name a child John Wesley Bell Webb? I Googled "John Wesley Bell" and all I found was an account of a nineteenth century slave owner named John Wesley Bell who was killed by two of his slaves. I doubt this incident was the basis for my grandfather's name. I suspect there is a Bell branch to the Webb family. It is possible that Confederate General John Bell Hood under whom William Morris Webb, Sr. had served in the Civil War may have been the source of this name. The Methodist theologian, John Wesley, was admired by many, and we know from the census report this family was Methodist.

We can trace William "Bill" Webb's migratory route by studying the census records. In 1870, William Webb was enumerated in the Gibson County, Tennessee (Jackson) federal census, and was described as nineteen years old, making the year of his birth 1851. William and Georgia Webb married about 1871 in Tennessee or Alabama when he was about twenty years old.

William and Georgia Webb relocated to Mississippi shortly after their marriage. My father always said the family came from Attala County, Mississippi, but I have been unable to pinpoint the years they were in Attala County; apparently, it was between census reports. Their first child, Amanda, was born in 1871 in Mississippi. Somewhere between the birth of John Webb in 1876 and his younger brother, Eugene, in 1879, William and Georgia Webb moved the family to Collin County, Texas, as evidenced by the federal census report. Sometime after 1880, the family relocated to Drew County, Arkansas.

William and Martha Camp Griffin had a daughter, Virginia, who married John Wesley Bell Webb, who had come to Drew County from Kosciusko, Mississippi (Attala County in central Mississippi) or Collin County, Texas, with his family.

Chapter 16
A Skeleton in the Closet: The Mysterious Disappearance of Georgia Webb

A manda, John B., Jim, and Eugene Webb, from all accounts, had an evil father, William M. Webb, Jr. I visited with my aunt, Maywood Webb Young, a few months prior to her death in 2001 and asked her about her grandfather, William M. Webb, Jr. Aunt May said she stayed away from him and was frightened of him when she was a child. She described him as a "mean old man." She knew little about him and did not even know his given name.

My father, Lewis French Webb, often told the story of the disappearance of his grandmother, Georgia Harris Webb. According to his account, she put her children to bed one night, and the next morning, their father told them she had run off with the doctor (or the preacher); the story varied. They never saw her again.

The family always believed the old man had murdered her and concealed her body in an abandoned well shaft. No one knew why. Perhaps it was in a jealous rage. To my knowledge, her disappearance was never investigated. I do not know if her disappearance occurred in Texas or Arkansas. I have found no record of her death, but I suspect she disappeared in Texas. Perhaps that is why William M. Webb, Jr. moved his family to Arkansas. My father told me his grandfather abused his children terribly. The general consensus of the family was that William Morris Webb, Jr. was destined to roast in hell. Amazingly, by all accounts, his sons John B., Jim, and Eugene Webb, were good men and kind fathers.

William M. Webb, Jr. is buried in Union Ridge Cemetery but, south of the Webb family plot. I had trouble locating his grave, because it is not with the other Webbs. I found his grave with that of his second wife, Harriet. William Morris Webb, Jr. and his second wife, Harriet, are buried next to a line of Jackson graves at Union Ridge Cemetery. Based on this, I believe Harriet was born a Jackson. William Morris Webb, Jr. died April 12, 1932 from a stroke, according to his death certificate. The headstone of Harriet M. Webb states that she is the wife of W. M. Webb, and died on December 25, 1915.

Allen Webb states that William M. Webb, Jr. may have had a second set of children by Harriet, but if so, neither Allen nor I have discovered their identities. William M. Webb, Jr. married again in 1906 to Emma Jackson who may have been a sister of Harriet Jackson. Drew County, Arkansas marriage records state William M. Webb married Emma Jackson on June 13, 1916. William M. Webb's third marriage was cut short by his death in 1932. Emma is not buried at Union Ridge Cemetery; her children probably buried her elsewhere.

The July 1894 edition of the *Advance Monticellonian* reported that W. M. Webb was appointed overseer of road district #4, Marion Township, Drew County, Arkansas. This was no doubt a very good job for that time, and probably a political "plum" of some sort.

Allen Webb believes that William M. Webb, Jr. was perhaps a member of the Masons, a fraternal order. If so, he was well networked with business and government leaders in Drew County. However, Allen also believes that William M. Webb, Jr. was a land surveyor, a skill that would have been useful for a road overseer.

John B. Webb and his older brother James William (Jim) Webb married first cousins, Virginia Griffin and Marietta Burks, respectively, giving this branch of the family an interesting and sometimes confusing twist. Jim Webb died at thirty-five years old, leaving Marietta Burks Webb a widow with seven children.

My father, Lewis French Webb, had double first cousins, Perry and Mattie Belle Webb. Double first cousins are the offspring of brothers who marry sisters. They were the children of Herman Eugene Webb, brother of John B. Webb, and Ina P. Griffin Webb, sister of Virginia Griffin Webb.

In our family plot at Union Ridge Cemetery, there are two headstones, H. E. Webb, born September 15, 1879, died August 7, 1915, and his wife Ina P. Webb, born May 19, 1882, died May 5, 1916. H. E. (Eugene) Webb died at approximately thirty-six years old, and his wife, Ina P. Webb, the sister of Virginia Griffin Webb, died at approximately thirty-four years old. This fits the story my father told about his double first cousins, Perry and Mattie Belle Webb, being orphaned at an early age.

Bob Lamb, a Webb family researcher, related an interesting story when he posted a reply April 7, 2001 to a question posed by another subscriber on a genealogy website message board. In his response, Lamb related the story of John Pinckney Webb (1866–1953?). I was intrigued to learn he had come from Attala County, Mississippi just as my great-grandfather's family, and during the same time frame. The following is the story of John Pinckney Webb as related by Bob Lamb (2001).

According to the 1870 federal census report for Yell County, Arkansas, John Pinckney Webb came from Attala County, Mississippi with his parents, John B. Webb (same name and middle initial as my grandfather) and Sarah F. Croft Webb, after his father, John B. Webb, lost everything during the Civil War. John Pinckney Webb lost both parents when he was a teenager, and lost his first wife in childbirth.

John Pinckney Webb, after a particularly nasty divorce in Perry County, Arkansas in 1919, disappeared forever from his family. After being arrested in 1925, during Prohibition, for making "moonshine" in the woods of Grant County, Arkansas, he broke out of jail by working some old bricks loose and climbing through the hole in the wall.

He hid out in the White River Refuge near Tichnor, Arkansas, where he lived on an old houseboat that was destroyed during the Great Flood of 1929. He, his mistress, and their illegitimate sons built a shanty of sorts on Big Island near the confluence of the White, Arkansas, and Mississippi Rivers. John Pinckney Webb adopted the alias "Kaiser Webb" but was found and arrested by federal authorities in the 1930s and jailed in Little Rock. Because he was an old man, the Federal authorities released him after a short while. He returned to Big Island and lived there until his death in the early 1950s. He is buried in an unmarked grave near Tichnor, located in Arkansas County, Arkansas, according to Bob Lamb's posting.

The account of John Pinckney Webb interests me for several reasons: (1) He came from Attala County, Mississippi during the same time frame as my great-grandfather and settled in southeast Arkansas just as my great-grandfather; my instinct tells me they must have been related, probably first cousins; (2) His behavior sounds similar to that of my great-grandfather, who allegedly murdered his wife. Neither of these men would have received a good citizenship award; (3) Lamb's posting states that John Pinckney Webb's roots go back to Anderson, South Carolina plantation owner, Charles Webb, who died there in 1831; (4) If my great-grandfather and "Moonshiner John" were related, that gives me a genealogical bridge to the past. However, I am still struggling to bridge the gap. My family is descended from John Wesley Bell Webb, son of William Webb, Jr. and Georgia Harris Webb who mysteriously disappeared when my grandfather was a child.

John Wesley Bell Webb and Virginia Griffin

John Wesley Bell Webb, known as J. B. Webb, was the third of four children born to William M. Webb, Jr. and Georgia Harris Webb. He married Virginia "Virgie" Griffin, daughter of William G. Griffin and Martha A. Camp Griffin. J. B. Webb did not beat his wife and children, but according to my mother, she witnessed him beating a horse unmercifully, an act she found almost unforgiveable. She told me this was the only act she really held against him. He was always good to my mother while she and my father lived in the same house with them. My grandmother was sometimes the recipient of a barrage of cursing from J. B. Webb.

According to my parents, Virginia Griffin Webb was aggravated that her husband, J. B. Webb, referred to her father, William Griffin, as "Billy." She believed that such familiarity showed a lack of respect for her father, indicating she may have had a more proper upbringing than her husband.

J. B. Webb did not approve of the custom of feeding children after the adults. He always wanted the children to eat first. He also did not enjoy feeding preachers, because he thought they were greedy. According to my mother, J. B. and Virginia Webb were not regular church goers but attended the annual Church of Christ revivals.

J. B. and Virginia Webb had twelve children. They lost six of them from birth to three years old. My father, Lewis French Webb, was one of the six children who lived to adulthood. My father and his siblings who survived to adulthood are listed below in their order of birth:

Julia Webb Barnette, born August 10, 1900, died December 5, 1995; married William Barnette; children, Earl Barnette, Derwood "Dink" Barnette, Patsy Barnette Kellum, Jan Barnette Tiner, and Betty Jean Barnette Carter. Derwood Barnette served in the United States Air Force. Julia and William Barnette are buried in Union Ridge Cemetery, Drew County, Arkansas.

Alvin Chance Webb, born February 20, 1908, died February 17, 1994; married Eathel Grant; children, Willie Eugene Webb, Loretta Webb Miller, and Gail Webb Pelley). Alvin and Eathel, along with their son, Willie Eugene Webb, are buried in Oakland Cemetery, Monticello, Arkansas.

Lewis French Webb, born August 16, 1910, died July 9, 1994; married Louise Hawkins; children, Arnold Ray Webb, Donald Roy Webb, Jo Ann Webb Morrison, and Judy Webb Hubbell. Lewis Webb is buried at Union Ridge Cemetery, Drew County, Arkansas. His son, Arnold Ray Webb is buried next to him.

Herman D. Webb, born September 14, 1914, died January 26, 1971; married Ruby Fuqua; children, James Jerry Webb, Herman Eugene Webb, Mary Sue Webb, and Martha Lou Webb. Herman Webb was a United States Navy Veteran of World War II, having served in the Pacific theatre of the war. Jerry Webb and Gene Webb served in the United States Army. Jerry Webb is a farmer, and Gene Webb is a disabled veteran. During World War II, the government censored letters written by servicemen to their families, to ensure that sensitive information did not fall into the hands of the enemy. When Herman Webb was deployed to the Philippines, he wrote to his family and asked about "Uncle Phillip." There was no "Uncle Phillip," so the family knew this was code, giving them the clue that he was in the Philippines.

Herman and Ruby Webb are buried in Union Ridge Cemetery, Drew County, Arkansas.

Ester Maywood Webb Young, born March 6, 1916, died March 13, 2001; married Jesse Leonard "Coon" Young; children, Rob Young and Tommy Young. Maywood and Leonard Young are buried in Wilmar Cemetery, Drew County, Arkansas. Leonard Young was one of the pioneers in the timber industry in south Arkansas. His sons, Rob and Tom, worked with him for many years. Tom and his son, Chance, are involved in the wood products industry. Tom owns Cypress Bend Chip Mill at Arkansas City.

Gertrude Webb Berryman, born January 7, 1921, died May 13, 1998, married Robert Berryman; children, Joe Berryman, Bob Berryman, and Mary Catherine Berryman. Gertrude and Robert Berryman are buried in the Green Hill Cemetery, Drew County, Arkansas.

Lewis French Webb and Louise Hawkins

J. B. and Virginia Webb had a son Lewis French Webb who was my father. He married Louise Hawkins after he proposed to her for the ninth time. Apparently, Daddy was a wild and handsome young man, but Mother eventually tamed him to some extent. They were married on June 17, 1939 by a Justice of the Peace in Monticello, Arkansas. They started out their marriage in a three-room "shotgun" house on the old home place in Green Hill. Their entire household inventory consisted of a bed and a table with two chairs. They farmed for a living.

Below is a picture of my father, Lewis French Webb, with several of his children, nephews, and niece at the old home place in Green Hill. The old house is in the background. I can remember playing under the big tree in the picture.

From left: Martha Jo Webb, Ray Webb with handkerchief, Joe Berryman, Rob Young, Derwood Barnette, Don Webb (with his back turned), Lewis Webb holding Perry Webb, Jerry Webb (on the rail), and Gene Webb.

My parents sold the place when I was about three years old and moved to Monticello. Their four children are as follows:

Arnold Ray Webb, born April 14, 1940, in Monticello, Arkansas; died July 15, 1998 in Little Rock, Arkansas; married Edith Rae Beard of Monticello. Ray is buried in Union Ridge Cemetery in Drew County, Arkansas. Their four children are David Michael Webb of Maumelle, Arkansas, Danny Scott Webb of Siloam Springs, Arkansas, Douglas Ray Webb of Siloam Springs, Arkansas, and D'Rae Leigh Krein of Gentry, Arkansas. Ray Webb died suddenly just as his father and grandfather had died, and was only fifty-eight years old when he died. Ray played full-court, "run and gun" basketball in a church league until the time of his death. He was a star basketball player in high school. Ray was a pharmacist at the University of Arkansas for Medical

Sciences and was a part-time instructor in the UAMS School of Pharmacy. All of Ray's children have careers in the medical profession. Ray's wife, Edie, is a registered nurse and lives in Siloam Springs, Arkansas. David is a respiratory therapist at Arkansas Children's Hospital in Little Rock. David's wife, Tammy, is a nurse who works in an administrative capacity at Arkansas Children's Hospital. David and Tammy have two daughters, Alex and Olivia; Danny and Doug are physical therapists, and D'Rae is a registered nurse. D'Rae's husband, Tom Krein, is also a registered nurse, and is a skilled knife-maker. They have three boys: Jake, Ben, and Zack. Danny's wife, Gina, is a nurse practitioner who commutes to Tulsa, Oklahoma to work; they have a daughter, Shelby. Doug's wife, Jennifer, is an elementary school teacher at a private school in Fayetteville, Arkansas. They have three boys, Cole, Cade, and Crew.

Donald Roy Webb was born September 30, 1943 in Monticello, Arkansas; he married Helen Hammil of Monticello, Arkansas. Their children are Marilyn Rebecca (Becky) Webb Rawls of Conway Arkansas, and Donald Ray Webb of Conway, Arkansas. Becky has two boys, Justin and Jesse Rawls. Both of Don's children have careers in the medical profession. Donald is a respiratory therapist at Arkansas Children's Hospital, working with his cousin, David Webb. Becky is a medical technologist at the Veterans Administration Hospital in Little Rock. Don served on active duty in the United States Army during the Vietnam Era, serving stateside and in Central America. The hospital incorrectly listed his middle name as Ray—it is actually Roy, after one of Daddy's brothers who died as an infant. The error proved difficult to correct, so Don now uses Donald Ray Webb as his legal name.

Jo Ann Webb Morrison, was born December 22, 1946, in Monticello, Arkansas; she married James E. Morrison III of

Monticello, Arkansas. Their children are Melanie Ann Morrison Arthur of The Woodlands, Texas, and James Andrew "Andy" Morrison of Little Rock, Arkansas. Jo Ann works as a medical technologist at Arkansas Children's hospital in Little Rock. Her daughter, Melanie, is married to Lee Eric Arthur, MD, an anesthesiologist in Conroe, Texas. Melanie is a medical technologist who is now a stay-at-home mother. They have two daughters, Annalese and Mariele. Andy recently graduated the University of Arkansas at Little Rock where he was a Dean's List Scholar, and is attending graduate school at UALR. He married Linda Burgess, a law student, on November 23, 2012 in Little Rock, Arkansas.

Judy Carol Webb Hubbell was born May 23, 1954 in Monticello, Arkansas; she married Billy James Hubbell, born May 21, 1949, in Pine Bluff, Arkansas, and grew up in Grady, Arkansas. Billy Hubbell served in the United States Army Reserve during the Vietnam Era. Their son is William Griffin Hubbell, born April 9, 1990, in Bastrop, Louisiana, and who now serves in the United States Army stationed in Germany. He completed a one-year tour of duty in Afghanistan. Judy and Billy own a forty-acre farm on Long Prairie in Drew County, and a forty-acre pine plantation in Ashley County. Billy is a lawyer and an Arkansas District Court Judge. Judy has her doctorate in education and has been an educator for twenty-seven years. She is now retired and devotes her time to writing.

Lewis French Webb and Louis Hawkins Webb

My father, Lewis French Webb, was the son of John Wesley Bell Webb and Virginia Griffin Webb. He was born August 16, 1910 in Drew County, Arkansas. He died suddenly, July 9, 1994, at his home. The doctor told us it was a massive heart attack, a massive stroke, or both. We allowed the doctors to harvest his corneas and skin for transplant purposes; Daddy was generous and would have liked that.

My mother, Louise Hawkins Webb, celebrated her 93rd birthday May 12, 2012. She is a remarkable person who keeps a sunny outlook. She has had a hard life in many ways. She lived through every parent's worst nightmare; she had to bury one of her children, my brother, Ray. She is an incredibly strong individual. Mother and my brother, Don, live with my sister, Jo Ann, in Little Rock so they can be near their doctors. Mother keeps a good attitude, and follows the Arkansas Razorbacks, the Dallas Cowboys, and the Chicago Cubs. She also enjoys horse racing at Oaklawn Park in Hot Springs. She learned to love the game of basketball when her sons played in school. She and Daddy never missed a game.

My father is the reason I am an historian today. He was forty-five years old when I was born, so instead of playing with me, he took me with him to visit the cemetery. We walked all over the cemetery, and he told me stories of the people buried there, many of whom were our relatives. He never tired of this, nor did I. I still enjoy visiting cemeteries; perhaps that sounds strange, but cemeteries are wonderful sources of family history. In Daddy's later years, we kept him entertained by visiting the cemetery.

When Daddy died, I visited with a staff member at the local funeral service when we were at Union Ridge Cemetery, picking the gravesite for Daddy's burial. The funeral home representative said it had always been assumed that our family's graves were some of the earliest at Union Ridge. The big, ancient cedar tree, located on the highest point of the cemetery, has stood as a silent sentinel over our dead loved ones for well over one hundred years. This grand old tree has weathered several severe ice storms and still stands firm. I would like to get a forestry expert to determine the approximate age of the tree. Daddy always said the tree was large when he was just a boy. If Daddy were still alive he would have been 103 years old on August 16, 2013, so it is a safe estimate that the tree is probably over two hundred years old.

During Daddy's later years, he worked for the City of Monticello as supervisor of the "Green Thumb" crew. One of his pet projects was the square in Monticello, and he kept it immaculately groomed. On the way to Daddy's funeral service, Charlie Dearman drove the family limousine around the square on the way from the house to the funeral home as a silent tribute to Daddy and his love for the square. Several policemen held the traffic lights and stood respectfully at parade rest as we passed.

Daddy loved his four children and shamelessly bragged on us. I have often heard him say that he was never happier than when he was doing something with his children, especially building or farming projects with his boys. Daddy and Ray built Mother and Daddy's house in 1962, and some years later, they built Ray and Edie's house, an accomplishment Ray alluded to in his eulogy at Daddy's funeral. Daddy loved his home and loved to be at home. Everyone in the family can vouch that Daddy was not a good traveler.

Lewis French Webb, Teller of Great Stories

My father was the consummate story-teller, and everyone loved it when he got wound up to tell tales. He often related the story of a preacher visiting his home when he was a teenager. He and his brothers were making "home brew" in the smoke house. As the homemade beer brewed, it blew the stoppers out of the jugs with a loud popping noise. The visiting preacher heard the corks popping, somewhat to J. B. Webb's embarrassment. His father pulled him and his brothers aside and told them, "Boys, do something with that damn beer!"

My father said that J. B. and Virginia Webb did not whip their children, a fact I find amazing considering how J. B. Webb was raised, but would use other forms of punishment. Daddy often told the story of a day when he had gotten home in the early morning hours "drunk as a skunk." John Webb knocked on the bedroom door at five o'clock in the morning and instructed my father to "scrap" cotton that day. Scrapping cotton consisted of going back over cotton that had already been picked to get what was missed, tedious "stoop" labor.

Daddy said he staggered to the field, picked enough cotton to make a pillow, and lay down under a peach tree. He said he lay in the hot sun all day, nursing a bad hangover and vomiting, with ants stinging him. He had a jug of water with him, and each time he took a drink, it made him drunk all over again. John Webb never asked my father how much cotton he scrapped, leading my father to believe that John Webb knew of the previous night's debauchery, and figured that a hangover in the early autumn heat, complete with stinging insects, was punishment enough.

The absolute funniest story about my daddy is told by my mother, and I laugh just as hard each time I hear the story because it is just so "Daddy." In his later years, he became hard of hearing, but he still liked to go to church, a big part of his reformation that can be attributed to my mother. Daddy was a deacon and an elder in the church, but he never let that interfere with his colorful language.

A husband and wife evangelistic team visited Mother and Daddy's church. The woman evangelist preached a long-winded sermon. Noon passed to one o'clock, then to close to two o'clock. Daddy turned to Mother and said, loudly as those hard of hearing tend to do, "Mama, do you reckon she is ever gonna shut up?" whereupon Mother whisked him out of the church and to the car. Mother cackles with laughter when she tells this story. Of course, it is much funnier to hear Mother tell it than to read about it. I guess I love this story because I too have often wanted to stand up in church, meetings at work, or class, or wherever I am held captive audience, and ask loudly, "Do you reckon he (or she) is ever gonna shut up?"

Some members of my family believe that another story about Daddy is the funniest, and I must admit, it is a strong contender. It seems that Daddy had a brother-in-law he was not fond of. We won't say which one. This particular brother-in-law died, and Daddy's classic comment was, "Well, he was a son-of-a-bitch all his life. Now he's a dead son-of-a-bitch."

Another amusing story told by Daddy, and retold wonderfully by my mother, was about one of his old flames who thought he was going to marry her. She was an extremely overweight spinster schoolteacher. When Daddy broke the news that he did not plan to marry her, she threatened to sue him for breach of promise.

Daddy laughed and said that Esther (I don't know her last name, but apparently it was never Webb) was so fat he had to hug half of her, mark the spot with chalk, walk around, and hug the other half of her. Again, it was much funnier when Daddy told it or Mother retells it. According to Mother, Fat Esther bragged that when she married Lewis Webb, she was *not* going to allow him to wear overalls. That was her first mistake, and the boast did not take Fat Esther down the road to matrimony. Mother said that Fat Esther stayed swelled-up for many years and did not speak to her or Daddy.

Daddy also told the story about getting caught stealing watermelons with one of his pals. The owner of the watermelons came to J. B. Webb and the father of the other boy and told of the theft that occurred the previous night. The other boy's father beat him severely with a leather plow line. My father got a short lecture, the essence of which was to be more careful next time or steal watermelons from someone else.

One particularly funny "Daddy" story was about me. When Daddy worked at MonArk Boat Company, a brash young man worked with him. He referred to Daddy as "old man" and was a smart-aleck. One day, he asked Daddy if he thought his daughter (me) would go out with him. Without missing a beat, Daddy replied, "Naw, she don't date stupid little bastards like you." Smart Aleck never asked me out on a date. Imagine that.

My father always told us the harshest thing his "Papa" ever did was to forbid his daughter, Julia, to marry a young man with whom she was deeply in love. It was a rift that was never fully mended between J. B. Webb and his daughter, Julia.

During World War II, Monticello was the site of a prisoner-of-war camp. One day, Daddy and his brother, Alvin Webb, picked up a hitchhiker. It did not take them long to determine that the man was an Italian POW who had escaped. They turned around and took him back to the camp with no resistance from the man. The camp was where the Drew County Fairgrounds is now located.

Daddy did not serve in World War II, because he was married with two children and was a farmer; this was considered to be an "essential occupation." He and Mother each had a sibling in the war, so they kept up with the radio news. I have often heard Daddy speak of the then-famous radio announcer, Gabriel Heeter. According to Daddy, Heeter put a negative spin on the news, and he always sounded as though America was losing the war. He said Heeter always depressed him. Mother remembers the war years as being a frightening time, especially when the horrors of the Nazi death camps were revealed. She had two small children and feared for the safety of her family if America lost the war.

My parents, Lewis and Louise Webb, lived with J. B. and Virginia Webb from the time of their marriage in 1939 to about 1957 when Virginia Griffin Webb died. It was a common practice at that time for several generations to inhabit the same home. At one time, four generations lived in the house at the same time: William Griffin; his daughter Virginia Webb and her husband, J. B. Webb; Lewis Webb, son of Virginia and J. B. Webb, and his wife, Louise, and their oldest child, Ray Webb. During my mother's first pregnancy, she developed toxemia and nearly died when my brother, Ray, was born. She was in a coma for several days.

The doctor told my father to take the baby home, because my mother was going to die. My grandfather, J. B. Webb, would not hear of this and refused to allow the baby to be sent home. I suppose he knew Mother was a fighter, because she eventually got well. During her second pregnancy, the doctor instructed her to walk each day to reduce the risk of developing toxemia. My grandfather saw to it that Mother walked each day, accompanying her most of the time.

J. B. Webb had a close friend who was one of Drew County's most beloved physicians, Dr. Johnnie Price. J. B. Webb developed heart problems, and Dr. Price told him that when he died, it would be suddenly and quickly. That was exactly how he died in 1943. Some of his hogs got out of the pen, and catching them proved difficult. He became agitated, had a heart attack, and died.

Union Ridge Cemetery

Union Ridge cemetery where the Camps, Griffins, and Webbs have been buried for at least six generations is a place of great significance to our family. It is an integral part of our family's history. I suppose it is a "Southern thing," but I find comfort in the fact that when I die, I will be buried under the big cedar at Union Ridge with several generations of my ancestors. Both my remaining siblings have also expressed the desire to be buried there.

Before my retirement, one of my favorite things to do was stop by the cemetery on my way to work and stroll through the grounds. It is so serene in the morning light, and the sounds of Monticello are muffled and distant. In the summers, the fragrances of freshly mown grass and honeysuckle take me back to the carefree summers of my youth. It was a time of reflection and helped me get centered for the work day ahead of me. Mother and I have taken lawn chairs and sat beneath the ancient cedar tree and enjoyed the tranquility of the setting. I have never been frightened or felt unsafe when I am alone in the cemetery. I have always heard it said that approximately seventy-five percent of the people buried in Union Ridge Cemetery are related. The old-timers still refer to it as "Scrouge Out" cemetery; it acquired this nickname because at one time, there was a church nearby that was too small for its congregation, and if you didn't get there early, you were "scrouged out."

According to a deed dated January 2, 1901, Lewis Butler Wilson gave the land for the Scrouge Out School across from the Union Ridge or "Scrouge Out" Cemetery (Drew County Deed Book TT, pg. 366). Preaching was allowed in the school house when it did not interfere with school. Wilson's grandson, Felton Wilson states (1982) that his grandfather also gave the land for the cemetery in the late 1800s.

The Baby Graves

One heartbreaking chapter of the Webb family history is contained in what we refer to as "the baby graves." J. B. and Virginia Griffin Webb had twelve children, six of whom died from birth to three years old. They entered the twentieth century losing three children during the year 1900. Julia was the first of their children who lived to adulthood. My father believed one of the children died of appendicitis.

The "baby graves" are all in a row under the big cedar tree at Union Ridge. According to my aunt, Maywood Webb Young, my grandmother nearly lost her mind during these tribulations. She said that after Virginia Griffin Webb had lost three children in one calendar year, she imagined she could hear them coo and toddle about the house. According to my parents, J. B. and Virginia Webb had little use for doctors and preachers. I suppose they felt that both had let them down, but they eventually adopted some form of religion before their deaths. Virginia Webb had been raised in the Christ of Christ where her father, William Griffin, was a charter member and elder.

The following are the birth and death dates of the six infants as recorded in *Drew County, Arkansas Cemetery Records, 3rd edition.* The date of birth is obviously wrong for Willie E. Webb or Roy B. Webb. The stones are difficult to read:

> **Willie E. Webb, born August 25, 1898, died April 11, 1900**

> **Roy B. Webb, born November 27, 1898, died May 16, 1900**

> **Infant Webb, born and died December 29, 1900**

> **Infant Webb, born and died March 7, 1904**

> **Earl Webb, born June 28, 1902 and died January 4, 1905**

> **Infant Webb, born and died January 6, 1912**

The "baby graves" were badly vandalized several years ago and received statewide news coverage. The little headstones have been repaired as well as possible; they are made of concrete and are crumbling with age. The cemetery association now locks the gate at night, and that has helped reduce vandalism at the cemetery.

There are now seven baby graves. Several years ago when my sister, Jo Ann Webb Morrison, was a department head at Drew Memorial Hospital in Monticello, a Hispanic woman came to the hospital and gave birth to a stillborn child. The family had fled political persecution from a South American country. They were utterly destitute. The hospital personnel took pity on their plight and took it upon themselves to help this family by taking donations for a funeral.

My mother, Louise Hawkins Webb, heard of their predicament and donated a cemetery plot to the family. The family could not speak English, so someone contacted a minister who spoke Spanish. A graveside funeral service was arranged with the preacher, my mother, my sister, the owner of Stephenson-Dearman Funeral Home, and some of the hospital personnel in attendance, all strangers to the grieving Hispanic couple. This story speaks volumes about the goodness of these Drew County people. The little grave has only an aluminum marker provided by the funeral home.

Chapter 17
The Dodsons and Hawkinses:
Two Southern Backcountry Clans

Direct Line of Descent for the Dodsons

John Dodson and Elizabeth (Unknown) were the parents of John Clayborn Dodson.

John Clayborn Dodson and Lydia Burks were the parents of Pleasant Riley Dodson.

Pleasant Riley Dodson and Margaret Addaline King were the parents of Sam Dodson.

Sam Dodson and Martha George were the parents of Omay Dodson.

Omay Dodson and Arthur Hawkins were the parents of Louise Hawkins.

Louise Hawkins and Lewis French Webb are the parents of Arnold Ray Webb, Donald Roy Webb, Jo Ann Webb Morrison, and Judy Carol Webb Hubbell.

Judy Carol Webb and Billy James Hubbell are the parents of William Griffin Hubbell.

Note: I would like to acknowledge the help I received from Martha Murel Forrest Reeme of Kingsland, Arkansas, in researching the Dodsons. She saw a query I had posted on a message board about Sam Dodson. She emailed me and told me things about herself and the Dodsons. In a letter postmarked October 19, 2009, she told me her parents were Frank Forrest and Florence Pearl Dodson Forrest. She sent me a stack of research and a picture of Sam Dodson with family members. She told me that she wanted a copy of the book when it was finished. I was saddened to learn that Martha died recently. Her research was a great help in writing this chapter.

I would like to relate some things about my mother, Louise Hawkins Webb, and her family even though this project is mainly about my father's family. Mother once told me a story that was a defining moment for me. She said that every time she filled out a job application, she put that she had finished the eighth grade; in reality, she finished the fourth grade. She told me she never wanted us children to be embarrassed by a lack of education as she was. She told me she studied our school books and educated herself as much as possible.

Ironically, Mother read to us all the time. Our favorite book was *Wild Creatures in Winter*; we never tired of it. Mother worked at Burlington Industries and in a sewing factory that had no air conditioning to help put us through school. When she worked at the sewing factory in Star City, she waited on tables at a café during the lunch hour in exchange for her lunches. She and Daddy preached education to us like religion.

Mother and Daddy always farmed at least part time. After they gave up cotton farming, they ran a dairy farm and also raised tomatoes for many years. Mother canned tomatoes and tomato juice using a big, black wash pot in the back yard. She built a wood fire beneath it, and this gave the tomatoes and the juice a rich, smoky flavor.

Mother and Daddy attended PTA meetings at school and made our education a priority. They were always interested in what we were doing in school. I fervently believe that rural southerners who weathered the Great Depression were made of tough stuff. My parents instilled in me a great respect for education and a strong work ethic; both priceless gifts. I weather adversity better than most people, and can I function in a crisis better than most. That is also a great gift and, to some degree, genetic, as illustrated in the family lineages in this book.

The Dodson Surname

My mother's mother was Omay Dodson Hawkins. The *Dodson* surname has several variants, as discussed in the following information (*Surname: Dodson*, 2007):

> *"One Aelfweard Dudd appears in the Old English Byname Register for Hampshire, circa 1030, and an Aluric Dod in*

the Domesday Book of 1086 for Dorset. The patronymic has the unusual distinction of also being first recorded in Domesday. Further early patronymic forms include: Aeluric Doddes, noted in Feudal Documents from the Abbey of Bury St. Edmonds, Suffold, and Magota Dodson, entered in the 1379 Poll Tax Returns of Yorkshire. In the modern idiom the patronymic takes seven variant forms: Dods, Dodds, Dadds, Dodson, Dudson, Dodding, and Dotson....The first recorded spelling of the name is shown to be that of Aluinus Dodeson, which was dated 1086 in the Domesday Book of Hertfordshire, during the reign of King William I, known as "William the Conquerer."

Jamestown, Virginia and John Dods(on)

The first Dodson in America is believed to have been John Dods; it is further believed that the surname evolved over time to Dodson, probably from the *son of Dod* or *"Dod's son."* John Dods(on) was one of one hundred forty-four English men and boys who, in 1607, set out to found the Jamestown Colony, a joint-stock company venture in the New World by the Virginia Company of London. In June 1606, King James I granted a charter to a group of London entrepreneurs to establish an English settlement in the Chesapeake region of North America (Arber, 1986); (Dorman, 2004–2007); (McCartney, 2007). The objectives of the venture were to find gold and silver, a passage to the Orient, the lost colony of Roanoke, and to convert the natives to Christianity (*Secrets of the Dead*, 2002).

The founding of Jamestown got off to a rocky start. The three ships that set sail in December 1606 carrying the adventurers became stranded for several weeks off the British coast, causing food supplies to be exhausted early in the voyage. Dozens perished during the journey, but one hundred four colonists survived the journey and reached the shores of Virginia on May 13, 1607 (*Secrets of the Dead*, 2002).

Three ships brought the adventurers to America. John Dods(on) came on the *Susan Constant* commanded by Captain Christopher Newport. The other two vessels were the *Godspeed* with Captain Bartholomew Gosnold, and the *Discovery* with Captain John Ratcliffe. The band of men reached the capes of Virginia in April 1607. The voyage across the ocean to Virginia usually took eight to twelve weeks (*Our Ancestors*, 2004). Many of these men were gentlemen of privilege who had no idea of the difficulties that lay ahead for the group and had few resources for survival. Among those surviving the voyage were artisans, crafts-men, and laborers (*Descendants of John Dods*, 2009); (Lavery, 1988); (*Virginia: Her History*, 2008).

John Dods(on), eighteen years old at the time, is listed in Captain John Smith's writing as one of the original group of settlers and as a "labourer" (McCartney, 2007); (*Virginia: Her History*, 2008). Many of the men were listed as "gentlemen" and made up the top tier of the settlers. It is interesting that the Webb branch of our family was also represented at Jamestown. Thomas Webbe was listed as one of the "gentlemen' in the original group of Jamestown settlers. The skilled craftsmen were listed next, representing the middle echelon of the settlers, and the next group listed was the "labourers." The last group was listed as "boyes" (*Original Settlers*, 2009).

John Dods(on) paid his own passage to Virginia, one of the requirements for receiving the designation of Ancient Planter, indicating that he was not indentured to a master who would have paid his fare (Dorman, 2007); (Kingsbury, n. d.).

Costly Mistakes

The group of explorers sailed up a river they found for about thirty-two miles and named it the James River, in honor of their king. Captain Newport left the one hundred four adventurers to form a settlement they called Jamestown, then Newport sailed to England. By September, only forty-six settlers survived (*Descendants of John Dods*, 2009).

Things went badly quickly in the venture. Living conditions were primitive and harsh. The men built crude cabins from poles and branches; some even dug caves for shelter (*Early Homes in the Colonies*, n. d.). The adventurers had picked a terrible location to settle; the marshy, malarial site proved to be unhealthy, and the number of deaths was staggering. Professor Ervin L. Jordan, Jr. of the University of Virginia wrote that the Jamestown settlers selected "perhaps the worst place in Virginia to establish a settlement." From 1606 to 1618, eighteen hundred immigrants came from England to Virginia. At the end of this period, only six hundred were alive. The "starving time" followed the departure of Captain Smith in 1609 (Jordan, n. d.).

The colony suffered starvation and illness. In 1607, about one-third of the population died from dysentery and typhoid fever (*Our Ancestors*, 2004), and the colonists did not always get along well because of problems inherent to holding property in common. The location chosen for the settlement could not have been worse. The site of the colony offered poor hunting and a shortage of drinking water. The fishing was not particularly good. The gentlemen colonists knew little about farming and, as a result, failed to plant crops early enough to ensure a successful harvest. To make matters worse, the region suffered the worst drought in eight hundred years. Many of the gentlemen were unaccustomed to manual labor and had visions of quick and easy riches (*A Brief History*, 1998); (*Secrets of the Dead*, 2002).

Strategically, the Virginia Company made a grave error in its dependence upon outside resources. It never planned to produce its own food but to trade with the Native American tribes between periodic supply ships from England. They mistakenly and arrogantly assumed they would be able to subjugate the natives into doing the farming for them. The Algonquian Native Americans were not welcoming to the Europeans and attacked the colony regularly. They killed the colonists if they found them in the woods hunting and raided their livestock (*Captain John Smith*, 2010); (Jordan, n. d.); (*Secrets of the Dead*, 2002).

Captain John Smith

A leader emerged among the colonists; Captain John Smith took over the government of the colony in 1608. Smith brought rigid discipline and instituted the simple rule "if you don't work, you don't eat." Many of the gentlemen still believed it was beneath their station in life to work, but Smith dispelled that notion when he proclaimed that every colonist must be engaged in agriculture at least four hours per day (*Jamestown Settlement*, 2007). Three absences from church services was a capital offense during this tyrannical rule (*Religion at Jamestown*, n. d.). Smith brokered an unsteady peace with the native people. Things were better until Smith was badly burned in an accident involving gunpowder and was forced to return to England for medical treatment in October 1609 (*Captain John Smith*, 2010); (Lossing, 1990).

The Starving Time: Winter of 1609–1610

After Smith's departure, the colony, now numbering about four hundred, was besieged by the Powhatan Confederation of Native Americans with the intent of starving out the colonists, an effective tactic that had been used for thousands of years. A hurricane helped the Native American cause by delaying and damaging a fleet of English ships bringing five hundred colonists and food supplies. Only part of the fleet arrived at Jamestown with relatively few supplies and more mouths to feed, about three hundred men, women, and children. No more supply ships came to Virginia that dreadful winter when frigid temperatures caused the James River to freeze (*A Brief History of Jamestown*, 1998); (Percy, 1624); (Smith, 1907).

The siege by the Powhaten Confederacy was successful; only sixty of the four hundred survived the winter, and John Dods(on) was one of the sixty survivors. The Powhatens worked the desperate situation to their advantage, trading a pittance of food for the colonists' valuable tools and weapons, causing the colonists to use their houses for firewood in a desperate attempt to stay warm. During this horrible time, two men were caught stealing from the common storehouse, and were tied to posts, and left to starve in an effort to restore some semblance of discipline (*Descendants of John Dods*, 2009); (*Explorers, Pioneers*, 2010).

The settlers ate their horses, and when the horses were gone, they resorted to eating dogs, cats, rats, snakes, frogs, and even leather (*A Brief History*, 1995); (*Captain John Smith*, n. d.); (Cotton, 1999); (Percy, 1624); (Ruane, 2007); (*Secrets of the Dead*, 2002).

They were forced to do the unspeakable. They robbed graves and ate the corpses. One man murdered his pregnant wife, cut out the fetus, threw it in the James River, and proceeded to salt down the body to preserve it. He had eaten all of the body except the head when it was discovered that he had resorted to cannibalism. He was tortured by being hung by his thumbs with weights on his ankles until he confessed his crime; he was then burned at the stake by the colonists (*A Brief History*, 1998). Captain Smith wrote this account of the starving time; it seems he found dark humor in the incident of the colonist eating his wife (Smith, 1907):

> "...there remained not past sixtie men, women and children, most miserable and poore creatures; and those were preserved for the most part, by roots, herbes, acornes, walnuts, berries, now and then a little fish: they that had startch in these extremities, made no small use of it; yea even the very skinnes of our horses. Nay, so great was our famine, that a Salvage we slew and buried, the poorer sort tooke him up againe and eat him; and so did divers one another boyled and stewed with roots and herbs: And one amongst the rest did kill his wife, powdered [i.e., salted] her,

and had eaten part of her before it was knowne; for which hee was executed, as hee well deserved: now whether shee was better roasted, boyled or carbonado'd [i.e., grilled], I know not; but of such a dish as powdered wife I never heard of."

Not surprisingly, it was decided to abandon the colony. Ninety percent of the Jamestown inhabitants perished during the "starving time." Only sixty gaunt survivors remained after that terrible winter, and John Dods(on) was one of them. George Percy (1624) wrote this eyewitness account:

"Finding of five hundred men we had only about sixty, the rest being either starved through famine or cut off by the savages, and those which were living were so meager and lean that it was lamentable to behold them, for many, through extreme hunger, have run out of their naked beds, being so lean that they looked like anomalies, crying out 'we are starved, we are starved'; others going to bed as we imagined in health were found dead the next morning."

On June 7, 1610, the survivors decided to abandon the settlement, and set sail down the James River for England. They were about ten miles downstream, when just like a scene from a movie, they were intercepted by three ships carrying more colonists, a doctor, food, and supplies. The ship brought the new governor of the colony, Lord De La Warr, who forced the deserters back to the colony, an unpopular order. Lord De La Warr, known as Lord Delaware in modern times, brought with him a substantial number of armed soldiers who launched a counter-offensive against the Powhatan Confederacy that proved to be effective (*A Brief History*, 1998); (Lossing, 1990); (*Secrets of the Dead*, 2002).

John Rolfe arrived on the scene in 1612. Rolfe, an Englishman, lost his wife and young son on the journey. He proved to be the economic savior of the Jamestown colony when he introduced tobacco farming as a cash crop; he introduced a sweeter tobacco that was a commercial success and ensured the permanency of the Virginia Colony. Rolfe became wealthy from this addictive plant and owned several plantations in Virginia (*A Brief History*, 1998); (Lossing, 1990).

In 1614, Rolfe married Pocahontas, daughter of the Algonquian Chief Powhatan, an act that gave the struggling colony about eight years of peace with the Native Americans. As an act of retaliation against the Native Americans who took several Englishmen captive, the colonists imprisoned Pocahontas. During her captivity, Pocahontas was given daily Bible lessons. She converted to Christianity and took the English name Rebecca. Their marriage helped bring about a short truce between the Powhatan Confederacy and the English (*A Brief History*, 1998); (Barbour, 1971); (Lossing, 1990); (Neill, 1869); (Roundtree, 1990); (Woodward, 1969).

John Rolfe took Pocahontas with him on a trip to England to discuss the commercial success of tobacco as a cash crop. Pocahontas was popular with the English. Unfortunately, she died during the visit to England at twenty-two years old. Some believe Pocahontas died from influenza, pneumonia, or perhaps smallpox. Rolfe and Pocahontas had a son, Thomas, whose grandfather, Chief Powhatan, had left him several thousand acres of land around Jamestown. He married an English woman and was a successful tobacco farmer (*A Brief History*, 1998); (Barbour, 1971); (Lossing, 1990); (Neill, 1869); (Roundtree, 1990); (Woodward, 1969).

John Dods(on) and Possible Wife or Wives

John Dods(on) was born around 1588 in Great Neck, Yorkshire, England, and died in 1659 in Jamestown, Virginia. There are three theories about the wife or wives of John Dods(on). It is commonly believed that he married the daughter of Chief Eagle Plume of the Iroquois Indian Nation, and she took the English name Jane. His possible marriage to Jane Eagle Plume could have at least partly accounted for his survival against such great odds, especially his survival of the Indian Massacre of 1622 (*Descendants of John Dods,* 2009).

Some believe that John Dods(on) brought two sons, Jesse, born around 1621, and William, born around 1623, with him from England after the death of their mother, or that they followed their father to Virginia at a later time. There is some speculation there was another son, Benjamin. There is further speculation that Jane Eagle Plume was the mother of Jesse and William Dods(on) and possibly Benjamin Dodson (*Descendants of John Dods,* 2009).

At least one scholar believes that John Dods(on) purchased a wife from one of the "bride ships," the *Marmaduke,* the *Warwick,* or the *Tiger.* David R. Ransome (2000) states that John Dods(on) married Jane Dier, one of the fifty-seven women sent to Jamestown on one of the "bride ships" that arrived in 1621. Jane was believed to be fifteen or sixteen years old when she arrived at Jamestown and was reported to be the youngest of the women (Ransome, 1991).

There were no women among the first group of Jamestown settlers. Mapp (2006) states, "…it was thought that women had no place in the grim and often grisly business of subduing a continent…." This changed in 1620 when a shipload of women, ninety to be exact, arrived for potential brides. In 1621, sixty more women arrived, and Jane Dier is believed to have been one of these women (Ransome, 1991). About thirteen hundred women and children arrived at Jamestown during this two-year period. The years 1618–1623 saw the population of Virginia climb from four hundred to about forty-five hundred settlers (Cridlin, 1922); (*Our Ancestors in Jamestown,* 2004); (Ransome, 1991).

The men had to acquire the women's permission to marry, and they had to pay for their transportation from England to Virginia in the amount of one hundred twenty pounds of tobacco, about five hundred dollars worth (Mapp, 2006); (*The Indispensable Role,* n.

d.). Jesse and William Dods(on) married women from the "bride ship" around 1630 (*Descendants of John Dods*, 2009).

John Dods(on) and his bride, whoever she was, survived starvation and the Indian massacre and settled in the Neck of Land community with the status of Original Settlers. The *Tax List of James City 16 Feb. 1623* (Coldham, 2009) lists John Dods(on) and his wife as inhabitants of the village, Neck of Land, along with forty other settlers. James City is now known as Chesterfield, Virginia.

The 1634 muster of the household of John and Jane Dods(on) lists the following provisions: ten barrels of corn, one-half bushel of peas, and fifty pounds of fish. Also listed were four pounds of gunpowder and thirty pounds of lead and bullets, two "peeces fixit," a coat of mail and headpiece (armor), one sword, two pigs, and twenty-five head of poultry (Dorman, 1987).

John Dods(on) survived all the hardships of the new colony and had the reputation as a great hunter and fur trader. By 1624, John Dods(on) was one of only three of the original group of settlers of 1607 still alive. He apparently had a good relationship with the Native Americans in Virginia. He traded with the tribes for large tracts of land (Dodson, 1965). John Dods(on) was apparently eager to acquire farmland. In the passage of text (McCartney, 2007) cited earlier in this chapter, we learn that John Dods(on) had acquired two hundred acres of land as a reward for settling in Jamestown. It seems that John Dods(on) had done well for himself in the New World.

John Dods(on) served with Captain Smith as a soldier in expeditions against the Native American tribes. He accompanied George Percy to visit Powhatan at the Indian village of Werowocomoco, and during this visit, Dods(on) used his building skills to construct a house for the tribal chief. In the following summary of the life of John Dods(on), McCartney (2007) discusses a land dispute involving Dods(on):

"John Dodd (Dodd, Dods), a laborer, came to Virginia in 1607 on the Susan Constant and was one of the first colonists. In 1608 John Dodd accompanied Captain John Smith on a voyage into the Pamunkey River, and on December 29, 1608, he was among the men who accompanied Smith to Werowocomoco, Powhatan's village on the York River. On February 16, 1624, John Dodd and his wife, Jane, were living at Bermuda Hundred. They were still there on January 24, 1625, at which time he was described as a 36-year-old household head who was very well supplied with stored food and defensive weaponry. In May, 1625, when a list of patented land was sent back to England, John Dodd was credited with 50 acres in Charles City and 150 acres in Tappahannah, land to which he was entitled as an ancient planter. On Janaury 11, 1627, Dodd appeared before the General Court where he testified that even though the late Luke Boise (also of Bermuda Hundred) had failed to make a will, he had said that he wanted his wife, Alice, and their child to have his estate. On February 9, 1628, John Dodd returned to court. This time the justices settled a land dispute he was having with William Vincent. The justices decided that each of them would have half of Joshua Chard's land and half of his house."

Order of Ancient Planters

John Dods(on)'s survival and perseverance made him a member of what was to become a very elite society. the *Order of Ancient Planters*. Ancient planters were defined as those who paid their own passage to Jamestown, Virginia before 1616, remained at least three years, and survived the 1622 Jamestown massacre (Bachelor, 2009). As a reward, the ancient planters received the first land grants in Virginia (Billings, 1975); (Boddie, 1974); (Campbell, 1860); (*Order of Descendants*, 2009).

Another significant turn of events for the colonists was the arrival of the first Africans to the colony in 1619. Twenty African were purchased from a passing Dutch ship as indentured servants. Technically, these Africans were not treated as slaves because they were baptized Christians. Many were literate, eventually worked off their indenture, and gained freedom (*History of Jamestown*, n. d); (Smiley, 2007).

Massacre of 1622

John Dods(on) survived a dangerous voyage to the New World, and he survived the starving time. He survived military actions against the Powhatan Confederacy, and perhaps took a Native American wife. He survived epidemics of deadly diseases such as malaria, typhoid, and smallpox. He also survived another major military blow to the colonists, the aforementioned Massacre of 1622. We know he survived the massacre because he is listed on the *Tax List of 1623* (Coldham, 2009).

On March 22, 1622, the Powhatan Confederacy attacked colonists in eastern Virginia and killed three hundred forty-seven, almost one-quarter of the English population in the colony of Virginia. A major cause of this conflict was the desire of the colonists to acquire more land to grow tobacco. The Powhatans were alarmed that the English were converting woodlands to farmland in their eagerness to acquire large tobacco plantations. The native tribes saw their hunting lands destroyed and stepped up efforts to expel the English. The spark that ignited the conflict was welcomed as an excuse for all-out war with the natives. Since the time of Columbus, Europeans had acquired land by right of conquest, but this was the first time English colonists employed that avenue of land acquisition (Fausz, 1978-1979); (Gleach, 1997); (Rountree, 1989, 1990, 1993).

Europeans had another powerful weapon that helped their cause in the New World. They unintentionally introduced European diseases such as smallpox to the natives who had no resistance to the often fatal diseases (*European Colonization*, 2008). The Powatan population of about twenty-five thousand in 1607 had dwindled to only a few thousand by the 1630s, largely due to these deadly diseases, but the natives did not give up. On April 18, 1644, they launched another attack on the colonists, killing over four hundred. This war lasted about two years, after which time Powhatan dominance in Virginia ended (Fausz, 1978, 1979); (Gleach, 1997); (Rountree 1989, 1990, 1994).

Hotten's *List* (1874) a compilation of the living and dead as of February 16, 1623, shows John Dods(on), Mrs. Dods(on), Goodman Webb, William Kemp, Stephen Webb, Thomas Webbe, and Thomas Hawkins as being among the living. Several branches of our family were well represented in Jamestown and appear to have acquired survival skills lacking in many of the Jamestown settlers. Even though I was a history minor in college, I did not realize the enormous hardships encountered by the Jamestown colonists until I researched this chapter. Our Jamestown origins probably explain why several branches of our family followed the Southern frontier. In Jamestown, they learned how row-crops such as tobacco could be very lucrative. They followed the Southern frontier seeking rich, available farmland. Instead of tobacco, many of them raised cotton as a lucrative cash crop. Our family mostly has been farmers, and many today still engage in farming. This has been a strong legacy.

The colony of Virginia attracted several of our ancestors to America. Hotten's *List* (1874) shows George Hawkins, eighteen years old, arriving in Virginia from England in June, 1635 on the ship *Thomas & John* after taking the required oath of allegiance. Thomas Webb, eighteen years old, arrived on July 4, 1635 on the ship *Transport*. Ann Griffin, twenty-six years old, arrived on the ship *Assurance de Lo*. Richard Webb and William Griffin arrived in Virginia on July 27, 1635 on the ship *Primrose*. James Hawkins arrived August 21, 1635 on the ship *George*. John Griffin, twenty-six years old, arrived in 1624 on the *William & John*. Arriving October 24, 1635 on the ship *Constance* was another young adventurer of the same name, John Griffin, twenty-six years old. William Kemp, his wife Margaret Kemp, and their seven-week-old son, Anthony Kemp, arrived in Virginia on January 30, 1624. My family is direct descendents of some of the first Europeans to set foot in America.

I have been unable to link John Dods(on) directly to our family, but the earliest Dodson I found, that I know for certain is in our direct line of descent, is John Dodson of Virginia, I feel reasonably sure this John Dodson was a descendent of John Dods(on) of Jamestown because of the naming tradition, the correct timeframe, geography, and the research of other Dodson genealogists.

John Dodson and Elizabeth (Unknown)

The 1850 federal census report for Jackson County, Alabama provides information about John and Elizabeth Dodson. According to the census report, John Dodson was seventy-three years old in 1850, making the year of his birth approximately 1777. Elizabeth is also described in the census as being seventy-three years old in 1850, making the year of her birth approximately 1777. Both were born in Virginia and, according to the census data, could read and write. The census further indicates that John and Elizabeth Dodson lived in the same household with their son, John Clayborn Dodson, and his wife, Lydia.

John Clayborn Dodson and (First) Lydia Burks (Second) Polly Cline / Kline)

The 1850 federal census report for Jackson County, Alabama described John C. Dodson as forty-four years old and a farmer born in Tennessee. The following is a list of his family members enumerated in the census report:

John C. Dodson, forty-four years old, and a farmer born in Tennessee

Lydia, forty-four years old, born in North Carolina

Pleasant R., twenty-two years old, and a farmer born in Tennessee

Rolly N(ewt), eighteen years old, and a laborer born in Tennessee

Sarah, fifteen years old, born in Alabama

Samuel, fourteen years old, born in Tennessee

John, seventy-three years old, born in Virginia

Elizabeth, seventy-three years old, born in Virginia

Elizabeth, twenty-four years old, born in Tennessee

Sivena, fourteen years old, born in Tennessee

It is interesting that one of the children, Sarah, was born in Alabama, indicating that the family must have settled in Alabama at one time, returned to Tennessee, and went back to Alabama. Two counties in Tennessee, Marion and Franklin, border Jackson County, Alabama. From studying the ages of the children, it appears that Samuel and Sivena may have been twins.

John Clayborn Dodson outlived his first wife, Lydia Burks Dodson. John Clayborn Dodson married Polly Cline/Kline), born around 1854 in Tennessee.

Pleasant Riley Dodson and Margaret Addaline King

My family is directly descended from the eldest son of John Clayborn Dodson and Lydia Burks Dodson, Pleasant Riley Dodson. Using the census data from 1850, Pleasant Riley Dodson was born around 1828 in Tennessee. He is buried in Miller Mount Cemetery in Jackson County, Alabama (*Family Group Record, Pleasant Riley Dodson,* 2008). He married Margaret Addaline King, born around 1826, on May 3, 1851 in Jackson County, Alabama. Margaret Addaline King died October 15, 1911 and is buried in Travis Cemetery, Jackson County, Tennessee.

When Pleasant Riley Dodson was ready to die, he went into the woods and died in the tradition of the Cherokee, a testament of his Cherokee ancestry. His body was found in a spring (Reeme, 2009).

Using the Jackson County, Alabama census data from 1850, Margaret King was born around 1826. The following is census information for her family; her father was John King and her mother was Sophiah King:

> **John King, fifty years old, a cooper (barrel-maker) born in North Carolina**
>
> **Sophiah King, forty-eight years old, born in North Carolina**
>
> **Margaret King, twenty-four years old, could read and write, born in North Carolina**
>
> John King, sixteen years old, born in Tennessee
>
> Jane King, eleven years old, born in Tennessee
>
> Elizabeth King, ten years old, born in Tennessee

William King, four years old, born in Alabama

The information shows how this family migrated through the Southern frontier from North Carolina, then to Tennessee, and then to Alabama. By the standards of that time, Margaret was probably considered a spinster at age twenty-four. There are eight years between her birth and the birth of her nearest sibling in age, indicating that her parents probably lost at least one child between Margaret's birth and the birth of her brother, John King. There is a five-year gap between the birth of John and his sister, Jane. There is a six-year gap between the birth of Elizabeth King and her little brother, William King. The census data indicate the family had been in Alabama fewer than ten years.

Pleasant Riley Dodson and Margaret King Dodson had a large family. The couple had ten children, all born in Alabama: William Dodson, born around 1846; Louisa, born around 1848; Thomas, born around 1850; Samuel, born around 1852; Nancy Dodson, born around 1854; James Riley Dodson, born around 1862; Peter Dodson, born around 1868; Seymore Dodson born around 1870; Jaley Ann Dodson, born May 10, 1860, and died March 6, 1944, Pisgah, Jackson County, Alabama, and buried in Travis Cemetery, Jackson County, Alabama; George Dodson, born December 22, 1867, and died October 7, 1922.

Pleasant Riley Dodson named one of his sons James Riley Dodson, and this son was called Riley by his family. This indicates there is probably a Riley branch of the family. My family is directly descended from Samuel Dodson and Martha Ann George Dodson.

Samuel Dodson's older brother, William, served as a private in the Confederate Army during the Civil War. He enlisted in Company K, Second Alabama Infantry, known as the Jackson County, Alabama Rifles.

Jackson County, Alabama

When the American Revolution came to a close in 1783, Great Britain had to cede to the new nation all lands east of the Mississippi River except Florida. In 1798, this became the Territory of Mississippi and included parts of present-day Alabama. Most of the territory was wilderness that supported a considerable fur trade. Cotton production had barely begun when it was interrupted by the War of 1812, during which time the Creek Confederacy of Native Americans was defeated by Andrew Jackson in 1814. Coupled with an increasing British demand for cotton, this brought about a period of heavy settlement into the Alabama region, especially from Georgia and Tennessee. Large cotton plantations based on slave labor were established in the fertile bottomlands. The population grew rapidly, and the Territory of Alabama was established in 1817 (Columbia, 2007).

Jackson County, Alabama is the northeastern most county in Alabama, bordering Tennessee to the north and Georgia to the east. Scottsboro is the county seat, and today it is considered to be in the Huntsville-Decatur metro area. Jackson County was established on December 13, 1819, and much of the county is located in the Appalachian Mountains. Adjacent counties are Marion County, Tennessee, Dade County, Georgia, Franklin County, Tennessee, DeKalb County, Alabama, Marshall County, Alabama, and Madison County, Alabama. Paint Rock is the small community located on the Paint Rock River in the southwestern corner of Jackson County, Alabama where my great-grandfather, Sam Dodson, and his family lived. Today it has a total population of one hundred eighty-five (*Paint Rock, Alabama Community Profile*, 2010).

Sam Dodson's migration to southeast Arkansas was probably motivated by the desire to acquire more fertile farmland where cotton could be cultivated. Only subsistence farming could be eked out of the thin, rocky, mountainous soil of Jackson County.

Sam Dodson and (First) Mary Frances George, (Second) Martha Ann George, (Third) Vinnie Atchley

According to his headstone and information supplied by his daughter, Omay Dodson Hawkins, Sam Dodson was born August 25, 1855 in Alabama, and died December 2, 1940 in Drew County, Arkansas. He is buried in Gaster Hill Cemetery, Drew County, Arkansas.

According to my mother, Louise Hawkins Webb, Sam Dodson was first married to a woman named Mary Frances George who died, leaving two small children, Monroe Dodson and Rosie Bell Dodson, known as "Sister Bell" to her family. Rosie Bell Dodson married a man named *Bateman*. There was another child, Grider, born to Sam and Frances Dodson, who died young. His name may indicate there is a Grider branch in the Dodson family.

According to my grandmother, Omay Dodson Hawkins, after the death of his first wife, Mary Frances, Sam returned to Alabama from Arkansas to marry her sister, Martha Ann George, because he felt she would be kind to her sister's children. Martha was the mother of Omay Lee Dodson Hawkins who was my grandmother, Lucy Dodson Forrest, and Daisy Dodson Sulzer.

There were three boys who apparently died young: Grider Dodson, born 1876, Jesse Dodson born 1883, and Lawrence Dodson, born 1884.

William George and Ann B. George

According to the 1870 federal census report for Jackson County, Alabama, the household of William and Ann George was as follows:

William George, forty-three years old, born in Alabama

Ann B. George, forty-three years old, born in South Carolina

Margaret George, twenty-seven years old, born in Tennessee

John George, twenty-two years old, born in Alabama

Mary F. George, seventeen years old, born in Alabama

William George, fifteen years old, born in Alabama

Raleigh George, thirteen years old, born in Alabama

Greene George, eleven years old, born in Alabama

Martha George, eight years old, born in Alabama

Nancy E. George, six years old, born in Alabama

Apparently, William and Ann George made a settlement in Tennessee prior to their removal to Jackson County, Alabama. By the 1880 federal census report for Jackson County, Alabama, Margaret George was no longer a member of the household.

Martha Ann George, my great-grandmother, was born in Alabama, and died in Monticello, Drew County, Arkansas. Martha George Dodson died young, from some epidemic, possibly small-pox, when my grandmother, Omay Dodson, was about three or four years old. Her grave and the grave of her sister, Mary Frances Dodson, have been lost. They are probably buried in Gaster Hill Cemetery in Drew County, Arkansas.

My grandmother, Omay Lee Dodson Hawkins, remembered that her mother broke out in sores and had a high fever before she died. Omay Lee Dodson Hawkins did not know her own date of birth as a result of being orphaned of her mother at such a young age. Her father, Sam Dodson, did not take note of such details. Omay Dodson knew she was born in October and could only approximate the year. By my mother's calculations, Omay Dodson Hawkins was between ninety-six and ninety-nine years old at the time of her death. For official records, my grandmother listed her birth date as October 23, 1894. Omay Dodson Hawkins died on January 19, 1994 after strangling on a dip of snuff at the nursing home where she was a resident.

My mother, Louise Hawkins Webb, related a sad story about Omay Dodson's little brother, Lawrence Dodson. Lawrence got sick at school one day, and Omay was going to take him home by riding him piggy-back. Before they left, he had to urinate, so Omay let him stand on the front porch of the school and relieve himself. The other children laughed and made fun of him. Omay rode him home on her back, and he died shortly thereafter. My mother believes that Lawrence Dodson's mother was Martha Ann George Dodson.

Omay Dodson Hawkins told the story of coming to Arkansas from Alabama in a covered wagon driven by her father, Sam Dodson. According to my mother, Sam Dodson also brought with them his grandmother who was a full-blooded Cherokee Native American. During this time, the Cherokee were driven off their land in Alabama and other states by the federal government. My mother states that the family took care of the old Cherokee woman and treated her with kindness. They fixed a bed for her to lie on in the back of the wagon during the trip to Arkansas. Omay Dodson Hawkins had strong Native American physical features, as did several of her children. She was at least one-quarter Cherokee. We always joked that "Mama Hawkins" needed a blanket wrapped around her and a feather stuck in her hair, and she would look every inch an Indian squaw.

Sam Dodson was an interesting character who had a weakness for women and flashy buggies. After the death of his second wife,

Martha Ann George, Dodson returned to Alabama in hopes of marrying a third George sister, Nancy. According to family stories, the father of the George sisters, William George, ran Dodson off his property and told him to never return (Reeme, 2009). He probably thought losing two daughters to Sam Dodson was enough.

Omay Dodson Hawkins related that Sam Dodson then "took up" with a young woman named Vinnie Atchley, born around 1864 in Jackson County, Alabama, who became pregnant with his child. She was only three years older than Sam Dodson's oldest child. As her pregnancy advanced, Sam Dodson showed no intention of marrying her until he was pressured to do so by his adult children. He finally married her, reluctantly. Vinnie was the mother of Ruby Dodson Stuart and Boyd Dodson. Vinnie Dodson is buried in Rough and Ready Cemetery in Drew County, Arkansas, but her headstone has been moved to Gaster Hill Cemetery and positioned in the family plot.

According to my mother, Sam Dodson's favorite wife was Martha Ann George, and each time my grandmother gave birth to a girl, Dodson wanted the child named Martha. One of my mother's sisters was named Martha Ann Hawkins. Ironically, Martha Ann Hawkins despised her grandfather and thought he was a mean old man. My mother, however, said Dodson was good to her. He encouraged his grandchildren to go to school, and if the weather was bad, he took them in his buggy, which was considered fancy for that time. He helped pack their lunches in lard buckets. Sadly, my grandparents did not value education for their children. I often heard my mother wonder aloud if she would ever have been sent to school had it not been for her grandfather, Sam Dodson. My mother admired and valued education and firmly instilled that attitude in her four children.

According to my mother, Sam Dodson had a brother who was a school teacher, but she does not know which brother. My mother remembers Dodson as having jet-black hair, a characteristic of his

Cherokee ancestry, that he had a good education for that time, and had beautiful penmanship, a talent valued by people of that generation.

Sam Dodson did not believe in God and would not allow the Bible to be read in his presence. He had a brother who was a preacher; my mother believes this brother was Seymore Dodson, who migrated to Chelsea, Oklahoma. Dodson did not tolerate prayer in his presence. On one occasion, Ethel and Bruce Smith, Arthur Hawkins's sister and brother-in-law, came to visit. They were saying their bedtime prayers, and Dodson overheard them. According to my mother, Dodson pitched a fit about the guests praying in the house where he lived and ridiculed them for it.

Ironically, Dodson had a large family Bible in which he kept important papers. He referred to it as his "record book" and kept it in a trunk. Unfortunately, that Bible was destroyed in a house fire, taking with it valuable genealogical information about the Dodson family. My mother does not think Dodson ever changed his anti-religion stance.

Martha Murel Forrest Reeme, another great-granddaughter of Dodson, told me in a letter (2009) that Dodson could be cruel to animals. He bragged that he could take a whip and in one stroke could cut the skin on a horse's back.

Sam Dodson and Martha Ann George Dodson had three daughters: Daisy, Lucy, and Omay, all born in Paint Rock, Alabama. My family is directly descended from Omay Dodson Hawkins and Arthur Hawkins.

Arthur Hawkins and Omay Lee Dodson Hawkins

My mother, Louise Hawkins Webb, was born to Arthur Hawkins and Omay Lee Dodson Hawkins in Prescott, Arkansas (Nevada County) on May 12, 1919. Arthur Hawkins had a job in Prescott building railroad tracks. His family was from the Hope, Arkansas, and the Prescott, Arkansas, vicinities.

When she was an infant, her parents relocated to Monticello where they had lived previously. Louise Hawkins and her mother did not go back to Monticello in a horse-drawn wagon with the rest of the family. She and her mother returned on the train. Her parents were afraid the wagon would be too rough and would make her sore. It was one of the few times in her life that she experienced nurturing of any sort from her parents.

Her mother, Omay Dodson Hawkins, was not good to her and was sometimes downright mean. Once during the worst of the Great Depression, Omay Hawkins got some sort of voucher from the government that allowed each child a new article of clothing. She took the voucher for my mother and used it on the other children. Lousie Hawkins was the oldest girl, and her mother told her that the younger ones needed the voucher more than she. Mother says that her father, Arthur Hawkins, was the one who got up with the children at night if they were sick.

From all accounts, Arthur Hawkins was kind to his children, but he did not provide well for his family. He preferred drinking, hunting, and fishing over work. However, he showed good judgment and refused to take his children to public hangings like his neighbors did. He did not want his children to witness such grisly events. According to my mother, public hangings were carried out somewhere around the Gaster Hill community, probably near Gaster Hill Cemetery.

Louise Hawkins was the third of nine children and the oldest girl. She was a child during the Great Depression, denied an education because of economic hardship, and denied a childhood. Each year, she could not enter school until after Christmas when the crops were harvested. She was absent each Thursday and Friday because she had to work at home. She cooked, washed clothes, worked in the fields, and tended the younger children.

She began sleeping with her infant brother, James Monroe Hawkins, when he was three days old; she was twelve years old at the time. She got up with him, fed, and changed him because her mother had a difficult pregnancy and delivery and was ill. I have often heard my mother complain that her mother was always either having a baby, a miscarriage, or recovering from one or the other. Not only did my mother care for her baby brother, James, but she carried out her other chores as well. After she married, her little brothers lived with her and Daddy so she could send them to school. Her siblings were Howard, Sammie, Bea, Martha, James, Otis, Harvey, and Patsy. All are dead from smoking-related illness except Patsy and Mother, neither of whom smoked.

Howard Lee Hawkins made a career of the army. During the Great Depression, he hopped freight trains and was a hobo. I suppose the army was a good career choice for someone from Depression-Era Arkansas who had little education and no job opportunities. He fought in World War II and Korea and decided to retire before he was sent to Vietnam.

Howard Hawkins was badly burned during the Japanese attack on Pearl Harbor, Hawaii, December 7, 1941. His ship was hit and sunk by the Japanese bombers. The oil on the water caught fire, and he was burned each time he came up for air. He was one of only a few survivors. The ranking officer gave Howard the job of making a list of the survivors, and he forgot to include his name on the list. Consequently, his parents received a telegram saying he was killed in the attack on Pearl Harbor. He quickly realized his error and sold his watch to buy a postage stamp, write his family, and tell them he was alive.

Hawkins was in an army hospital in Hot Springs, Arkansas, for several months receiving treatment for his burns. He received skin grafts over parts of his body. My mother said that the family never went to visit him because at that time, a trip to Hot Springs from Monticello was the equivalent of journeying to the moon today.

During his combat duty in World War II, the ship on which Hawkins served picked up several Japanese sailors as prisoners-of-war after their vessel sank. Hawkins took pity on one of the exhausted prisoners and told him to rest in his bunk. That simple act of kindness saved Hawkins's life. A large artillery shell from the enemy whistled through the air and hit squarely in the center of the bunk where the Japanese sailor lay resting. Howard Hawkins did not marry until late in life when he married Raye Robbins. He had no children.

James Hawkins, mother's little brother that she cared for from three days old, joined the army toward the end of World War II. By the time he received his training, the war had ended, but he was sent to Germany as part of the American occupation of Europe. There he met his wife, Ann, a survivor of Hitler's regime. Her family lost everything, and their property was in what became Communist-controlled East Germany.

Ann was pressed into service as part of Hitler's Youth, and did hard, physical labor on German railroads. As a result, she never had a successful pregnancy. She and James had twins who were born dead or died shortly after birth. I have heard Ann tell of how German soldiers terrorized her home; she and the other children would hide under the bed, and the soldiers stuck their bayonets into the mattress to frighten the children. She also said that James often spoke of his sister, Louise. At first she thought Louise was James's mother. Howard, Sammie, Martha, and Harvey are buried in Gaster Hill Cemetery in Monticello. My mother's parents are also buried at Gaster Hill.

My mother did not allow emotional negatives to shape her life. She and Daddy loved us and told us so, something they never experienced from their parents. We were dressed cleanly and neatly, sent to school, and taken to church. We were expected to amount to something, and we did. We are blessed to have such wonderful parents. We may not have had enough money, but we were rich in many ways. As a teenager, I ran with a group of boys and girls in Monticello who had much more materially than my family, and I envied them for that. Several of them have made devastating life choices that money cannot repair. It took me until I was about forty years old to grasp that I was the blessed one all along.

Robert Hawkins and Mary Adams

Arthur Hawkins's father was Robert Hawkins. His mother's name was Mary Adams. The 1880 federal census report for Missouri Township, Nevada County, Arkansas described Robert Hawkins as twenty-six years old, and a farmer married to Mary Hawkins, twenty-four years old. Both were born in Tennessee. Mary Adams's year of birth was 1876.

Robert Hawkins was born September 10, 1853 in Arkansas and died February 20, 1927. John Hawkins, born 1821 in Mississippi, and Susan Hunter, born 1820 in Tennessee, were the parents of Robert Hawkins. Robert Hawkins settled on eighty acres of government land in southwest Arkansas. Land Records reveal the following information:

Land Records: Alabama, Arkansas, FL, LA, MI, MN, OH, WI, 1790–1907

Document number: 1787 Description number: 1

Number of acres: 80.0000 Accession number: AR1500__.234

Patentee Surname: Hawkins Patentee given name: Robert

State name: Arkansas

Volume: 1500 Page number: 234

Land office: Camden Aliquot part reference: S½SW

Section number: 3

Township: 11 South Range: 22 West

Meridian or special survey area: Fifth Principal Meridian

Misc. document number: 43468

Title transfer authority: Homestead Entry Orig.

Combined signature date: Aug. 30, 1882

Multiple patentees: N Multiple warrantees: N

Signature: Y Canceled document: N Subsurface rights reserved: N

Metes and bounds: N Fractional section: N

At the time of the 1880 census, Robert and Mary Hawkins had two sons: John, two years old, named for Robert's father and born in Arkansas, and Hosea, two months old and born in Arkansas. According to my mother, Louise Hawkins Webb, John Hawkins died as a teenager. My mother's father, Arthur Hawkins, was born in 1891. The following are the children of Robert and Mary Hawkins:

> **John Hawkins, born around 1878/1879; died young, probably in Arkansas**

> **Hosea Hawkins, born May 20, 1881 in Prescott, Nevada County, Arkansas; died 1981 in California or Arizona**

> **Birton B. Hawkins, born November 3, 1887 in Prescott, Nevada County Arkansas; died October 6, 1976 in Chico, Calfornia**

> **Hubert Hawkins, born March 1889 in Arkansas; died November 13, 1968 in Calfornia or Arizona**

Arthur Hawkins, born August 24, 1891 in Arkansas; died of stomach cancer May 1972 in Monticello, Drew County, Arkansas

Carlisle Hawkins, born August 11, 1892 in Arkansas; died May 1973 in Merced, Calfornia

Ethel Rean Hawkins, born February 28, 1894 in Prescott, Nevada County, Arkansas; married Bruce Smith; died March 27, 1983 in Calfornia or Arizona

Robert Hawkins and all his sons except Arthur, my mother's father, pushed westward to acquire government land, first in Arizona and then in California. They became prosperous farmers. Today, their descendants grow almonds around Chico, California.

Arthur Hawkins was married to Omay Lee Dodson by the time of the western migration of his family. Omay did not want to leave her father, Sam Dodson, and move to Arizona, so Arthur did not join his family in the move west. My mother was never around her Hawkins grandparents, so she has little knowledge of them.

John Hawkins and Susan Hunter

The 1880 federal census report for Missouri Township, Nevada County, Arkansas, provides information about John Hawkins and his family. In it, John Hawkins is described as fifty-nine years old, married, and a hotel keeper. Working my way back in time, I came upon more information about the life of John and Susan Hawkins in the 1860 federal census report for Ouachita County, Arkansas. John Hawkins was described in the census data as a farmer, thirty-nine years old, and born in Mississippi. Enumerated in his household were his wife, Susan, thirty-nine years old, and his son, Robert, seven years old.

John Hawkins was born July 8, 1821 in Monroe County, Mississippi, located in the northeast part of the state. The county seat is Columbus, and it borders the Alabama state line. John Hawkins married Susan Hunter, January 16, 1841 in Lowndes County, Mississippi. Lowndes County borders Monroe County to the south.

Robert Hawkins and Elizabeth Hickman

From the 1830 federal census, it can be determined that John Hawkins's parents were Robert Hawkins and Elizabeth Hickman. Robert Hawkins was born in 1795 in Lowndes County, Mississippi. He married Elizabeth Hickman in 1816 in Monroe County, Mississippi. Elizabeth Hickman was born September 12, 1803 in Tennessee. If these dates are correct, Elizabeth Hickman was a thirteen-year-old bride. She died August 3, 1883 in Fayette, Alabama. Her parents were John Hickman, born July 19, 1835 in Monroe, Mississippi. Her mother was Polly (Unknown), born June 18, 1837.

Robert Hawkins died at about forty years old on October 7, 1835. The federal census data for Lowndes County, Mississippi give us insight into the life of Elizabeth Hickman Hawkins after the death of her husband, Robert Hawkins. This census enumerated Elizabeth Hawkins as the head of her household consisting of five females older than sixteen, one female younger than sixteen, and two male slaves. She owned one acre of cultivated land. She was listed on the 1837 tax list for Lowndes County, Mississippi. Apparently her son, John Hawkins, about sixteen years old in 1837 had already set out on his own. Elizabeth Hawkins and her house full of daughters probably had a difficult life and had to produce most of their food. Elizabeth Hawkins died in 1883 at about sixty-seven years old.

The naming tradition is evident in the Hawkins generations with a "Robert, John, Robert, John" pattern. John Hawkins named his oldest son Robert and his oldest daughter Elizabeth after his parents, Robert Hawkins and Elizabeth Hickman. Recall from an earlier chapter in this narrative that Fischer (1989) identified the Hawkinses and Alexanders as two of the leading Southern backcountry clans, and Tennessee was definitely considered the backcountry.

My grandfather, Arthur Hawkins, told the story that his grandfather or great-grandfather had arrived in America as a child on a ship that had sailed from Holland. The boy arrived in America alone and with no recollection of how he got on board the ship. Undoubtedly, he had experienced some horrific event. I searched the passenger lists of ships entering this country during that time, but, so far, have uncovered nothing. He was probably a stowaway. I do not know if this ancestor was on the paternal or maternal side of the family of Arthur Hawkins, but I have learned that the surname Hawkins is Dutch in origin. I wish I knew more about the little Dutch boy. I am sure it would be a great story.

Chapter 18
Concluding Remarks

Judy Carol Webb Hubbell and Billy James Hubbell

I, Judy Carol Webb Hubbell, was born May 23, 1954 at the old Drew Memorial Hospital in Monticello, Arkansas. My father was Lewis French Webb, and my mother is Louise Hawkins Webb. Dr. Lewis Hyatt delivered me. We lived on the old home place in the Green Hill community of Drew County, Arkansas until 1957 when we moved closer to Monticello.

I married Billy James Hubbell, a native of Grady, Lincoln County, Arkansas, on February 21, 1981 at the Rose Hill Cumberland Presbyterian Church in Drew County, Arkansas. Reverend Dale Gentry, a beloved minister in south Arkansas, officiated at the nuptials.

I went to McGehee (Desha County) as a bride in 1981. We lived there where Billy practiced law for three years and then relocated to Crossett in Ashley County, Arkansas. Billy and I have one son, William Griffin Hubbell, named for his great-great-grandfather, William Griffin. We call him Griffin.

I was educated in the Monticello public schools and received a college degree in English with a minor in history from the University of Arkansas at Monticello in May 1974. I earned a master's degree in 1976 and a doctoral degree in 2004 from the University of Louisiana at Monroe. Billy and I own forty acres of land on Long Prairie (Midway Route) in Drew County where we plan to build a home someday. Billy Hubbell is an Arkansas district court judge and a practicing attorney. Our son, Griffin Hubbell, is currently serving in the United States Army. He is stationed in Germany and has completed a tour of duty in Afghanistan. He was injured in Afghanistan; both ear drums were perforated from the loud artillery.

Looking Back

I was three years old when we moved from Green Hill, but my earliest memories are of the old home place where I can remember my parents raising cotton. I recall that Daddy iced down a number three wash tub full of Cokes for the field hands to have each day at lunch. I can remember being pulled along on a cotton sack in the field.

I vividly remember going with Daddy to the cotton gin on one occasion. The gin used a big vacuum device to suck the cotton out of the cotton trailer. Daddy's cap got knocked off and was sucked into the vacuum along with the cotton. As many of you will remember, Daddy always wore overalls and a cap. I remember Daddy and I had a good laugh about the cap. With the advent of mechanized farming, he stopped raising cotton. The equipment was too expensive for small farmers to purchase and make a profit.

Most of my memories of living in Green Hill are sketchy. I can remember going to Soap Chatman's store with my parents and my siblings, and buying "short" Cokes, the 6-½ oz. bottles that came in a twelve pack, and, yes, short Cokes taste best.

I also remember Mr. Hogue's grocery truck. My cousins, Sue and Lou Webb, and my sister, Jo Ann, and I often got to buy candy from Mr. Hogue. He allowed my brothers to swap eggs for candy. "Rolling grocery stores" were common in rural Arkansas at that time. I remember seeing a bobcat run across the road in front of the house. I remember following my mother about the place while she did chores. I remember her wearing blue jeans cuffed up to the length we currently refer to as "capri pants." I remember my cat finding an entire family of mice in an empty canning jar stored in the barn. I have no idea why I remember these things.

It was interesting, as a three-year-old, to watch my mother kill chickens. Killing and cleaning chickens is an experience that will turn one into a vegetarian. Mother wrung their necks, and they flopped around until they were dead. She put them in a tub of scalding water to remove the feathers, and she gutted and cooked them. The odor was awful during the scalding process. I am sure PETA would condemn my mother's chicken-killing techniques.

Our parents took up a lot of time with the four of us. We didn't have a great deal of money, but we were loved. We did not acquire a television until I was about six years old, and we did not have indoor plumbing or have a telephone until I was about seven. We did not have air-conditioning in our home until I was in the tenth grade.

I remember taking walks with my parents and seeing wildlife. Sometimes Daddy burned a brush pile in the pasture in the late evening, and we roasted marshmallows or hot dogs. Of course, there were outings to Ozment's Bluff on the Saline River, a favorite recreational spot for Drew Countians. The water is shallow in the summer, and you can walk across to the sandbar on the other side. The water is clear due to the gravel bottom of the Saline River.

The worst sunburn I ever got was at Ozment's Bluff when I was a teenager. My best friend, Pam Allen (born Dec. 21, 1953 to Curtis Allen and Irene Leonard Allen in Monticello, Arkansas) and I spent the day at the Bluff one Fourth of July. We placed folding lounge chairs midstream and lay in the sun all day without benefit of sunscreen. My fair skin was cooked. Even the part in my red hair was sunburned, but we had a good time.

My mother often made tomato soup and chocolate pudding from scratch, favorite dishes of my cousin, Gene Webb. Daddy's brother, Herman Webb, lived close by, so we four children and Uncle Herman's four children were often together. Mother also made biscuits from scratch for every meal. Her dough tray was a section of a hollowed-out maple log, left to her by my grandmother, Virginia Griffin Webb. I remember a conversation Daddy and I had concerning the age of the dough tray. If memory serves me, Virginia Webb inherited the tray from her mother, Martha Camp Griffin. The tray is over one hundred years old and possibly older. I do not know the date of the marriage of John Webb and Virginia Griffin Webb, but they started having children in the late 1890s. My grandmother probably acquired the tray at the time of her marriage. There is no telling how many dozens of biscuits have been made in that old tray!

Mother gave the maple tray to her grandson and his wife, Danny and Gina Webb of Siloam Springs, Arkansas. They have it on the island in their kitchen and keep fruit in it. It is quite a conversation piece, according to Gina, and a designer has questioned them about it. It is an authentic "primitive" artifact from frontier America and may be valuable; it is certainly valuable from an heirloom perspective. Maple trees, beautiful hardwoods, at one time grew abundantly in Arkansas and were used to make furniture, but they have been eradicated by insects and timber companies whose fortunes lie in pine timber.

Modern Americans often do not realize that frontiersmen made most of their dishes from wood. Plates and bowls were fashioned from circular sections of smaller trees. Spoons and forks were carved from wood; some spoons were fashioned from horn. Drinking mugs and dippers were made from dry gourds. Fine china had no place in the backwoods of the American frontier, and metal was scarce. Door hinges were made of leather, and wooden pins were often used in place of nails. In *History of Western North Carolina* (1914), John Preston Arthur discusses "nailless" houses that were held together with wooden pins.

More Memories

Charlie Taylor lived with us in Green Hill, because there were no nursing homes in Monticello. I am not sure how Charlie came to live with us, but I remember being scared to death of him. Mother tells of one occasion when Charlie got into bad trouble with her. My brother, Don, aggravated Charlie about something, and Charlie grabbed a clothesline pole with the intention of hitting Don. Mother intervened. Charlie did not hit Don or ever cross Mother again.

My grandmother, Virginia Griffin Webb, lived with us at the old home place. I vaguely remember her rocking me beside a window. The window screen had a hole in it. My grandmother dipped snuff and would spit through the hole, which, at three years old, I found fascinating.

No one had air-conditioning at that time. Mother and Daddy sometimes took the beds outside in the hot summer months, and we slept outdoors to escape the stifling heat. I remember that it was a treat to go in the air-conditioned Safeway store in Monticello.

Many of you probably remember Trotter's store on the square. It was in operation until I was in high school—I loved to go in there; it was like stepping back in time. Monticello was segregated until I was in junior high school. The doctors and dentists had segregated waiting rooms and bathrooms. I remember being in the old Van Atkins store with my mother and Aunt Ruby Webb. The water fountains were segregated; the "colored" fountain was lower, so I was going to drink from it. I was scolded by a white lady for using the "colored" fountain.

I started first grade at Wilmar, Arkansas, where my teacher was Mrs. Maxine Jacks. Mrs. Jacks taught first and second grade in the same room. I remember the first day of school when she taught us our first lesson. She marched us single file to the restroom and explained how to use a commode and how to flush it. Many of us, myself included, had never seen such a thing.

We moved to town later that year, and I entered the Monticello public schools. I can well remember the tension of the Cuban Missile Crisis even though I was only in the third grade. Mrs. Jane Garrett was my third grade teacher. That morning, when we always had a prayer, she told us we needed to pray for our country and explained the missile crisis to us. I remember all the adults being tense that day.

Exactly thirteen months later, on November 22, 1963, President John Kennedy was shot dead in Dallas, Texas. I was nine years old and in Mrs. Helen Stuckey's fourth grade class at W. C. Whaley Elementary School in Monticello. She and several other teachers brought a radio into the classroom, and we listened to the news stories. My family and I were glued to the television for the next few days. My parents were apprehensive of President Kennedy because he was a Catholic; this troubled many Americans at the time. I vividly remember the assassinations of Robert F. Kennedy and Martin Luther King, Jr.

I remember the first "moon walk" when I was a ninth grader at Monticello High School. I also remember being in Mrs. Pat Groce's physical education class where we learned what to do in case of a nuclear attack; it was a grim lesson.

Many of us will recall Bee Dee's, a popular drive-in restaurant located on the corner of Gaines and Hyatt Streets in Monticello. The business was owned by the Gladden family, and used carhops to serve their customers. They had wonderful burgers topped with Velvetta cheese.

When I was in the eleventh grade, I witnessed another Monticello restaurant owner refuse to seat a group of blacks. That same year, the Monticello public schools became completely integrated. We had a race riot in the spring of that year, resulting in injuries for several students. School closed for a couple of days; upon our return, we had to go straight to class, students could not bring fingernail files or any sharp objects that could be used as a weapon. It created a dismal atmosphere and brought me to a major decision. I had enough credits to start to college at the end of the eleventh grade, and that is what I did. It seems that going to school is what I do best.

Of course, the Vietnam War defined my generation. During this era, Daddy dug graves for the local funeral home to earn extra money. I remember his bringing home some scrap lumber from a wooden crate containing the coffin of a Drew County man killed in combat in Vietnam. His name, rank, and serial number were stenciled on the wood. That made an impression on me for some reason, I suppose because this young man died needlessly in an unpopular war, and the wooden crate he was shipped home in was used to build a chicken coop.

Each night, the national news gave a body count of American soldiers killed in Vietnam. I remember my parents being sick with worry that my brothers would have to go to Vietnam. Neither had to go, for which we were all thankful; however, Don served on active duty in the Army during the Vietnam era. Ray was never called.

In many ways, I have lived a normal, small-town life, but I have witnessed a great deal of history. It is a different world today than the one found by Hans Michael Gebert when he first arrived in Philadelphia. The terrorist attack of September 11, 2001 is the most shocking thing I have witnessed via television. It was a beautiful, clear, late summer day. I recall feeling grateful that I lived in a small town in southeast Arkansas. It seemed unbelievable that such an event had occurred.

I have seen Arkansas Governor Bill Clinton elected to two terms as President of the United States. I am an unapologetic fan of Bill and Hillary Clinton, a member of the Democratic National Committee, a self-described "Yellow Dog Democrat," and I couldn't care less about Monica Lewinsky.

I have witnessed a milestone in our nation's history when Barrack Obama was elected President of the United States, and re-elected to a second term, making him the first African-American president. I supported Hillary Clinton in the Democratic primary and was bitterly disappointed when she failed to win the nomination, but I am pleased that President O'bama appointed her to the office of Secretary of State.

I have watched a war being played out on television. When the Iraqis invaded our ally, Kuwait, in 1991, television stations filmed the American bombing attacks. It was truly amazing to see a war on live television.

I have seen medical knowledge increase by leaps and bounds, and I have watched the sun set on the twentieth century while eating in a restaurant in Monroe, Louisiana. My life has spanned two centuries.

Rebels to the Core

Our family came to this country in much the same manner as many other American families. We were fleeing religious and political persecution in Europe and looking for a better way of life. We followed the usual migration patterns, moving westward as the frontier moved westward. We were some of the first white people to arrive in the wilderness that would become the Arkansas Territory.

We represent contradictions. Our ancestors owned slaves in the antebellum South and fought for the Confederacy, but at the same time, one of our ancestors showed great compassion toward a freed slave who needed help. We are guilty of helping build this nation from land taken away from the Native Americans, but we also married into the Native American tribes.

We are rebels to the core. We broke from the Roman Catholic Church, which at the time was risky business, and we clung to our religious beliefs even when such beliefs were outlawed. Some of us totally rebelled against religion. We rebelled against Great Britain and fought and won the American Revolutionary War. At least one of us rebelled against rebellion and fought on the side of the British. We fought the British again in the War of 1812, and we prevailed.

We pushed westward to avoid the tax collector. We rebelled against the federal government and joined the Confederacy. We endured hardship and punishment during Radical Reconstruction in the South, and survived. We have picked a lot of cotton. We traveled in horse-drawn wagons to carve out homes on government land. Somehow, we managed to get those horses and wagons across the Mississippi River—I marvel at that each time I drive across the Greenville, Mississippi River Bridge.

We survived the Great Depression by hard work and sheer perseverance. We showed up for World War II and helped save the world. We survived great personal loss, an example of which is the mute testament of the six "baby graves" at Union Ridge Cemetery.

We are made of "tough stuff." I am reminded of a line from a Hank Williams, Jr. song: "country boys (and country girls) can survive." We are survivors—that is our legacy. We have the "gift of bravery"—geb hard(t). That is how we became who we are, and what a journey it has been!

References

A Brief History of Jamestown, Virginia. (n. d.). Accessed March 5, 2010, at http://www.tobacco.org/History/Jamestown.html.

A Flawed History of American Tax Revolts. (n. d.). Tax History Project. Accessed January 9, 2009, at http://www.taxhistory.org/thp/readings.nsf?ArtWeb/76A0C2C03BC180B885256E430079327E?OpenDocument

A Little History of Tennessee. (n. d.). Accessed January 17, 2009, at http://homepages.rootsweb.ancestry.com/~bridgett/tennhist.htm

A Nation Divided: The U. S. Civil War 1861–1865. (1997). Accessed August 30, 2010, at http://www.historyplace.com/civilwar/.

Adair, R. (1995). *An Account of the Harbour, Radford, and Watters Families of E. T. Harbour, and the History of the 8th Alabama Volunteer Infantry.* Baton Rouge, LA: privately published.

Advance Monticellonian. (1892). Editorial comments, October 4.

Advance Monticellonian. (1892). News article, October 5.

Advance Monticellonian. (1894). Vol. 5: 3.

Alagna, M. (2003). *The Great Fire of London of 1666.* New York: Rosen Publishing Group.

Alderman, P. (1986). *The Overmountain Men.* Johnson City, TN: Overmountain Press.

Allen, V. (1984). *Five Family Reunion.* Unpublished research.

Alexanders Descending from James and Mary Peden Alexander. (n. d.). Alexander Board. Accessed September 9, 2007, at http://boards.rootsweb.com/surnames.alexander/4184.1.1.1.1.1.1.1.1/mb.ashx.

Alexander Genealogy. (n. d.). Accessed January 26, 2009, at http://wc.rootsweb.ancestry.com/cgi-bin/igm./cgi?op=GET&db=alexander1&id=116430.

Alexander Genealogy Chart: 40 Generations, ca. 675 to ca. 1783. (n. d.). Accessed February 18, 2007, at http://freepages.genealogy.rootsweb.com/~sassytazzy/family/surnames/alexander/docs/alexanderchart40gensogrl.html.

Alexander, J. B. (1897). *Biographical Sketches of the Early Settlers of the Hopewell Section and Reminiscences of the Pioneers and their Descendants by Families with Some Historical Facts and Incidents of the Times in Which They Lived.* Charlotte, NC: Observer Printing and Publishing House.

Alexander, J. B. (1902). *The History of Mecklenburg County from 1740–1900.* Charlotte, NC: Privately published.

Alexander, J. B. (1908). *Reminiscences of the Past Sixty Years.* Privately published.

Alexander-Name Meaning & Origin. (n. d.). Accessed January 6, 2009, at http://genealogy.about.com/library/surnames/a/bl_name-ALEXANDER.htm.

American Revolution, the South Carolina Infantry. (n. d.). Accessed July 25, 2011, at http://sciway3.net/proctor/marion/military/revwar/RevWarSC_muster_grenadiers.html

Ancestors of Edward A. Pereira: Fourteenth Generation. Accessed October 3, 2010, at http://freepages.genealogy.rootsweb.ancestry.com/~seamonkey/pafg14.htm#19186.

Ancestors of Jason Richard Cassell: 25 Generations Only. Accessed December 15, 2008, at http://familytreemaker.genealogy.com/users/c/a/s/Margaret-T-Cassell/GENE20-0022.html.

Ancestors of Kevin Dexter Marshall. Accessed October 15, 2007, at http://familytreemaker.genealogy.com/users/m/a/r/Kevin-D-Marshall/GENE7-0021.html.

Ancestors of Kevin Dexter Marshall,Generation No. 6. Accessed October 8, 2007, at http://familytreemaker.genealogy.com/users/m/a/r/Kevin-D-Marshall/GENE7-0008.html.

Ancestors of Kevin Dexter Marshall, Generation No. 7. Accessed January 29, 2007, at http://familytreemaker.genealogy.com/users/m/a/r/Kevin-D-Marshall/GENE7-0010.html.

Ancestors of Richard Landon Miller. Accessed August 30, 2011, at familytreemaker.genealogy.com/users/m/i/l/Cathy-J-Miller/GENE16-0001.html.

Ancestors of Susannah Gabbert. Generation No. 3. Accessed December 2, 2008, at http://130.94.183.233/txt/gabbert.rtf.

Ancestors of Susannah Gabbert. Generation No. 4. Accessed December 2, 2008, at http://130.94.183.233/txt/gabbert.rtf.

Ancestors of Susannah Gabbert. Generation No. 5. Accessed December 2, 2008, at http://130.94.183.233/txt/gabbert.rtf.

Ancestors of Susannah Gabbert. Generation No. 6. Accessed December 2, 2008, at http://130.94.183.233/txt/gabbert.rtf.

Ancestors of Susannah Gabbert, Alex Gabbard. Accessed December 1, 2008, at http://130.94.183.233/txt/gabbert.rtf.

Ancestors of Susannah Gabbert, T. Giancola. Accessed December 1, 2008, at http://130.94.183.233/txt/gabbert.rtf.

Ancestors of William Kirk Kottmeyer Generation No. 15. Accessed June 4, 2007, at http://familytreemaker.genealogy.com/users/k/o/t/William–K-Kottmeyer-jr/GENE1-0021.html

Ancestral Rolls, South Carolina Daughters of the American Revolution. (1938). Compiled by Mrs. E. T. Crawford, State Registrar.

Anderson, J. (n. d.). *Rial Family Genealogy.* Accessed May 29, 2011, at http://www.megjohn.info/genealogy/uncleged/com919.html

Anderson, W. (n. d.). *Notes about Scotch-Irish and German Settlers in Virginia and theCarolinas.* Accessed December 3, 2009, at http://home.earthlink.net/~historycarolina/ScotchIrish.pdf

Andrea, L. (1947). Camp and Kemp manuscript prepared by a professional genealogist, South Carolina.

Arber, E. (ed.). (2006). *Travels and Works of Captain John Smith, President of Virginia and Admiral of New England.* Whitefish, MT: Kessinger Publishing.

Arkansas Confederate Pension Records, Arkansas History Commission, Little Rock, Arkansas, accessed August 31, 2010, at http://www.ark-ives.net/documenting/confed_pensions.asp.

Arkansas Court Clerk's Office Index, Bk C, p. 412.

Arkansas Land Records Little Rock, Document no. 2353, issue date July 28, 1838.

Arkansas Land Records, Champagnolle, Document no. 8594, issue date July 1, 1859.

Arkansas Territory Tax List. (1814).

Auditor General Account Book. (1778-1780). South Carolina Department of Archives and History.

Baird, R. (1985). *Huskey Miscellany 1700–1800s.* Personal correspondence to Jimmy L. Berry.

Bancroft, G. (1842). *History of the United States.* Boston: Charles C. Little & James Brown.

Bancroft, H. (ed.). (n.d.). *The Great Republic by the Master Historians, Vol. II.* Accessed December 20, 2008, at http://www.publicbookshelf.com/public_html/The_Great_Republic_By_the_Master_Historians_Vol_II/northcaro_cb_html.

Bannerman, J. (1977). *The Lordship of the Isles, in Scottish Society in the Fifteenth Century.* J. M. Brown, ed. London: Edward Arnold.

Barbour, P. (1971). *Pocahontas and Her World.* London: Robert Hale Ltd.

Barbour, P., ed. (1986). *Travels and Works of Captain John Smith, President of Virginia and Admiral of New England, 1580–1631, Vol. 1.* Chapel Hill, NC: University of North Carolina Press.

Battle of Cowpens. (n. d.). Accessed August 1, 2010, at http://www.statemaster.com/encyclopedia/Battle-of-Cowpens.

Battle of Vicksburg. (n. d.). New World Encyclopedia. Accessed April 19, 2010, at http://www.newworldencyclopedia.org/entry/Battle_of_Vicksburg

Beech Branch Baptist Church Records. (n. d.). Accessed August 30, 2010, at http://www.usgennet.org/ga/state1/burke/sardis.htm.

Berkeley, W. (1914). *A Discourse and View of Virginia.* Norwalk, CT: William H. Smith, Jr.

Bishop, D. (1999). *Descendants of Bartholomew Stovall (1665–1722).* Laurel, MS: Stovall Family Association.

Billings, W. (1975). *The Old Dominion in the Seventeenth Century.* Chapel Hill, NC: UNC Press.

Boddie, J. (1974). *Colonial Surry.* Toronto: General Publishing Co.

Bodnar, J. (1973). *The Ethnic Experience in Pennsylvania.* Lewisburg, PA: Bucknell University Press.

Boettner, L. (n. d.). *Calvinism in History: Calvinism in America.* Accessed January 13, 2009, at http://www.graceonlinelibrary.org/etc/printer-friendly.asp?ID=868.

Bogan, D. (2004). *Political History of Tennessee Began in 1772 with Adoption of "Written Articles of Association."* Accessed February 18, 2012, at http://www.tngenweb.org/campbell/hist-bogan. Campbell County, Tennessee Genweb.

Boit, R. (n. d.). *Chronicles of the Boit Family and Their Descendants and Other Allied Families.*

Bolton, S. (n. d.). *Louisiana Purchase through Early Statehood, 1803–1860.* Accessed July 13, 2009, at http://www.encyclopediaofarkansas.net/encyclopedia/entry-detail.aspx?search=1&entryID=398.

Boyd, W. K. (1929). *William Byrd's History of the Dividing Line.* Raleigh, NC.

Boyer, C. (2009). *Ship Passenger Lists, the South (1538–1825).* Westminster, MD: Heritage Books.

Bradley, H. (1918). *The Enclosures in England: An Economic Reconstruction.* Ontario, Canada: Batoche Books.

Bradley, S., Brunswick County, Virginia Deed Books Volume 5, 1770-1775 FHL# 975.5575 R2bs Document #11.

Breed, W. P. (1876). *Presbyterians and the Revolution.* Philadelphia, PA: Presbyterian Board of Publication.

Brice, D. (1987). *The Great Comanche Raid: Boldest Indian Attack on the Texas Republic.* Weldon, NC: McGowan Book Company.

Brightwell, L. (2008). *Individual Record Robert Hawkins.* FamilySearch Pedigree Resource File.

Brobst, W. (n. d.). *The History of the German Immigration to America in The BrobstChronicles: A history of the early Brobst/Probst families in Pennsylvania. Kitty Hawk, North Carolina: Brobst Family Historical Registry.* Accessed October 18, 2007, at http://homepage.rootsweb.com/~brobst/chronicles/chap2.htm.

Brock, R. (1886). Virginia Historical Society. Documents relating to the Huegenot Emigration and the Settlement at Manakin-Town, chiefly unpublished.

Brown, K. (n. d.). *Women in Early Jamestown.* Accessed December 28, 2008, at http://www.virtualjamestown.org/essays/brown_essay.html.

Brown, W. (1847). *Narrative of William W. Brown, an American Slave.* London: Charles Gilpin, Bishopgate-St. Accessed October 23, 2011, at docsouth.unc.edu/fpn/brownw/brown.html.

Brunswick County, Virginia Deed Books 1770-1775 Abstracts. FHL# 975.5575 R2bs Vol. 5.

Brunswick County, Virginia Deed Book 30:243 FHL #30653, Document #7.

Brunswick County, Virginia Will Book Abstracts 6 1795-1804 (Reel 22). FHL# 975.5575 P2br.

Building the New World: The Women of Jamestown Settlement. (n. d.). National Women's History Museum. Accessed December 28, 2008, at http://nwhm.org/exhibits/jamestownwomen/index.htm.

Bureau of Land Management General Land Office Records, accessed June 5, 2010, http://www.glorecords.blm.gov/.

Burgert, A. K. (1983). *Eighteenth Century Emigrants from German-Speaking Lands to North America.* Publication of the Pennsylvania German Society, 16/19. Birdsboro, PA: The Pennsylvania German Society. Vol. I: The Northern Kraichgau.

Burke County, North Carolina Land Record 901, p. 278.

Burke, J. (1805). *History of Virginia.* 2 vols. Petersburg, VA: Dickson & Pescud.

Burke, J. (1832). *A General and Heraldic Dictionary of the Peerage and Baronetage of the British Empire.* Vol. 2, 5th ed. London: Colburn and Bentley.

Byars Family History. (n. d.). Accessed Nov. 15, 2010, at http://critterranch.freeservers.com/FamHis/byars.htm.

Caldwell County Texas Genweb Project. (2011). Accessed April 8, 2011, at http://www.txgenweb5.org/txcaldwell//index.htm.

Caldwell County Texas Marriage Book B, Vol. 31.

Camp Family Bulletin, Vol. 1(n. 2), August 1924, published by the Camp Association.

Camp Family Bulletin, Vol. 1 (n. 17), August 1932, published by the Camp Association.

Campbell, C. (1860). *History of the Colony and Dominion of Virginia.* Philadelphia: J. B. Lippincott.

Cannon, J., and A. Hargreaves. (2002). *The Kings & Queens of Britain.* London: Oxford University Press.

Canny, N. (2003). *Making Ireland British, 1580–1650.* London: Oxford University Press.

Cappon, L., ed. (1988). The *Adams-Jefferson Letters: The Complete Correspondence Between Thomas Jefferson and Abigail and John Adams.* Chapel Hill, NC: The University of North Carolina Press.

Captain John Smith. (n. d.). Accessed March 9, 2010, at http://www. preservationvirginia.org/rediscovery/page.php?page_id=25.

Captain John Smith and the Virginia Company (2010). Accessed March 9, 2010, at http://www.smithtrail.net/pdf/Hist_Narr_ SmithVaCo.pdf.

Carlson, M. (n. d.). *Witches and Witch Trials in England, the Channel Islands, Ireland, and Scotland.* Accessed January 5, 2009, at http://www. personal.utulsa.edu/~marc-carlson/witchtrials/eis.html.

Carpenter, D. (2001). *Huskey Family History.* A Family History Report Prepared for Jimmy Berry by D. Jane Carpenter, MLS, Professional Genealogist, Heritage Consulting and Services, Salt Lake, City, Utah.

Carpenter, D. (2002). *Huskey & Allied Families.* A Family History Report Prepared for Jimmy Berry by D. Jane Carpenter, MLS, Professional Genealogist, Heritage Consulting and Services, Salt Lake City, UT.

Carpenter and Garrett Family. (2002). Index of Individuals. Thomas Campe (b. abt. 1633, d. date unknown)," accessed December 28, 2008, at http://familytreemaker.genealogy.com/users/ c/a/r/Misty-Autumn-Carpenter/WEBSITE-0001/UHP-0808.html.

Carpenter and Garrett Family. (2002). Index of Individuals. Thomas Camp (b. 1661, d. 1711). Accessed December 28, 2008, at http://familytreemaker.genealogy.com/users/c/a/r/Misty-Autumn-Carpenter/WEBSITE-0001/UHP-0377.html.

Cecil (Cecilius) Calvert, Second Lord Baltimore (1605—1675). Accessed January 8, 2009, at http://mdroots.thinkport.org/library/cecilcalvert.asp.

Celebrating the Mecklenburg Declaration of Independence: A Look at the History of a Most Controversial Document. (n. d.). Accessed January 9, 2009, at http://www.cmstory.net/meckdec/main.htm.

Certificate of Death: State of Arkansas. (1932). William M. Webb.

Chamberlayne, C. (n. d.). *St. Peter's Church, St. Peter's Parish, New Kent County, Virginia.* Accessed October 4, 2010, at http://genealogytrails.com/vir/newkent/church_stpeterschurch.html

Charles, Prince of Wales. (n. d.). Britannica Concise Encyclopedia. Accessed February 5, 2009, at http://www.answers.com/topic/charles-prince-of-wales.

Chronicles of the Scotch-Irish Settlement in Virginia, Vol. I pp. 525-526. Baltimore, MD: Genealogical Publishing Company, L. Chalkley, accessed December 8, 2008, at http://www.rootsweb.ancestry.com/~chalkley.

Chapman, S. (1939). *A History of Chapman and Alexander Families.* Berryville, VA: Virginia Book Company.

Charter Members of the Wolf Creek United Baptist Church. (n. d.). Accessed December 22, 2008, at http://homepages.rootweb.com/~sabthomp/TNWolf1821.htm.

Chartulary of Cambuskenneth Abbey, p. 86.

Childress/Mathis Family Tree (2008). Accessed August 15, 2007, at http://worldconnect.genealogy.rootsweb.com/cgi-bin/igm.cgi?op=GET&db=patchildress&id=10089.

Church of Jesus Christ of Latter-day Saints, "Family Group Record: Elias Alexander and Nancy Agnes McCall," accessed June 14, 2010, at http://www.familysearch.org/eng/search/frameset_search.asp?PAGE=/eng/search/ancestorsearchresults.asp.

Church of Jesus Christ of Latter-day Saints, "Family Group Record: James McCall and Janet Harris," accessed June 16, 2010, at http://www.familysearch.org/eng/search/frameset_search.asp?PAGE=/eng/search/ancestorsearchresults.asp.

Church of Jesus Christ of Latter-day Saints, "Family Group Record: John Byars and Elizabeth Glen," accessed November 16, 2010, at http://www.familysearch.org/eng/search/frameset_search.asp?PAGE=/eng/search/ancestorsearchresults.asp.

Church of Jesus Christ of Latter-day Saints, "Family Group Record: John C. Dodson and Lydia Burks," accessed September 20, 2009, at http://www.familysearch.org/eng/search/ancestorsearchresults.asp.

Church of Jesus Christ of Latter-day Saints, "Family Group Record: John Webb and Sarah Cocke," accessed October 3, 2010, at http://www.familysearch.org/eng/search/ancestorsearchresults.asp.

Church of Jesus Christ of Latter-day Saints, "Family Group Record: Pleasant Riley Dodson and Margaret Addaline King," accessed April 16, 2010, at http://www.familysearch.org/search/frameset_search.asp?n99=John.

Church of Jesus Christ of Latter-day Saints, "Family Group Record: Johann Michael Gebert and Agnes Maria Boger," accessed October 15, 2007, at http://www.familysearch.org/Eng/search/AF/family_group_record.asp?familyid=609923.

Church of Jesus Christ of Latter-day Saints, "Family Group Record: Mathaus Gebhard and Margaretha Mueller," accessed December 1, 2008, at http://www.familysearch.org/default.asp.

Church of Jesus Christ of Latter-day Saints, "Family Group Record: Petrus "Peter" Gebhard "Gebert," accessed October 15, 2007, at http://www.familysearch.org/Eng/search?AFk/family_group.asp?familyid=609923.

Church of Jesus Christ of Latter-day Saints, "Family Group Record: Stephen Camp and Anne Alexander," accessed January 7, 2009, at http:www.familysearch.org/eng/default.asp.

Church of Jesus Christ of Latter-day Saints, "Family Group Record: Thomas Marshall and Mary Fitzgerald," accessed June 4, 2007, at http://www.familysearch.org/eng/default.asp.

Church of Jesus Christ of Latter-day Saints, "Family Group Record: John Marshall and Jane McCarthy," accessed January 6, 2009, at http://www.familysearch.org/eng/default.asp.

Church of Jesus Christ of Latter-day Saints, "Family Group Record: Nicholas Marshall," accessed June 4, 2007, at http://www.familysearch.org/eng/default.asp.

Church of Jesus Christ of Latter-day Saints, "Family Group Record: Sam Dodson," accessed April 20, 2010, at http://www.familysearch.org/eng/search/frameset_search.asp?PAGE=/eng/search/ancestorsearch.results.asp.

Church of Jesus Christ of Latter-day Saints, Family Group Record: Thomas Marshall, accessed January 6, 2009, at http://www.familysearch.org/eng/default.asp.

Church of Jesus Christ of Latter-day Saints, Family Group Record: Michael Gebert Gabhart and Catherine Grindstaff, accessed January 29, 2007, at http://www.familysearch.org/default.asp.

Churches of Christ. (n. d.). The Concise Oxford Dictionary of World Religions. Accessed December 28, 2008, at http://www.encyclopedia.com/doc/1O1O1-ChurchesofChrist.html.

Civil War 1625-1649, Irish Plantations. (n. d.). Accessed January 29, 2009, at http://www.open2.net/civilwar/irishplantations.html.

Civil War Soldiers and Sailors System, National Park Service. (n. d.). Accessed August 25, 2010, at http://www.itd.nps.gov/cwss/soldiers.cfm.

Clemens, W. (1914). *Alexander Family Records: An Account of the First American Settlers and Colonial Families of the Name Alexander, and Other Genealogical and Historical Data, Mostly New and Original Material, Including Early Wills and Marriages Heretofore Unpublished.* New York: W. M. Clemens.

Cleveland County, Arkansas Marriage Records (1873-1880), Book A-1, accessed October 9, 2011, at http://files.usgwarchives.org/ar/cleveland/vitals/marriage/earlybrides.txt.

Coffey, R. (n. d.). *Genealogical Notes on Ezra Alexander.* Accessed January 11, 2009, at http://freepages.family.rootsweb.ancestry.com/~josephkennedy/genealogical_notes_ezra_alexander.htm.

Coldham, P. (1990). *Child Apprentices in America from Christ's Hospital, London, 1617–1778.* Baltimore, MD: Genealogical Publishing Company.

Coldham, P. (2009). *The Complete Book of Emigrants 1607–1660.* Baltimore, MD: Genealogical Publishing Company.

Collins, B. (1967). *Penguin Dictionary of Surnames.* Baltimore, MD: Penguin Books.

Colonial Records of Virginia. (1874). Lists of the Living & Dead in Virginia, February 16, 1623. Richmond, VA: public printing. pp. 37-66. p. 55.

Columbia Electronic Encyclopedia, (n. d.). Accessed October 15, 2009, at http://www.infoplease.com/ce6/us/A0856532.html.

Commonwealth-Subjugation of Ireland and Scotland (n. d.). American Encyclopedia. Accessed January 8, 2009, at http://encyclo-paedic.net/american-encyclopedia/the-commonwealth-subju-gation-of-ireland-and-scotland.html.

Congress of the United States, 109th Congress, First Session, H. Con. Res. 148, accessed January 11, 2009, at http://bulk.resource.org/gpo.gov/bills/109/hc148ih.txt.pdf.

Connor, S. (2006). *The Peters Colony of Texas: A History and Biographical Sketches of the Early Settlers.* Denton, TX: Texas State Historical Association.

Cooke, J. (n. d.). *Old St. Peter's Church.* Appleton's Journal. Vol. XII, No. 297. Accessed October 3, 2010, at http://vagenweb.org/newkent/appleto1.txt.

Copinger, W. (1904). *County of Suffolk.* Vol. 3, p. 385. London: Henry Sotheran.

Crawley, R. (n. d.). *James McCall, Sr. and sons in the American Revolution* accessed June 16, 2010, at http://www.schistory.net/3CLD/Articles/mccall%20family.html.

Crawley, R. (n. d.). *Military Exploits of James McCall.* Accessed August 1, 2010, at http://www.schistory.net/3CLD/Articles/exploits.html.

Cridlin, W. (1922). *A History of Colonial Virginia: The First Permanent Colony in America.* Richmond, VA: Williams Printing Company.

Culp Notes (2001). Alexander Genealogy. Accessed January 29, 2009, at http://wc.rootsweb.ancestry.com/cgi-bin/igm.cgi?op=GET&db=alexander1&id=18944.

Cumberland County, KY Archives, Church Records Index. Clear Fork United Baptist Church, April (1821) Minutes, accessed December 26, 2008, at http://www.usgwarchives.org/ky/cumberland/churches.html.

Cumberland Presbyterian. (Nov. 30, 1893). p. 319.

Cumberland Presbyterian. (Oct. 19, 1939). p. 14.

Cunfer, D. (1987). *The Early Brobst-Probst Family. In The Brobst Chronicles.* Kitty Hawk, NC: Brobst Family Historical Registry.

Daniel Gookin Muster in *Daniel Gookin, 1612–1687.* (1912). Chicago: Privately printed, pp. 47-48.

Daniels, M. (transcribed). (n. d.). *Walton County Marriages,1833.* Accessed July 12, 2011, at http://www.usgennet.org/usa/ga/county/fulton/walton/waltonmarriages.pdf *of London and the Plantation of Ulster,*BBCi History Online accessed July 25, 2010, at http://www.bbc.co.uk/history/war/plantation.

Daughters of the American Revolution Magazine. (1952), pp. 311–315.

David Gabbert and Kate Giles, Ancestors of Kevin Dexter Marshall, Generation No. 6, H. M. Gabbert II. Accessed December 26, 2008, at http://familytreemaker.genealogy.com/users/m/a/r/Kevin-D-Marshall/GENE7.0008.html.

Davis, B. (n. d.). *The Civil War: Strange and Fascinating Facts.* Accessed May 7, 2010, at http://www.civilwarhome.com/casualties.htm.

Davis, B. (n. d.). *Biography of Louisiana Governor William Wright Heard, Native of Shiloh, Union Parish Louisiana.* Accessed July 26, 2011, at http://files.usgwarchives.org/la/union/bios/heard-ww.txt

DeArmond, R. (1980). *Old Times Not Forgotten: A History of Drew County.* Little Rock, AR: Rose Publishing.

Delfino, S., Gillespie, M. & Kyriakoudes, L. (2011). *Southern Society and its Transformations, 1790–1860.* Columbia, MS and London: University of Missouri Press.

Descendants Chart. (n. d.). Accessed January 31, 2011, at home.earthlink.net/~kmcgee03/dtadsyr.html#top.

Descendants of James Alexander. (n. d.). Accessed January 8, 2009, at http://familytreemaker.genealogy.com/users/p/a/r/L-Parker/GENE2-0001.html.

Descendants of John Dods. (n. d.). Accessed October 10, 2009, at http://familytreemaker.genealogy.com/users/b/e/c/Teresa-Beckelheimer-Colorado/GENE1-0001.html.

Descendents of Sir Henry Webb. (n. d.). Accessed September 18, 2010, at http://jimwebb.rootsweb.ancestry.com/webb/pafg01.htm.

Descendents of Sir Henry Webb. (n. d.). Accessed September 13, 2010, at http://www.oocities.com/exira2000/sir_henry_webb5.html?20105.

Descendants of John Webb. Accessed January 31, 2011, at http://familytreemaker.genealogy.com/users/m/a/y/Lyndall-J-Mayes/BOOK-0001/0026-0002.html.

DeSoto County, Mississippi Marriage Records Book 1 (1845-1847). Accessed January 18, 2007, at http://www.rootsweb.com/~msdesoto/vitalrecs/marriages/mar1845-1847.htm.

Didama Townsend. (n. d.). Accessed January 31, 2011, at http://www.windypeak.com/genealogy/individual.php?pid=1475&ged=Family.GED.

Dorman, J., ed. (1987). *Adventures of Purse and Person 1607–1624/5, Vol. 1.* Baltimore: Genealogical Publishing Company.

Drew County, Arkansas Cemetery Records, 3rd ed. (2002). Crossett, Arkansas: Nowlin Printing.

Drew County, Arkansas Deed Book TT, p. 366.

Drew County, Arkansas Marriage Book C: 168 FHL # 986551 Document #6.

Drew County, Arkansas Sale Bills of Personal Estates (1870-1899).

Dickson, D. (1997). *Arctic Ice: The Extrordinary Story of the Great Frost and Forgotten Famine of 1740–41.* Belfast, Ireland: White Row Press.

Dixon, M. (1989). *The Wataugans: First Free and Independent Community on the Continent.* Johnson City: The Overmountain Press.

Dodson, C. (1965). *Ancestors of Robert Dodson and His Descendants.*

Dorman, J., ed. (1987). *Adventures of Purse and Person, Virginia 1607-1624/5, 3rd Ed.* Baltimore: Genealogical Publishing Company.

Dunbar, J. (1981). *The Lordship of the Isles in the Middle Ages in the Highlands.* Inverness, Scotland: Inverness Field Club.

Early Homes in the Colonies. (n. d.). Accessed March 5, 2010, at http://www.scarborough.k12.me.us/wis/teachers/dtewhey/webquest/colonial/early_homes.htm.

Eddis, W. (1792). *Letters from America, Historical and Descriptive: Comprising Occurrences from 1769–1777 Inclusive.* London.

Elias Alexander, Sr. (n. d.). Accessed June 14, 2010, at http://mytree.net/gen/getperson.php?personID=12096&tree=MAST.

Elliot, C. (n. d.). *Leathercoat: The Life History of a Texas Patriot, Contained in Handbook of Texas.* Accessed July 17, 2009, at http://www.tshaonline.org/handbook/online/articles/TT/fth36.html.

Emmison, F., ed. (1982). *Essex Wills (England) Vol. 1, 1558–1565.*

Encyclopedia of Arkansas History and Culture. (n. d.). Accessed July 13, 2009, at http://www.encyclopediaofarkansas.net/.

English Camp/Kempe Ancestors. Accessed February 15, 2007, at http://www.next1000.com/family/EC/camp.english.html.

Eochaid the Venomous of Dalriada. (n. d.). Accessed January 8, 2009, at http://www.geocities.com/mcnaughtonofdunderave/eochaid_the_venomous_of_dalriada.htm.

Ervin, S. (1971). *South Carolinians in the Revolution: With Service Records and Miscellaneous Data, Also Abstracts of Wills, Laurens County (Ninety-six District) 1755–1855.* Baltimore. MD: Genealogical Publishing Company.

Estes, R. (n. d.). *The Story of Roanoke, Sir Walter Raleigh's Lost Colony.* Accessed July 31, 2011, at http://www.rootsweb.ancestry.com/~molcgdrg/faqslcstory.htm.

European Colonization of the Americas. (n. d.). New World Encyclopedia. Accessed April 16, 2010, at http://www.newworldencyclopedia.org/entry/European_Colonization_of_the_ Americas.

Explorers, Pioneers, and Frontiersmen, Jamestown, 1609-10. (n. d.). Accessed March 9, 2010, at http://www.u-s-history.com/pages/h533.html.

Eyewitness to History, Aboard the Mayflower, 1620. (n. d.). Accessed December 28, 2008, at http://www.eyewitnesstohistory.com/mayflower.htm

Falley, M. (1981). Irish and Scotch-Irish Ancestral Research, Vol. I, Repositories and Records. Baltimore, MD: Genealogical Publishing, Inc.

Family History of Giles Kelly. (n. d.). Accessed December 27, 2002, at http://genforum.genealogy.com/cgi-bin/print.cgi?HUSKEY::191.html.

Fausz, J. (1978). *The Barbarous Massacre"Reconsidered: The Powhatan Uprising of 1622 and the Historians.* Explorations in Ethnic Studies I.

Fausz, J. (1979). *George Thorpe, Nemattanew, and Powhatan Uprising of 1622.Virginia Cavalcade 28.*

Federal Census. 1790. Rutherford County, North Carolina.

Federal Census. 1800. Rutherford County, North Carolina.

Federal Census. 1810. Brunswick County, Meherrin District, Virginia.

Federal Census. 1850. Desoto County, Mississippi.

Federal Census. 1850. Marion County, Tennessee.

Federal Census. 1860. Davidson County, Tennessee.

Federal Census. 1870. Bartholomew Township, Drew County Arkansas.

Federal Census. 1870. Veasey Township, Drew County, Arkansas.

Federal Census. 1850. Jackson County, Alabama.

Federal Census. 1860. of Kemper County, Mississippi.

Federal Census. 1860. Mecklenburg County, North Carolina.

Federal Census 1870, Drew County, Arkansas. Veasey Township. Accessed April 7, 2005, at http://www.rootsweb.com/~ardrew/1870vea.html.

Federal Census 1850. Desoto County, Mississippi Northern Division. Accessed December 27, 2008, at http://ftp.us-census.org/pub/usgenweb/census/ms/desoto/1850/pg0401a.txt.

Federal Census. 1840. Shelby County, Tennessee.

Federal Census. 1850. Victoria County, Texas.

Federal Census. 1870. Yell County, Arkansas

Federal Census of the United States. 1790.

First Church of the First First-Lady. (n. d.). Accessed October 3, 2010, at http://www.oocities.com/stpeterstc/sphist.html.

First Generation of the Joseph Alexander Line in America to Grace Williams Alexander. (n. d.). Accessed January 8, 2009, at http://freepages.genealogy.rootsweb.ancestry.com/~sassytazzy/family/surnames/alexander/docs/alexjoseph1.html.

Fischer, D. (1989). *Albion's Seed: Four British Folkways in America.* New York and London: Oxford University Press.

Foote, S. (1974). *The Civil War, A Narrative: Fredericksburg to Meridian.* New York: Random House.

Foote, W. (1846). *Sketches of North Carolina, Historical and Biographical, Illustrative of the Principles of a Portion of her Early Settlers.* New York: Craighead's Power Press.

Ford, H. J. (1915). *The Scotch-Irish in America.* Princeton: Princeton University Press.

Frazier, H. (2009). *Slavery and Crime in Missouri, 1773–1865.* Jefferson, NC: McFarland Publishing.

Free Dictionary. (n. d.). Accessed April 8, 2011, at http://acronyms.thefreedictionary.com/VDM.

Gabbert-Giancola Family Tree Pages: Information about Petrus Gebhard, accessed, at http://familytreemaker.genealogy.com/users/g/i/a/Tammy-L-Giancola/WEBSITE-0001/U.

Gabbert, H. (n. d.). *Notes for Michael Gabbert, Ancestors of Kevin Dexter Marshall, Generation No. 7.* Accessed January 29, 2007, at http://familytreemaker.genealogy.com/users/m/a/r/Kevin-D-Marshall/GENE7-0010.html.

Gabbert, J. (n. d.). Electronic mail response to query, accessed, http://www.familytreemaker.genealogy.com/users/g/i/a/Tammy-L-Giancola/WEBSITE-0001/U.

Gallagher, G. (1997). *The Confederate War.* Boston: Harvard University Press.

Ganis, J. (n. d.). *Hamilton-Griffin Cemetery, Union County, North Carolina.* Accessed July 4, 2009, at http://freepages.genealogy.rootsweb.ancestry.com/~jganis/unionco/HamiltonCemetery.htm.

Gard's Grassroots Genealogy: James Webb's Bio. (n. d.). Accessed January 31, 2011, at http://home.pacbell.net/gardm/jameswebbbio.html.

Gard's Grassroots Genealogy: Webb Family. (n. d.). Accessed January 31, 2011, at http://home.pacbell.net/gardm/webb.htm.

Garman, G. (n. d.). *The Poor Palatines.* (n. d.). Accessed February 7, 2007, at http://www.sunnetworks.net/-ggarman/palatine.html.

Gary, K. (1954). *Freedom's Shrine Fading into Time, The Charlotte Observer,* May 17, 1954.

Genealogy of Mecklenburg County North Carolina. (n. d.). Accessed January 9, 2009, at http://www.usgennet.org/usa/nc/county/mecklenburg/.

Georgia Land Lotteries. (n. d.). Accessed December 26, 2008, at http://www.lineages.com/InfoCenter/Records/georgialand.cfm.

Georgia Land Lottery Act (1821). Accessed December 26, 2008, at http://georgiainfo.usg.edu/1821act-1.htm.

Gerdes, E. (n. d.). *Company B Hardy's Arkansas Infantry Regiment Confederate States of America.* Accessed August 26, 2010, at http://www.couchgenweb.com/civilwar/hardycob.html.

Gerdes, E. (n. d.). *First Arkansas Infantry, CSA: Company -I-Monticello Guards.* Accessed September 2, 2010, at http://www.couchgenweb.com/civilwar/1infcoi.html.

Gerdes, E. (n. d.). *First Arkansas Mounted Confederate Rifles Company A "Chicot Rangers," Chicot County.* Accessed August 26, 2010, at http://www.couchgenweb.com/civilwar/1stmtcoa.htm.

Gerdes, E. (n. d.). *Nineth Regiment Arkansas Infantry.* Accessed August 30, 2010, at http://www.couchgenweb.com/civilwar/9thinf_hist.html.

Gerena, C. (n. d.). *Germany: Historical Setting, the Peace of Westphalia.* Accessed October 15, 2007, at http://historymedren.about.com/library/text/bltxtgermany16.htm.

Gerson, M. (n. d.). *Norman's Conquest.* Policy Review, 74(3). Accessed January 5, 2009, at http://www.hoover.org/publications/policyreview/3564402.html.

Gilliam, B. (2012). Personal communication to Judy Hubbell via electronic mail, February 12.

Gleach, F. (1997). *Powhatan's World and Colonial Virginia: A Conflict of Cultures.* Norman, OK: University of Oklahoma Press.

Golden, R. (n. d.). *About North Georgia. The Battle of Allatoona Pass.* Accessed April 19, 2010, at http://ngeorgia.com/history/allapass.html.

Goodspeed's History of Hamilton, Knox, and Shelby Counties of Tennessee. (1974). Goodspeed Publishing Company.

Graham, G. (1905). *The Mecklenburg Declaration of Independence May 20, 1775 and Lives of Its Signers.* New York and Washington: The Neale Publishing Company.

Graham, R. (n. d.). *The Carved Stones of Islay-Part III History.* Accessed February 2, 2009 from http://www.islayinfo.com/carved_stones_islay_history.html.

Grant, A. & Davies, R., eds. (1988). *Scotland's "Celtic Fringe" in the Late Middle Ages: The MacDonald Lords of the Isles and the Kingdom of Scotland, in the British Isles, 1100–1500.*

Green, M. L. (1904). *The Palatines as Founders and Patriots: An Address at a Meeting of the Connecticut Society of the Order of the Founders and Patriots of America, September 7, 1907.* New Haven: The Tuttle, Morehouse & Taylor Co.

Greer, G. (1982). *Early Virginia Immigrants, 1623–1666.* Baltimore, MD: Genealogical Publishing Company.

Gregory, D. (1975). *History of the Western Highlands and the Islands of Scotland, 1493-1625.* 2nd ed. Edinburgh: John Donald Publishers, Ltd.

Griffin, L. (2011). Personal communication to Judy Hubbell via electronic mail.

Griffin/Findeisen, Hartman/Palmer/Young Tree. (n. d.). Accessed May 25, 2011, at http/wc.rootsweb.ancestry.com/cgi-bin/img.cgi?op=GET&db=updatedjan&id=16154.

Griffin, J. & Griffen, Z. (1912). *The Griffin-Griffen-Griffith Immigrants from England to America 1600–1700.* Privately printed.

Grubb, F. (1986). *Redemptioner immigration to Pennsylvania: Evidence on contract choice and profitability.* The Journal of Economic History, 46(2), 407–418.

Haisty, C. (n. d.). *Selma Arkansas the Early Years.,* Accessed June 5, 2010, at http://backwardbranch.com/ardrew/dcselma.html.

Haisty, C. (n. d.). *Selma Methodist Church.* Accessed June 5, 2010, at http://backwardbranch.com/ardrew/dcselma.html.

Hammett, C. (n. d.). *The Battle of King's Mountain.* Accessed December 15, 2008, at http://www.tngenweb.org/revwar/kingsmountain.html.

Hand, G. (n. d.). Electronic mail message posted in TXVICTOR-L Archives. Accessed August 23, 2011, at archiver.rootswe.ancestry.com/th/read/TXVICTOR/2001-01/0979695203.

Hanes, T. ed. (1997). *World History: Continuity & Change.* Holt, Rinehart and Winston.

Hanks, P., ed. (2003). *Dictionary of American Family Names.* New York: Oxford University Press.

Henahan, S. (n. d.). *The Great Famine: Gone, but not Forgotten.* Accessed January 6, 2009, at http://www.accessexcellence.org/WN/SUA03/great_famine.php.

Henry Campe Family History Wiki. Accessed July 26, 2011, at http://www.wikitree.com/wiki/Campe-14.

Hicks, P. (n. d.). Church of Jesus Christ of Latter-Day Saints, Family Group Record. Microfilm: 1394191. Submission AF83-042571, accessed September 20, 2009, at http://www.familysearch.org/eng/search/AF/family_group_record.asp?familyid=12430&fr.

Historical Statements Concerning the Battle of Kings Mountain and the Battle of Cowpens South Carolina. Part I: The Subjugation of South Carolina. (n. d.).United States Government Printing Office. Accessed December 15, 2008, at http://www.history.army.mil/books/RevWar/KM-Cpns/AWC-KM-FM.htm.

History of Jamestown. (n. d.). Accessed April 6, 2010, at http://www.preservationvirginia.org/rediscovery/page.php?page_id=6.

History of Pine Bluff. (n. d.). Accessed July 4, 2011, at http://www.cityofpinebluff.com/history.htm.

Holley, D. (2001). *A Look behind the Masks: The 1920s Ku Klux Klan in Monticello, Arkansas.* Arkansas Historical Quarterly 60, no. 2 (2001), 131.

Hooker, R., ed. (1953). *The Carolina Backcountry on the Eve of Revolution: The Journal and Other Writings of Charles Woodmason, Anglican Itinerant.* Chapel Hill, NC: University of North Carolina Press.

Hooker, R. (n. d.). *Absolutism.* Accessed October 15, 2007, http://www.wwsu.edu/-dee/GLOSSARY/ABSOLUTE.HTM.

Hooker, R. (n. d.). *Counter Reformation.* Accessed December 1, 2008, at http://www.wwsu.edu/-dee/REFORM/ENGLAND.HTM.

Hooker, R. (n. d.). *Protestant England.* Accessed October 15, 2007, at http://www.wwsu.edu/-dee/REFORM/ENGLAND.HTM.

Hornets' Nest: The Story of Charlotte and Mecklenburg County, Chapter 9: A Trifling Place. (n. d.). Accessed January 12, 2009, at http://www.cmstory.org/history/hornet/trifling.htm.

Hotten, J. ed. (1874). *The Original Lists of Persons of Quality; Emigrants; Religious Exiles; Political Rebels; Serving Men Sold for a Term of Years; Apprentices; Children Stolen; Maidens Pressed; and Others Who Went from Great Britain to the American Plantations 1600–1700.* London: Chatto and Windus, Publishers.

Howell, K. (2008). *Texas Confederate, Reconstruction Governor: James Webb Throckmorton.* College Station, TX: Texas A&M University.

Howerton, B. (n. d.). *Monticello Home Guard.* Accessed August 25, 2010, http://www.couchgenweb.com/civilwar/mont-hg.html.

Hoyt, W. H. (1907). *The Mecklenburg Declaration of Independence. A Study of Evidence Showing that the Alleged Early Declaration of Independence by Mecklenburg County, North Carolina, on May 20, 1775, Is Spurious.* New York: G. P. Putnam's Sons.

Huguenots, an Introduction. (n. d.). Accessed October 15, 2007, at http://www.ferdinando.org.uk/huguenots.htm.

Human, C. (n. d.). *Pioneers of Freethought in North Carolina.* Accessed January 11, 2009, at http://htomc.dns2go.com/atheism/pioneers.htm.

Hume, I. (1994). *The Virginia Adventure: Roanoke to Jamestowne.* New York: Alfred A. Knopf.

Hunter-Blair, O. (n. d.). *Holyrood Abbey.* The Catholic Encyclopedia. Accessed February 4, 2009, at http://www.newadvent.org/cathen/07423a.htm.

Huskey Family Crest and Name History. (n. d.). Accessed February 5, 2010, at mhtml:file://J:\Huskey%20Crest.mht.

Huskey, W. (2009). Personal correspondence to Judy Webb Hubbell.

Indispensable Role of Women at Jamestown. (n. d.). United States National Park Service, United States Department of the Interior. Accessed April 5, 2010, at http://www.nps.gov/jame/historyculture/the-indispensible-role-of-women-at-jamestown.htm.

Individual Record: Geoffrey Webb. (n. d.). Church of Jesus Christ of Latter-day Saints. Accessed August 25, 2010, at http://www.familysearch.org/eng/search/frameset_search.asp?PAGE=/eng/search/ancestorsearchresults.asp.

Individual Record: Henry Webb. (n. d.). Church of Jesus Christ of Latter-day Saints. Accessed August 25, 2010, at http://www.familysearch.org/eng/search/frameset_search.asp?PAGE=/eng/search/ancestorsearchresults.asp.

Individual Record: James Huskey. (n. d.). Church of Jesus Christ of Latter-day Saints. Accessed August 25, 2010, at http://www.familysearch.org/eng/search/frameset_search.asp?PAGE=/eng/search/ancestorsearchresults.asp.

Individual Record: John Webb. (n. d.). Church of Jesus Christ of Latter-day Saints. Accessed August 25, 2010, at http://www.familysearch.org/eng/search/frameset_search.asp?PAGE=/eng/search/ancestorsearchresults.asp.

Individual Record: Lafayette Gabbert.(n. d.). Church of Jesus Christ of Latter-day Saints. Accessed June 5, 2010, at http://www.familysearch.org/eng/search/frameset_search.asp?PAGE=/eng/search/ancestorsearchresults.asp.

Individual Record: John Marshall. (n. d.). Church of Jesus Christ of Latter-day Saints. Accessed January 6, 2009, at http://www.familysearch.org/eng/default.asp.

Individual Record: Julia Ann Gabbert. (n. d.). Church of Jesus Christ of Latter-day Saints. Accessed December 27, 2008, at http://www.familysearch.org/eng/default.asp.

Individual Record: Mathaus Gebhard. (n. d.). Church of Jesus Christ of Latter-day Saints. Accessed December 1, 2008, at http://www.familysearch.org/eng/default.asp.

Individual Record: George Gabbert. (n. d.). Church of Jesus Christ of Latter-day Saints. Accessed December 26, 2008, at http://www.familysearch.org/eng/default.asp.

Individual Record: Michael Gebert. (n. d.). Church of Jesus Christ of Latter-day Saints. Accessed June 5, 2010, at http://www.familysearch.org/eng/search/frameset_search.asp?PAGE=/eng/search/ancestorsearchresults.asp.

Individual Record: Petrus Gebhard. (n. d.). Church of Jesus Christ of Latter-day Saints. Accessed June 5, 2010, at http://www.familysearch.org/eng/search/frameset_search.asp?PAGE=/eng/search/ancestorsearchresults.asp.

Individual Record: William Webb. (n. d.). Church of Jesus Christ of Latter-day Saints. Accessed June 5, 2010, at http://www.familysearch.org/eng/search/frameset_search.asp?PAGE=/eng/search/ancestorsearchresults.asp.

Internet Surname Database. (n. d.). Accessed September 6, 2010, at http://www.surnamedb.com.

Irish Information Guide. (n. d.). Accessed January 26, 2009, at http://www.irishinformationguide.com/Bog.

Irwin, H. (1882). *History of Charlotte, North Carolina.* Privately published: Charlotte, North Carolina. p. 29.

James Huskey, Will, 1843, Will Book 14, pp. 231–232, Brunswick County, Virginia.

Jamestown. (n. d.). United States Department of State. Accessed December 28, 2008, at http://countrystudies.us/united-states/history-6.htm.

Jamestown. (n. d.). Accessed February 15, 2007, at http://www.next1000.com/family/EC/jamestown.hist.html.

Jamestown Settlement and the "Starving Time." Accessed March 9, 2010, at http://www.beyondbooks.com/ush72/2c.asp?pf=on.

John Camp Family: Virginia, South Carolina, and Georgia. (n. d.). Accessed April 23, 2007, at http://www.next1000.com/family/EC/camp.john.html.

Jokinen, A. (n. d.). *Oath of Supremacy.* Accessed December 31, 2008, at http://www.luminarium.org/encyclopedia/supremacy.htm.

Jordan, E. (n. d.). *Jamestown, Virginia, 1607–1907: An Overview.* Accessed March 5, 2010, at http://curry.edschool.virginia.edu/socialstudies/projects/jvc/overview.html.

Journal of the House of Commons: Volume 7: 1651–1660, pp. 204-208. Accessed November 7, 2006, at http://www.british-history.ac.uk/report.asp?compid=24095&strquery=webbe.

Kemp, F. (1902). *A General History of the Kemp and Kempe Families of Great Britain and Her Colonies.* London: Charles Scribner's Sons.

Kerchner, C. (n. d.). *Pennsylvania Dutch are German Heritage, not Dutch.* Accessed December 16, 2008, at http://www.kerchner.com/padutch.htm.

Kidd, C. and Williamson, D., eds. (1990). *Debrett's Peerage and Baronetage.* New York: St. Martin's Press.

Kindig, T. (n. d.). *Proclamation of 1763.* Accessed December 15, 2008, at http://www.ushistory.org/declaration/related/proc63.htm.

Kingsbury, S., ed. (1906-1935). *Records of the Virginia Company of London.* 4 vols. Washington DC: Government Printing Office.

Kirsch, J. (n. d.). The Catholic Encyclopedia. *The Reformation*. Accessed December 30, 2008, at http://www.newadvent.org/cathen/12700b.htm.

Knauss, W. (2010). *The Story of Camp Chase*. San Francisco: Nabu Press.

Knight, L. (n. d.). *Georgia's Roster of the Revolution, Containing a List of the State's Defenders; Officers and Men; Soldiers and Sailors; Partisans and Regulars; Whether Enlisted from Georgia or Settled in Georgia After the Close of Hostilities*. Accessed August 24, 2010, at http://www.archive.org/stream/georgiarosterrev00knigrich/georgiarosterrev00knigrich_djvu.txt.

Knittle, W. (1937). *Early Eighteenth Century Palatine Emigration*. Philadelphia: Dorrance & Company.

Kolchin, P. (2003). *American Slavery: 1619–1877*. New York: Hill and Wang.

Lamb, B. (2009). Personal correspondence to Judy Webb Hubbell.

Lambert, T. (n. d.). *England in the Seventeenth Century*. Accessed January 5, 2009, at http://www.localhistories.org/17thcent.html.

Lampkin, S. (2010). *From the Museum*, Advance Monticellonian, July 21, 2010.

Land Office Patents No. 37, 1767–1768, p. 287 (Reel 37).

Land Records Georgia Land Lottery. (n. d.). Accessed December 27, 2008, at http://files.usgwarchives.org/ga/deeds/1821/1821eg.txt.

Landrum, L. (1900). *History of Spartanburg County, South Carolina*. Baltimore, MD: Clearfield Publishing.

Langland, W. (2006). *Piers Plowman.* London: W. W. Norton & Company.

Lavery, B. (1988). *History of the Clan MacDonald, McDonald and McDonnell. Ships of the World.* Annapolis: Naval Institute Press.

Life-rent. (n. d.). Free Dictionary. Accessed February 6, 2009, at http://legal-dictionary.thefreedictionary.com/Life-rent.

Linder, D. (n. d.). *The Witchcraft Trials in Salem: A Commentary.* Accessed January 5, 2009, at http://www.law.umkc.edu/faculty/projects/ftrials/salem/SAL_ACCT.HTM.

Lipscomb, T. (1976). *Names in South Carolina, XXIII, Winter 1976, pp. 33–34, "South Carolina Revolutionary Battles-Part Four.*

List of Lord Mayors of the City of London. (n. d.). Accessed October 1, 2010, at http://www.barryoneoff.co.uk/html/lord_mayors.html.

Loiselle, L. (n. d.). *Martin Webb 1737-1815.* Accessed July 4, 2011, at http://genforum.genealogy.com/nc/surry/messages/505.html.

Lossing, B. (n. d.). *Our Country: Vol. 1: Chap. XV.* Accessed March 9, 2010, at http://www.highbeam.com/doc/1P1-28036971.htm.

Lost Colony Research Group. (n. d.). Accessed July 31, 2011, at http://www.rootsweb.ancestry.com/~molcgdrg/sur/1surnames.htm.

Louisiana Purchase through Early Statehood, 1803 through 1860. (n. d.). Encyclopedia of Arkansas History & Culture. Accessed July 4, 2011, at http://www.encyclopediaofarkansas.net/encyclopedia/entry-details.aspx?entryID=398.

Louisiana Purchase Treaty; April 30, 1803. Treaties and Other International Acts of the United States of America, Vol. 2. Documents I-40: 1776-1818. Washington: Government Printing Office," Miller, H. ed. Accessed December 31, 2008, at http://avalon.yale.law.edu/19th_century/louis1.asp.

Lunenburg County, Virginia Will Book I, p. 31.

Macaulay, T. (1900). *The History of England.* Boston: Houghton, Mifflin and Company.

MacDonald, C. (1950). *The History of Argyll.*

MacDonald, H. (1914). *History of the MacDonald's* in *Highland Papers I.* Westminster, MD: Heritage Books.

MacDonald, N. (n. d.). *Clan Donald: An Introductory History.* Accessed February 2, 2009, at http://www.clandonaldchiefs.org.uk/history/history.htm.

Mack, T. (n. d.). *Menstrie Castle.* Accessed January 20, 2009, at http://www.menstrie.org/hist_cas.html.

MacPhail, N. (n. d.). *The Lord of the Isles.* Accessed January 31, 2009, at http://www.linneberg.com/skye/all.html.

MacPhee, K. (2004). *Somerled: Hammer of the Norse.* Glasgow, Scotland: Neil Wilson Publishing.

Mann, C. (n. d.). *America Found and Lost.* National Geographic. Accessed December 28, 2008, at http://ngm.nationalgeographic.com/2007/05/jamestown/charles-mann-text.

Manuscript of the Minutes of the Old Florence Church of Drew County, Arkansas. Accessed December 27, 2008, at http://files.usgwarchives.org/ar/drew.churches/florence.txt.

Mapp, A. (2006). *The Virginia Experiment: The Old Dominion's Role in the Making of America 1607–1781.* New York: Backinprint. com.

Marion County History. (n. d.). Accessed July 12, 2011, at http://www.rootsweb.ancestry.com/~tnmarion/history.htm.

Marjorie Mae Bond: February 1, 1921–April 9, 2011. (n. d.). Accessed October, 9, 2011, at stephensondearman.com/services.asp.

Marshall Family Crest and Name History. (n. d.). Accessed January 5, 2009, at http://www.houseofnames.com/xq/asp.fc/qx/marshall-family-crest.htm.

Marshall-Name Meaning & Origin. (n. d.). Accessed January 5, 2009, at http://genealogy.about.com/library/surname/m/bl_name-MARSHALL.htm.

McCall, H. (1811). *The History of Georgia.* Atlanta, GA: Cherokee Publishing.

McCall, M. (n. d.). *My McCall Family Scotland and Ireland to America; Pennsylvania, Georgia, Alabama, and Florida.* Accessed August 1, 2010, at http://www.redbirdacres.net/McCall.html.

McCartney, M. (2007). *Virginia Immigrants and Adventurers, 1607–1635.* Baltimore, MD: Genealogical Publishing Co.

McDonald, J. (1907). *Life in Old Virginia.* Norfolk, VA: Old Virginia Publishing Company, Inc.

McIlwaine, H., ed. (1979). *Minutes of the Council and General Court of Colonial Virginia.* Richmond, VA: Virginia State Library.

McFarland, J. (n. d.). *Bounty Land Warrants for Military Service in the War of 1812.* Accessed October 3, 2011, at http://www.direct-linesofsoftware.com/bounty.htm.

McPherson, J. (2005). *The Atlas of the Civil War.* Philadelphia, PA: Running Press.

Meddaugh, G. (n. d.). *Gard's Grassroots Genealogy: Webb Family.* Accessed October 4, 2010, at http://home.pacbell.net/gardm/webb.htm.

Merry Webb, Will. (1774). Will Book I, pp. 17–18, Henry County, Virginia.

Medieval Tymes, 1100-1199. (n. d.). Accessed January 7, 2009, at http://www.medievaltymes.com/courtyard/1100_-_1199.htm.

Michael Gebert (b. November 23, 1735; d. 1790. (n. d.). Genealogy. com FamilyTreeMaker Online. Accessed January 29, 2007, at http://www.familytreemaker.genealogy.com/users/g/i/a/ Tammy-L-Giancola/WEBSITE-0001/U.

MilitaryHistoryOnline, "31st Louisiana Infantry CSA. (n. d.). Accessed December 28, 2008, at http://www.militaryhistoryonline. com/genealogy/ancestor comments.aspx?id=2360&state=Lo uisiana&type=4&rid=2264#a.

Military Records of William Morris Webb, Sr. Acquired from the National Archives.

Mini Biographies of Scots and Scots Descendants: Hezekiah Alexander. (n. d.). Accessed January 8, 2009, at http://www.electricscotland. com/webclans/minibios/a/alexander_hezekiah.htm.

Minutes of the General Assembly of the Cumberland Presbyterian Church. (1890-1891).

Minor, D. (n. d.). *Throckmorton, James Webb.* Texas State Historical Association, Handbook of Texas Online. Accessed July 5, 2011, at http://www.tshaonline.org/handbook/online/ articles/fth36.

Mobley, J., ed. (n. d.). *The Way We Lived in North Carolina.* Accessed January 12, 2009, at http://www.waywelivednc.com/1770-1820/planters-slaves.htm.

Moore, A. (1924). *Conscription and Conflict in the Confederacy.* Columbia, SC: University of South Carolina Press.

Morgan District North Carolina Superior Court of Law & Equity, Misc. Records, Book III. (1782).

Morgan, M. (n. d.). *My McCall Family from Scotland and Ireland to America: Pennsylvania, Georgia, Alabama, & Florida.* Accessed August 24, 2010, at http://www.redbirdacres.net/mccall. html.

Morrill, D. (n. d.). *Independence and Revolution.* Accessed June 14, 2010, at http://www.danandmary.com/historyofcharlottech-ap2replace.htm.

Morris, R. B. (1963). *The Life History of the United States.* New York: Time-Life Books.

Muhlberger, S. (n. d.). *The Early Modern Witch-Hunt.* Accessed January 5, 2009, at http://www.nipissingu.california/history/MUHLBERGER/2155/witch.htm.

Mullis, C. (2010). Personal communication to Judy Webb Hubbell.

Munro, J. (1986). *The Earldom of Ross and the Lordship of the Isles,* in J. R. Baldwin, ed. *Firthlands of Ross and Sutherland.*

National Library of Scotland, Map of Scotland Showing the Historic District of Lochaber, accessed March 23, 2009, at http://en.wikipedia.org/wiki/Lochaber.

Neill, E. (1869). *Pocahontas and Her Companions.* Albany, NY: Joel Munsell.

New Kent County, Virginia Genealogy Project. (n. d.). Accessed October 3, 2010, at http://www.vagenweb.org/newkent/index.html.

News from Massachusetts. (n. d.). Accessed January 12, 2009, at http://www.cmstory.org/meckdec/chainOfError/change_ch02.pdf.

Northern, W., ed. (2007). *Men of Mark in Georgia: A Complete and Elaborate History of the State from Its Settlement to the Present Time, Chiefly Told in Biographies and Autobiographies.* Whitefist, MT: Kessinger Publishing.

Nugent, N. (1987). *Cavaliers and Pioneers: Abstracts of Virginia Land Patents and Grants, 1623–1666.* Baltimore, MD: Genealogical Publishing Company.

O'Kelly, P. (2005). *Nothing but Blood and Slaughter. The Revolutionary War in the Carolinas, Vol. 3.* Bangor, ME: Booklocker.com.

O'Laughlin, M. (1997). *The Book of Irish Families: Great & Small.* 2nd ed., vol. I. Kansas City, MO: Irish Genealogical Foundation.

Old Bildad Church, microfilm roll 703, vol I., Tennessee State Library and Archives.

One Great Family. (n. d.). Accessed August 3, 2011, at http://www.onegreatfamily.com/Home.aspx.

Orange County, Georgia Land Records (1769).

Order of Battle-Confederates. (n. d.). United States Department of the Interior, National Park Service. Accessed July 4, 2011, at http://www.nps.gov/vick/historyculture/order-of-battle-confederate.htm.

Order of Descendants of Ancient Planters 1606–1616. (n. d.). Accessed March 19, 2010, at http://ancientplanters.org/about.htm.

Original Settlers. (n. d.). Preservation Virginia. Accessed March 5, 2010, at http://www.preservationvirginia.org/rediscovery/page.php?page_id=31.

Origins of English Surnames. (n. d.). Accessed December 18, 2012 at http://www.ramsdale.org.

Otterness, P. (2004). *The 1709 Palatine Migration and the Formation of GermanImmigrant Identity in London and New York.* Itaca and London: Cornell University Press.

Our Family Tree. (n. d.). Accessed October 3, 2010, at http://wc.rootsweb.ancestry.com/.cgi-bin/igm.cgi?op=GET&db=g_o_brown&id=10852.

Our Jamestown Ancestors. (n. d.). Accessed April 5, 2010, at http://www.genealogical-gleanings.com/Jamestcwn.htm.

Paint Rock, Alabama Community Profile. Accessed April 20, 2010, at http://alabama.hometownlocator.com/al/jackson/paint-rock.cfm.

Parish Register of Saint Peter's Church New Kent County, Virginia 1680-1787. (2004). National Society of the Colonial Dames of America.

Parkes, N. (1979). *Mississippi Daughters and Their Ancestors.* Daughters of the American Revolution: Privately printed.

Parran, A. (1935). *Register of Maryland's Heraldic Families, 1634–1935.* Series 2. Baltimore, MD: H. G. Roebuck and Sons.

Passenger List 1731 Pennsylvania Merchant. (n. d.). ProGenealogists Family History Research Group. Accessed October 15, 2007, at http://progenealogists.com/palproject/pa/1731pmer.htm.

Paul, J., ed. (1908). *The Scots Peerage Founded on Wood's Edition of Sir RobertDouglas's Peerage of Scotland.* Edinburgh, Scotland: David Douglas.

Percy, G. (1606). *Discourse of the Plantation of the Southerne Colonie in Virginia by the English.*

Percy, G. (1624). *George Percy: A True Relation of the Proceedings and Occurances of Moment which have happened in Virginia from the Time Sir Thomas Gates shipwrecked upon the Bermudes Anno 1609 until my Departure out of theCountry which was in Anno Domini 1612.* London: Author.

Person Sheet: Thomas Campe. (n. d.). Accessed July 26, 2011, at http://www.tomcamp.org/ps01/ps01_145.html.

Peters, J. & Peters, D. (n. d.). *Carter County, Tennessee Genealogy. Sycomore Shoals.* Accessed December 15, 2008, at http://www.tngenweb.org/#HISTORY.

Places to Visit near Stirling. (n. d.). Accessed January 26, 2009, at http://www.instirling.com/sight/menstrie.htm.

Pledge, L. & Foley, H. (2009). *Early Virginia Families Along the James River: Their Deep Roots and Tangled Branches, Vol. 3: James City County & Surry County, Virginia.* Baltimore, MD: Clearfield Publishing.

Pollen, J. (n. d.). The Catholic Encyclopedia. *The Counter Reformation.* Accessed December 30, 2008, at http://www.newadvent.org/cathen/04437a.htm.

Portraits of Texas Governors: War, Ruin, and Reconstruction 1866-1876, James Webb Throckmorton. (n. d.). Texas State Archives and History Commission.

Powell, W. (n. d.). Encyclopedia of North Carolina. *Regulator Movement.* Accessed December 20, 2008, at http://www.unc-press.unc.edu/nc_encyclopedia/regulator.html.

Pray, F. (n. d.). The Gibbs Magazine. *The Palatine Emigration to America.* Accessed October 15, 2007, at http://knoxcotn.org/history/gibbs/palatine.html.

Presbyter. (n. d.). Merriam-Webster Online Dictionary. Accessed February 6, 2009, at http://www.merriam-webster.com/dictionary/presbyter.

Price, Z. (1963). *Of Whom I Came; From Whence I Came-Wells-Wise, Rish-Wise, and Otherwise,* vol. 6. Greenville, MS: author.

Primogeniture. (n. d.). Merriam-Webster Online Dictionary. Accessed December 26, 2008, at http://www.merriam-webster.com/dictionary/primogeniture.

Pritchett, W. (2000). *Civil War Soldiers from Brunswick County, Virginia.* Murphys, CA: Gateway Press.

Professional Census of Drew County Arkansas. (n. d.). Accessed December 27, 2008, at http://backwardbranch.com/ardrew/drewcountyprofessionals.pdf.

Protestant Reformation (n. d.). Hanover College History Department Internet Archives of Texts and Documents. Accessed October 15, 2007, at http://history.hanover.edu/early/prot.html.

Ramsey, J. (n. d.). *Annals of Tennessee to the End of the Eighteenth Century.* Accessed December 15, 2008, at http://www.roanetnhistory.org/ramseysannals.php?loc=RamseysAnnals&pgid=42.

Ransome, D. (1991). Wives for Virginia, 1621. *William and Mary Quarterly.* 3rd ser., p. 48.

Ransome, D. (2000). Village Tensions in Early Virginia: Sex, Land, and Status at theNeck of Land in the 1620s. *The Historical Journal* 43, no. 2: 365–381.

Reagan, D. (1978). *Smoky Mountain Clans.* Knoxville, TN: Author.

Reeme, M. (2009). Personal Correspondence to Judy Webb Hubbell, Oct. 19, 2009.

Regulator Movement. (n. d.). Accessed January 17, 2009, at http://www.geocities.com/qatballou_laura/history/history_north_carolina_regulators.htm.

Regulator Movement. (n. d.). The Columbia Encyclopedia. Accessed September 30, 2011 at http://www.bartleby.com/65/Regulator.html.

Reich, E., ed. (n. d.). *The Religious Peace of Augsburg, 1555, Select Documents,* 230–232. Acessed October 15, 2007, at http://www.uoregon.edu/-sshoemak/323/texts/augsburg.htm.

Religion at Jamestown. (n. d.). Accessed March 9, 2010, at http://www.historyisfun.org/pdf/Background-Essays/ReligionatJamestown.pdf.

Revolutionary War Pension Abstracts. (n. d.). USGenWebArchives Mercer County, Kentucky. Accessed December 20, 2008, at http://www.usgwarchives.org/ky/mercer.html.

Rich Man's War Poor Man's Fight: The Draft and the Civil War. (n. d.). Accessed August 31, 2010, at http://www.thecivilwaromni-bus.com/articles/84.

Richmond County, Virginia Deed Book I, 1692–1693, p.16.

Richmond, Virginia County Records 1704–1724, p. 19.

Robinson, C. (n. d.). *Chronological History of Lochaber.* Accessed February 5, 2009, at http://www.lochaber.com/history/chronology.htm.

Robinson, C. (n. d.). *London's burning: The Great Fire.* Accessed December 31, 2008, at http://www.bbc.co.uk/history/british/civil_war_revolution/great_fire_05.shtml.

Robinson, P. (1994). *The Plantation of Ulster: British Settlement in an Irish Landscape.* Belfast, Northern Ireland: Ulster Historical Foundation.

Rogers, C. (1877). *Memorials of the Earl of Stirling and of the House of Alexander.* Vol. 1. Edinburgh, Scotland: William Paterson.

Rogers, C. (1877). *Memorials of the Earl of Stirling and of the House of Alexander.* Vol. 2. Edinburgh, Scotland: William Paterson.

Rountree, H. (1989). *Pocahontas's People: The Powhatan Indians of Virginia.* Norman, OK: University of Oklahoma Press.

Rountree, H. (1990). *Pocahontas' People: The Powhatan Indians of Virginia through Four Centuries.* Norman, OK: University of Oklahoma Press.

Rountree, H., ed. (1993). *Powhatan Foreign Relations, 1500–1722.* Charlottesville, VA: University Press of Virginia.

Ruane, M. (2007). Jamestown's "Starving Time" Reveals Unsavory Tales of Cannibalism. *Washington Post,* May 10, 2007.

Rupp, D. (n. d.). *History of the Palentine Immigration to Pennsylvania.* Accessed October 15, 2007, at http://www.searchforancestors.com/passengerlists/history.htm.

Rutherford County Wills, 1784-1833, Ace-Haw, Vao. I, p. 29. North Carolina Archives: Raleigh, NC.

Sage of Monticello, June 15, 1961.

Sasine. (n. d.). The Free Online Dictionary. Accessed February 6, 2009, at http://legal-dictionary.thefreedictionary.com/Sasine.

Scots-Irish from Ulster and the Great Philadelphia Wagon Road. (n. d.). Accessed January 9, 2009, at http://www.electricscotland.com/history/america/wagon_road.htm.

Scott, R. (1880). *War of the Rebellion: A Compilation of the Official Records of the Union and Confederate Armies.* Washington, DC: Government Printing Office.

Scottish Weights and Measures: Capacity. (n. d.). SCAN Weights and Measures Guide. Accessed February 7, 2009, at http://www.scan.org.uk/measures/capacity.asp.

Secrets of the Dead, Case File: Death at Jamestown. (n. d.). Accessed October 11, 2009, at http://www.pbs.org/wnet/secrets/previous_seasons/case_jamestown/index.html.

Sellar, W. (1966). *The Origins and Ancestry of Somerled.* Scottish Historical Review 45: 123–142.

Sharpe, R., ed. (n. d.). *Folios xxx-xxxix, Calendar of Letter-books of the City of London: C: 1291-1309.* , pp. 40-57. London: Center for Metropolitan History. Accessed September 7, 2010, at http://www.british-history.ac.uk/report.aspx?compid=33056&strquery=simon+le+webbe#s36.

Shaw, W. (1962). *The American Journal of Legal History* 6, no. 4: 368–405.

Sherrill, C. (1987). *Tennessee Convicts Early Records of the State Penitentiary, vol. 1, 1831–1850.*

Slater, G. (1907). *The English Peasantry and the Enclosure of Common Fields.* London: Archibald Constable & Company, Ltd.

Slater, G. (1913). *The Land: The Report of the Land Enquiry Committee.* London: Hodder & Stoughton.

Smiley, T. (n. d.). *400th Anniversary of Jamestown, Virginia: Where African Culture First Became American Culture.* Accessed April 6, 2010, at http://www.pbs.org.kcet.tavissmiley/special/jamestown.html.

Smith, D. (n. d.). *Dragging Canoe, Cherokee War Chief.* Accessed December 15, 2008, at http:members.tripod.com/~SmithDRay/draggingcanoe-index-9.html#tp.

Smith, J. (1907). *The Generall Historie of Virginia, New England & the Summer Isles.* Vol. I. Glasgow, Scotland: James MacLehose and Sons.

Smith, J. (2002). *Grant.* New York: Simon and Schuster.

Smith, N. & Eppich, B. (n. d.). Family Search: Church of Jesus Christ of Latter-Day Saints. Accessed March 2, 2010, at http://www.familysearch.org/eng/search/frameset_search.asp?PAGE=/eng/searchresults.asp.

Smith, W. (1954). *A Genealogy Compiled by W. P. Smith of Parkersburg, West Virginia.*

Some Notes on Medieval English Genealogy: Public Record: Pipe Roll. (n. d.). Accessed September 9, 2010, at http://www.medievalgenealogy.org.uk/guide/pip.shtml.

Somerled. (n. d.). Accessed February 1, 2009, at http://www.undiscoveredscotland.co.uk/usbiography/stu/somerled.html.

Somerled, Lord of the Isles. (n. d.). Accessed February 1, 2009, at http://web.archive.org/web/20050218075118/http://www.tartans.com/articles/famscots/somerled.html.

Southern Campaign Revolutionary War Pension Statements & Rosters. (n. d.). Accessed June 14, 2010, at http://www.southerncampaign. org/pen/s6487.pdf.

Southern Colonies: Colonial Life: 1700–1763: U. S. History: Colonial Period through 1865. (n. d.). Accessed January 6, 2009, at http://www.sparknotes.com/101/us_history_one/colonial_ life/southern_colonies.html.

Spaeth, A., Reed, L. & Jacobs, H., Trans. (n. d.). *Disputation of Doctor Martin Luther on the Power and Efficacy of Indulgences.* Accessed October 15, 2007, at http://www.iclnet.org/pub/ resources/text/wittenberg/luther/web/ninetyfive.html.

Speer, L. (1997). *Portals to Hell: The Military Prisons of the Civil War.* Mechanicsburg, PA: Stackpole Books.

Spidell, D. (n. d.). *The Great Palatine Migration.* Accessed February 7, 2007, at http://www.amethystrealty.com/famsearch/pala- tine.html.

Spahn, M. (n. d.). *The Thirty Years War.* The Catholic Encyclopedia. Accessed December 30, 2008, at http://www.newadvent.org/ cathen/14648b.htm.

State Records of North Carolina, vol. 22. Oxford, NC: Richard Thornton Library.

Stevens, W. B. (1847). *A History of Georgia, from its First Discovery by Europeans to the Adoption of the Present Constitution in MDCCXCVIII.* 2 vols. Savannah, GA: Beehive Press.

Stewart, J. R., ed. (1918). *A Standard History of Champaign County Illinois.* Vol. I. Chicago: The Lewis Publishing Company.

St. Peter's Episcopal Church, New Kent County, Virginia. (n. d.). Accessed October 3, 2010, at http://www.boatwrightgenealogy.com/church2.html.

Surname: Dodson. (n. d.). Accessed November 16, 2009, at http://www.surnamedb.com/surname.aspx?name=Dodson.

Sussex County, Virginia Will Book C (1776) p. 217.

Suzerainty. (n. d.). Merriam-Webster Online Dictionary. Accessed February 6, 2009, at http://www.merriam-webster.com/dictionary/suzerainty.

Sweeny, W. (1998). *Wills of Rappahannock County, Virginia 1656–1692.* Greenville, SC: Southern Historical Press.

Thane. (n. d.). Merriam-Webster Online Dictionary. Accessed February 3, 2009, at http://www.merriam-webster.com/dictionary/thane.

Thomas Camp Family: Virginia, South Carolina, and Georgia. (n. d.). Accessed February 15, 2007, at http://www.next1000.com/family/EC/camp.thom.html.

Thomas Camp I Family: England & Virginia. (n. d.). Accessed February 15, 2007, at http://www.next1000.com/family/EC/camp.thomI.html.

Thomas Camp II Family: Virginia, South Carolina, and Georgia. (n. d.). Accessed February 15, 2007, at http://www.next1000.com/family/EC/camp.thomII.html.

Thomas, S. (n. d.). *The 1780 Presbyterian Rebellion and the Battle of Huck's Defeat.* Accessed August 3, 2009 at http://www.sciway3.net/revolutionarywar/1780-Huck_noframes.html.

Thompson, C. (n. d.). *Miscellaneous Revolutionary War Veterans of Union County, North Carolina, Anson County, North Carolina, Stanly County, North Carolina, Cabarrus County, North Carolina and Surrounding Areas.* Accessed August 30, 2010, at http://freepages.genealogy.rootsweb.ancestry.com/~jganis/unionco/HamiltonCemetery.htlm.

Thompson, N. (1993). *The Family of Bartholomew Stovall: Eight Generations of Stovalls in England and America.* Fort Worth, TX: Stovall Family Association.

Thorlton, F. (n. d.). *They Came from Ireland: Seven Brothers from Ireland.* Accessed January 6, 2007, at http://www.hartslog.org/7%20brothers.htm.

Thorlton, F. (n. d.). *The Mecklenburg Declaration of Independence.* (n. d.). Accessed January 9, 2009, at http://www.hartslog.org/declar/1775.htm.

Toleration Act. (n. d.). Microsoft Encarta Online Encyclopedia. Accessed January 8, 2009, at http://uk.encarta.msn.com.

Transylvania Company. (2008). The Colombia Encyclopedia, 6th ed. Columbia University Press.

Turner, R. (2007). *Webb Families of the Virginias.* Manassas, VA: The author.

Tyler, L. (1897). Education in Colonial Virginia, Part III: Free Schools. *William and Mary College Quarterly Historical Magazine* (1897): 70–85.

UK Genealogy Archives. (n. d.). Accessed January 5, 2009, at http://www.uk/england/Essex/gazetteer.html.

United States Department of the Interior, Bureau of Land Management: General Land Office. (n. d.). Accessed August 22, 2011, at http://www.glorecords.blm.gov

U. S. History Pre-Columbian to the New Millennium: Indentured Servants. (n. d.). Accessed March 15, 2010, at http://www.ushistory.org.us/5b.asp.

Van Ells, M. (n. d.). *The Establishment of English Colonies.* Accessed January 6, 2009, at http://www.vanells.com/125-05.pdf.

Vestry Book of Saint Peter's Parish (New Kent County, Virginia). (1905). National Society of the Colonial Dames of America in the Commonwealth of Virginia. Richmond, VA: W. E. Jones.

Virginia: Her History and Her Families. (n. d.). Accessed March 5, 2010, at http://www.virginiadescendants.com/historyandfamilies/1606-1607vavoyage.htm.

Virginia Patent Book 37, Brunswick County, July 20, 1768, p. 287.

Von Rintein, D. (n. d.). *Lt. Col. James McCall, Revolutionary War Hero of Old Ninety-Six South Carolina.* Accessed August 1, 2010, at http://boards.ancestry.com/surnames.mccall/1018.2/mb.ashx.

Von Rintein, D. *Re: Private John C. Spivey, 2nd Georgia Infantry.* Accessed January 12, 2009, at http://history-sites.com/cgi-bin/bbs53x/gacwmb/webbbs_config.pl?noframes;read=9295.

Voss, J. (n. d.). *Re: Vass, Sharp(e) et al., Essex Co. Virginia 1600s, 1700s.* Accessed October 3, 2010, at http://genforum.genealogy. com/vass/messages/553.html.

Wade, H. (n. d.). *Peters Colony.* Texas State Historical Association, Handbook of Texas Online. Accessed July 5, 2011, at http:// www.tshaonline.org/handbook/online/articles/uep02.

Wallace, E. & Hoebel, E. (1952). *The Comanches: Lords of the Southern Plains.* Norman, OK: University of Oklahoma Press.

War of the Grand Alliance. (n. d.). Columbia Electronic Encyclopedia. Accessed December 30, 2008, at http://www.infoplease.com/ ce6/history/a0821511.html.

Warren County, Tennessee. (n. d.). Accessed July 4, 2011, at https://wiki. familysearch.org/en/Warren_County,_Tennessee#Taxation.

Warren County, Tennessee Will Book 1. (1835). p. 101.

Waters, H. (2010). *Genealogical Gleanings in England.* Vol. I. New York: Schuyler Press.

Webb-Lucas, R. (n. d.). *Descendents of Sir Henry Webb.* Accessed September 19, 2010, at http://www.texgenweb2.org/txguad-alupe/trees/webb.html.

Webb, B. (1895). *Notes on the Webb Family,* vol. XXVI. The New York Genealogical and Biographical Record. New York: The Society.

Webb-L Archives. (n. d.). Accessed October 4, 2010, at http://archiver.rootsweb.ancestry.com/th/read/WEBB/ 2000-01/0948320045.

Webb, L. (2009). Personal Communication of Louise Webb to Judy Webb Hubbell.

Webb, N. (n. d.). *Webb Families Henrico/New Kent #II John 1664-1726.* Electronic mail message at http://newsarch.rootsweb. com/th/read/WEBB/1998-09/0905182039.

Webb, N. (n. d.). *Webbs Henrico/New Kent Continued: #II John 1664.* Electronic mail message, http://newsarch.rootsweb.com/th/ read/WEBB/1998-09/0905190046.

Webb, R. (1894). *The Webb Family.* Yazoo City, MS: Author.

Webb, T. (1994). *Julius Webb and Wife Hannah Watkins.* Warren County Genealogical Association 3, no. I: 22.

Webb, T. (2002). *The Webb Families of DeKalb County Tennessee and 23 Related Families.* Smithville, TN: Bradley Printing Company.

Webb Coat of Arms/Webb Family Crest. (2010). Accessed September 6, 2010, at http://www.4crests.com/webb-coat-of-arms. html.

Webb Family Genealogy: Life in the Past Lane. Accessed April 8, 2008, at http://kyusa.addr.com/-Webb/.

Webb Surname DNA Project. (2004). Accessed September 18, 2010, at http://www.webbdnaproject.org/newsletter/WSDP_Newsletter_ May_to_Aug_2004.pdf.

Webb Surname DNA Project. (2006). Accessed October I, 2010, at http://www.webbsurnamedna.org/newsletter/WebbSurname DNANewsletter_11292006.pdf.

Wheat, J. (n. d.). *Postmasters & Post Offices of Victoria County, Texas 1846-1930*. Accessed August 23, 2011, at www.rootsweb. ancestry.com/~txpost/victoria.html.

White, V. (1995). *Index to Revolutionary War Service Records.* Waynesboro, TN: National Historical Publishing Company.

Whitley, E. (1982). *Marriages of Shelby County, Tennessee, 1820–1858.* Baltimore, MD: Genealogical Publishing Company.

Wilderness Road. (2007). *Columbia Electronic Encyclopedia.* 6th ed. New York: Columbia University Press.

William Campe Family History Wiki. Accessed July 26, 2010, at http://www.wikitree.com/wiki/Campe-16.

Willis, J. (1998). *Arkansas Confederates in the Western Theatre.* Alexandria, VA: American Society for Training and Development.

Wilson, F. (1982). Quoted in *Drew County, Arkansas Cemetery Records.* 3rd ed. Crossett, AR: Nowlin Printing, Inc.

Wiltshire. (n. d.). Accessed January 5, 2009, at http://www.genuki.org.uk/big/eng/WIL/.

Williams, R. (1992). *The Kemp, Turner, and Roberts Families on Little Silver Creek, Washington Parish, Louisiana: The Story of Three Pioneer Families of Early Louisiana, Their Ancestors and Progeny.* Monroe, LA: Williams Genealogical Printing.

Williams, R. (1999). *The Lord of the Isles: The Donald Clan and the Early Kingdom of the Scots.* Colonsay, Scotland: House of Lochar.

Woodward, G. (1969). *Pocahontas.* Norman, OK: University of Oklahoma Press.